T0331130

The English East India Company's Silk Enterprise in Bengal, 1750–1850

WORLDS OF THE EAST INDIA COMPANY

ISSN 1752-5667

This series offers high-quality studies of the East India Company, drawn from across a broad chronological, geographical and thematic range. The rich history of the Company has long been of interest to those who engage in the study of Britain's commercial, imperial, maritime and military past, but in recent years it has also attracted considerable attention from those who explore art, cultural and social themes within an historical context. The series will thus provide a forum for scholars from different disciplinary backgrounds, and for those whose have interests in the history of Britain (London and the regions), India, China, Indonesia, as well as the seas and oceans.

The editors welcome submissions from both established scholars and those beginning their career; monographs are particularly encouraged but volumes of essays will also be considered. All submissions will receive rapid, informed attention. They should be sent in the first instance to:

Professor H. V. Bowen, Department of History and Classics, Swansea University, Swansea SA2 8PP

Previously published titles are listed at the back of this volume

THE ENGLISH EAST INDIA COMPANY'S SILK ENTERPRISE IN BENGAL, 1750–1850

Economy, Empire and Business

Karolina Hutková

THE BOYDELL PRESS

First published 2019
The Boydell Press, Woodbridge

ISBN 978-1-78327-394-2

The Boydell Press is an imprint of Boydell & Brewer Ltd
PO Box 9, Woodbridge, Suffolk IP12 3DF, UK
and of Boydell & Brewer Inc.
668 Mt Hope Avenue, Rochester, NY 14620–2731, USA
website: www.boydellandbrewer.com

A catalogue record for this title is available from the British Library

The publisher has no responsibility for the continued existence or accuracy of URLs for external or third-party internet websites referred to in this book, and does not guarantee that any content on such websites is, or will remain, accurate or appropriate

This publication is printed on acid-free paper

CONTENTS

ILLUSTRATIONS

Figures

Tables

The author and publisher are grateful to all the institutions and individuals listed for permission to reproduce the materials in which they hold copyright. Every effort has been made to trace the copyright holders; apologies are offered for any omission, and the publisher will be pleased to add any necessary acknowledgement in subsequent editions.

ACKNOWLEDGEMENTS

This monograph is the outcome of a number of years of research, which would not have been possible without funding from the University of Warwick and the Centre of Textile Research (CTR), University of Copenhagen. At CTR, I need to thank especially Marie-Louise Nosch. I am particularly grateful to the Economic History Society (EHS) for a postdoctoral scholarship that provided me with the opportunity to expand my research. Studying the Bengal silk industry over a longer time period helped me to increase my understanding of the development of the sector and shaped my arguments. The majority of this book was written in the Economic History Department of the London School of Economics, and I am thankful that I was able to spend my EHS fellowship there and then continue as an LSE Fellow in Economic History. I would also like to thank the LSE Economic History Department for financial support with the publication of this book.

Several people offered support and research guidance. First and foremost I must thank Giorgio Riello for all his invaluable help. He read multiple versions of many of the chapters, and offered constructive suggestions and beneficial advice. I sincerely appreciate his efforts and the time he invested. I want to thank Maxine Berg and Anne Gerritsen for their helpful suggestions. John Styles and Luca Molà provided significant insights into the history of the silk industry and consumption. Michael Aldous contributed invaluable information about entrepreneurship in Bengal. A number of the members of the Economic History Department at the LSE provided helpful comments; the extensive knowledge of both Debin Ma with regard to the economic history of the silk industry and Tirthankar Roy on Indian economic history were essential. David Chilosi kindly shared his silk price data. I am grateful to Patrick Wallis and Jordan Claridge, it was a pleasure to teach EH482 with them; Jordan also offered advice and deciphered some illegible but valuable data. Patrick Wallis's module EH466 Labour and Work in Preindustrial Europe introduced me to premodern economic history during my MSc studies at the LSE and was an important foundation for this research. I also want to thank Michael Middeke and Megan Milan at Boydell & Brewer, who provided vital support during the publication process.

The research benefited from comments and suggestions from participants at the EHS conferences in Warwick, Wolverhampton, and Royal Holloway,

University of London, the Association of Business Historians Conference in Glasgow, the ENIUGH Congress in Paris, the BHC/EBHA conference in Miami, the Economic and Social History of the Early Modern World IHR Seminar, Pasold Conference, workshops at the LSE, the University of Bern, and the Textile Research Centre at the University of Copenhagen, and summer schools in Paris and Florence.

Last but not least I want to thank my friends and family. David Hagebölling was nice enough to visit, Aditi Sahni was a great support (and provided help with Excel), Anna Shabalova helped me with the images, Alice Dolan read parts of the text and offered support, Tang Hui was a great counterpart for (non)academic debates and Hui Yi Foo helped me with the bibliography. I would like to thank Ania Husak for producing the index. Thanks to any others not mentioned who also contributed.

ABBREVIATIONS

BL	British Library, London
BoT	Board of Trade
EEIC	English East India Company
GL	Goldsmiths Library, London
IOR	India Office Records and Private Papers, British Library, London
LSE	London School of Economics and Political Science
RSA	Royal Society of Arts, London
TNA	The National Archives, Kew, London
WBSA	West Bengal State Archive

MEASURES AND CURRENCIES

Unless otherwise stated, prices in this book are converted from Sicca Rupees into pounds sterling, shillings and pence (£ s. d.), where £1 (one pound sterling) was equal to 20s. (twenty shillings) and 1s. (one shilling) contained 12d. (twelve pence). The conversion rate used was one Sicca Rupee equal to 2s. 2d. until 1799 and to 2s. subsequently. One Sicca Rupee contained 16 Annas, and 1 Anna contained 12 Pices. One current Rupee was equal to 2s. The conversion used for liras was £1 equal to 25 liras. One lira contained 20 soldi, and one soldo contained 12 denari.

Measures of weight in this book are either in small pounds (sm. lbs.) of 16 oz or great pounds (gr. lbs.) of 24 oz. The figures are converted from weights used in Bengal. Seer was a unit of weight common throughout India. In Bengal 40 Seers equalled one Maund and one Maund equalled 75 sm. lbs., thus one Seer was approximately 1.88 sm. lbs, and one Seer contained 16 Chattaks.

Further measures include begah, where one begah (or beegah) equated to $\frac{1}{3}$ acre, depending on the province.

Introduction

COMPANIES, POLITICAL ECONOMY AND THE GREAT DIVERGENCE

This book focuses on the English East India Company's venture into silk manufacturing in Bengal and presents the Company as a manufacturer that invested over £1 million in developing raw silk production in India. The book thus complements two bodies of literature – the strand that portrays the English East India Company (EEIC) as a commercial monopolistic entity or power structure, and the one that explains the rise of European manufacturing in terms of import substitution.[1] This book studies the activities of the EEIC in adapting Bengal raw silk production to meet the demands of British silk weavers. Central to this was the transfer of silk technologies from the West to the East – this was one of the first transfers from Europe to Asia rather than vice versa. The transfer occurred in a mercantilist framework, and the transferred technologies connected trade and manufacturing. The outcome of this venture was influenced by the business and management capacities of the EEIC and by British, and eventually imperial, policies. This book ultimately presents a case of manufacturing failure: it argues that rather than being a failure of colonial economies, it was a failure of British imperial policies. Such a failure produced negative consequences for the Indian economy and stifled Indian economic development. By studying a specific case of manufacturing

---

[1] K. N. Chaudhuri, *The Trading World of Asia and the English East India Company, 1660–1760* (Cambridge: Cambridge University Press, 1978); Huw Bowen, *Business of Empire: The East India Company and Imperial Britain, 1756–1833* (Cambridge: Cambridge University Press, 2006); Maxine Berg, 'In Pursuit of Luxury: Global History and British Consumer Goods in the Eighteenth Century', *Past and Present* 182 (1), 2004, pp. 85–142; Giorgio Riello, 'Asian Knowledge and the Development of Calico Printing in Europe in the Seventeenth and Eighteenth Centuries', *Journal of Global History* 5 (1), 2010, pp. 1–6. This book uses the title English East India Company rather than British East India Company, as the Company itself drew on its English connection as can be seen from its official name, United Company of Merchants of England Trading to the East Indies, which was used in the period 1708–1873. Furthermore, from the viewpoint of the EEIC, the union with Scotland meant an extension of its existing monopoly to Scotland rather than including the Company of Scotland in the trade with the East Indies.

failure this book also contributes to our understanding of the involution of the Indian economy.

Silk never achieved a high share of the global fibre market, and yet the economic, social and cultural role of silk in pre-industrial societies far outweighed its quantitative importance.[2] Due to its high value and low volume, silk became one of the first globally traded commodities. Silk reeling – the process of silk thread production – and silk throwing – the process of making silk yarn from silk thread – were mechanised in Italy as early as the seventeenth and fourteenth century, respectively. As a labour-intensive industry, silk manufacturing had potential for employing the poor, produced goods of high value and generated state revenues through taxation. It thus attained the position of a strategic industry in many economies in Eurasia. The silk industry was also an important sector in Britain; although unable to produce raw silk domestically, Britain considered acquiring supplies of raw silk from its colonies and those territories under its influence. The most successful of such attempts was carried out by the EEIC in Bengal.

The silk industry had a long tradition in India; however, there was little demand from the weaving sector for producing silk thread of a high quality and fineness. Consequently, Indian raw silk, that is silk thread, was of a lower quality than other raw silks on the global market. The main region of raw silk production in India was Bengal, by coincidence the region over which the EEIC first gained control. The victory at the Battle of Plassey (1757) and the acquisition of the Diwani (tax revenues) of Bengal, Bihar and Orissa (1765) gave the Company a financial incentive to expand its export trade. Since transferring the tax revenues through the export of bullion or bills of exchange would involve high transaction costs, the only feasible option was to use the tax revenues to buy Indian goods and sell them in Europe. Raw silk was the second most important Bengal export item after cotton cloth and thus deemed by the EEIC as worthy of investment.[3] Yet since the quality of Bengal raw silk was low and could not be easily used by British weavers, the EEIC decided to get directly involved in silk manufacturing. In order to improve the quality of the raw silk the EEIC adopted the Piedmontese system of silk reeling – the most advanced reeling system in Europe. This book explores this colonial project from the point of view of organisation and management, technology, and political economy, and the connections between the British, Bengal and Piedmontese silk industries. It shows that this new system of reeling was profitable under the Company's management and that the venture's success was shaped by the contemporary political economy

[2]   Dagmar Schäfer, Giorgio Riello and Luca Molà, 'Introduction: Silk in the Pre-Modern World', in Dagmar Schäfer, Giorgio Riello and Luca Molà (eds), *Threads of Global Desire: Silk in the Pre-Modern World* (Woodbridge: Boydell Press, 2018), pp. 1–18.

[3]   Chaudhuri, *Trading World of Asia*, pp. 510 and 534.

in Britain. After 1833 the British government banned the EEIC from direct involvement in economic activity in India and made the Company sell its silk factories. This event marked a technological falling behind; raw silk production became unprofitable, and exports to Europe declined to trivial numbers.

The East India Company's venture into Bengal raw silk needs to be considered as an imperial project influenced by the contemporary political economy. The expansion of the British Empire was accompanied by a range of imperial projects shaped by mercantilist principles. With the rise of Britain as a colonial power, the British political economy provided a framework for the economic activities of overseas colonies. This happened directly with the implementation of economic projects as well as indirectly through alterations in the institutional framework that regulated economic activity. Whether this influence was deliberate or not, it had long-lasting impacts on the institutions, economic environment and the way business activity was organised in colonial settlements such as Bengal.

With its various commercial and military projects, the English East India Company played an important role in the expansion of the British Empire. The Company's venture into raw silk manufacturing in Bengal illustrates the effects of shifts in the British political economy on economic activity in India. Whereas seventeenth- and eighteenth-century policies favoured import substitution and importation of raw materials from dependent territories, and lent privileges to trading companies, by the nineteenth century a consensus that private individuals could carry out trade more efficiently won through and import substitution policies were disbanded. By situating the late-eighteenth- and nineteenth-century development of the Bengal silk industry within the context of the Company's policies and the British political economy, this research seeks to contribute to a new understanding of the political economy environment and of institutions conducive to development.

India was one of the most advanced manufacturing regions of the premodern world,[4] and the subcontinent was unrivalled in the production of textiles that were exported worldwide. Bengal was one of the key centres of textile production and trade, and one of the best examples of export-stimulated economic growth in the seventeenth and eighteenth centuries. However, during the eighteenth century, Indian leadership slowly faded away and by the early nineteenth century the Indian textile industry was lagging behind that of Britain.[5] Such decline was most prominent in regions such as Bengal and is often presented as a 'reversal of fortunes' facilitated by

---

4   Tirthankar Roy, 'Where Is Bengal: Situating an Indian Region in the Early Modern World Economy', *Past and Present* 213 (1), 2011, pp. 115–18.

5   Stephen Broadberry and Bishnupriya Gupta, 'Lancashire, India, and Shifting Competitive Advantage in Cotton Textiles, 1700–1850: The Neglected Role of Factor Prices', *Economic History Review* 62 (2), 2009, pp. 279–305.

the long-term action of colonial institutions unconducive to development.[6] Drawing on Gareth Austin's criticism of the 'reversal of fortunes' thesis, I show that a lack of endorsement of private property rights was not the point at issue in the case of Bengal raw silk production.[7] This book instead argues that the expansion of Bengal raw silk manufacturing and exports in the late eighteenth century, and the demise of production of raw silk for exports in the nineteenth century, was driven by the switch from mercantilism to laissez-faire policies in Britain.

My methodological approach is informed by recent developments in global history, which emphasise the necessity of exploring global connections and interactions instead of focusing on European exceptionalism. My research examines the influence of British mercantilism and laissez-faire policies from this perspective. It also relies on new institutional economics, factor price theory, and global value and commodity chain approaches, as well as business history, especially entrepreneurship and business models.

The English East India Company's Silk Enterprise puts forward two main arguments. First, that the eighteenth-century political economy of mercantilism represented a framework that was supportive of the EEIC's venture into Bengal raw silk manufacturing. Similarly, as the British government supported manufacturing in Britain, the same policies provided incentives for the EEIC to invest in raw silk manufacturing in Bengal. Thanks to economies of scale and learning-by-doing, by the end of the eighteenth century the EEIC developed a business model that allowed it to export raw silk profitably to the British market. Second, that the nineteenth-century decline in raw silk production for export was an unintended result of the shift to laissez-faire policies in Britain which had repercussions in India. Thus, my research challenges the perception that deindustrialisation was the outcome of exploitative British institutions. Overall, my book argues that it is necessary to include studies of successful business models in discussion of the political economy environment and institutions that are conducive to development. In the case of Bengal raw silk, production efficiency was undermined by the radical shift in business structure and organisation after 1833. Private entrepreneurs had little access to specialised knowledge and skills, and could not take advantage of economies of scale. Hence, without establishing a value chain, private entrepreneurs were unable to produce raw silk as efficiently as the Company.

---

6   Daron Acemoglu, Simon Johnson and James A. Robinson, 'Reversal of Fortune: Geography and Institutions in the Making of the Modern World Income Distribution', *Quarterly Journal of Economics* 117 (4), 2002, pp. 1231–94.

7   Gareth Austin, 'The 'Reversal of Fortunes' Thesis and the Compression of History: Perspectives from African and Comparative Economic History, *Journal of International Development* 20 (8), 2008, pp. 996–1027.

Historical Perspectives and Directions of Inquiry

This book focuses solely on raw silk production in India and therefore does not address the production of Indian silk textiles, which anyway could not have been legally imported into Britain in the eighteenth century. The key strands of literature this book refers to are scholarship on the silk industry, the English East India Company, and British political economy.

The Silk Industry

The silk industry has never received as much scholarly attention as the cotton industry. Existing literature focuses predominantly on the history of silk production, consumption, and silk textile designs in Europe, especially in Italy, and France, as well as in China.

Scholarly interest in the Indian silk industry focused on the origins of sericulture and silk production, and those communities involved in silk weaving.[8] Alternatively, it explored the unsuccessful attempts to set up silk production on the Coromandel Coast and in western India.[9] Literature that refers to the Bengal silk industry focuses mostly on trade and the role of merchants, and on deindustrialisation in the nineteenth century.[10] Rila Mukherjee and Sushil Chaudhury have examined the position of Indian silk merchants in the Bengal silk trade in the eighteenth century and concluded that their influence declined in the second part of the century.[11] Gautam Bhadra has studied the diffusion of the EEIC's silk filatures (factory-like establishments) in Bengal with a focus on the role of the Bengalese merchants.[12]

8　Vijaya Ramaswamy, 'Silk and Weavers of Silk in Medieval Peninsular India', *Medieval History Journal* 17 (1), 2014, pp. 145–69; Lotika Varadajan, 'Silk in Northeastern and Eastern India: The Indigenous Tradition', *Modern Asian Studies* 22 (3), 1988, pp. 561–70.

9　Maxine Berg, 'Passionate Projectors: Savants and Silk on the Coromandel Coast 1780–1798', *Journal of Colonialism and Colonial History* 14 (3), 2013, pp. 1–24; Claudio Zanier, 'Silk Culture in Western India: The 'Mutti Experiment' (1830–47)', *Indian Economic and Social History Review* 21 (4), 1984, pp. 463–96.

10　Abhay Kumar Singh presents an overview of the development of Bengal silk production from Mughal times. Abhay Kumar Singh, *Modern World System and Indian Proto-Industrialization: Bengal 1650–1800* (New Delhi: Northern Book Centre, 2006), vol. 1, pp. 173–201.

11　Rila Mukherjee, 'The Story of Kasimbazar: Silk Merchants and Commerce in Eighteenth-Century India', *Review Fernand Braudel Center* 17 (4), 1994, pp. 499–554; Rila Mukherjee, *Merchants and Companies in Bengal: Kasimbazar and Jugdia* (New Delhi: India Pragati Publications 2006); Sushil Chaudhury, 'International Trade in Bengal Silk and the Comparative Role of Asians and Europeans, circa. 1700–1757', *Modern Asian Studies* 29 (2), 1995, pp. 373–86.

12　Gautam Bhadra noted that in the late eighteenth century most of the silk filatures were owned by the Company or English private proprietors. Only 18 per cent of the total number of basins was in filatures owned by gomasta merchants, paid agents who procured goods for the EEIC. Gautam Bhadra, 'Silk Filature and Silk Production: Technological Development in the Early Colonial Context, 1768–1833', in Deepak Kumar (ed.), *Science and Empire: Essays in Indian Context, 1700–1947* (Delhi: Anamika Prakashan, 1991), pp. 59–87. Bhadra also focused

An important contribution was made by Harbans Mukhia, who observed that the Bengal reelers resisted the winding methods implemented by the EEIC for economic reasons as they were less profitable for reelers than the local methods.[13] Indrajit Ray has explored the Bengal silk industry in the period 1650–1875 and considered alternative hypotheses for the demise of the industry in the late nineteenth century.[14] Ray argues that the nineteenth-century decline of the industry was caused by the inability of the Bengal silk industry to catch up with the technological innovations of the sector at the global scale. A more detailed picture of the Bengal silk industry was presented by Roberto Davini who studied the industry in his dissertation and in several papers.[15] Although the literature pays attention to the EEIC's involvement in the Bengal silk industry, a comprehensive study is missing. Moreover, none of the previous studies considered the internal approaches and business strategies of the Company with regard to its silk venture. Furthermore, our understanding of the success and subsequent failure of the venture cannot be complete if shifts in British political economy are not considered.

The economic history of the British silk industry in the eighteenth and early nineteenth centuries was studied by Frank Warner, Gerald Hertz and J. H. Clapham, who focused on the system of production, regulation and protection of the silk industry in London.[16] The regional distribution of silk production was explored by Gail Malmgreen and Jean-François Fava-Verde.[17]

on the role of Pykars – intermediary merchants who advanced payments to peasants and procured reeled silk and cocoons. Gautam Bhadra, 'The Role of Pykars in the Silk Industry of Bengal (c.1765–1830)', *Studies in History* 3 (1), 1987, pp. 155–85; Gautam Bhadra, 'The Role of Pykars in the Silk Industry of Bengal (c.1765–1830) Part 2', *Studies in History* 4 (1/2), 1988, pp. 1–35.

13   Harbans Mukhia, 'Social Resistance to Superior Technology: The Filature in Eighteenth-Century Bengal', *Indian Historical Review* 11 (1/2), 1984, pp. 56–64.

14   Indrajit Ray, 'The Silk Industry in Bengal during Colonial Rule: The 'De-Industrialisation' Thesis Revisited', *Indian Economic and Social History Review* 42 (3), 2005, pp. 339–75.

15   Roberto Davini, 'Una Conquista Incerta. La Compagnia Inglese delle Indie e la Seta del Bengala, 1769–1833', (unpublished Ph.D. thesis, European University Institute, 2004). See also: Roberto Davini, 'A Global Supremacy: The Worldwide Hegemony of the Piedmontese Reeling Technologies, 1720s–1830s', in Anna Guagnini and Luca Molà (eds), *History of Technology*, vol. 32 (London: Bloomsbury Publishing, 2014), pp. 87–105; Roberto Davini, 'Bengali Raw Silk, the East India Company and the European Global Market, 1770–1833', *Journal of Global History* 4 (1), 2009, pp. 57–79.

16   Gerald B. Hertz, 'The English Silk Industry in the Eighteenth Century', *English Historical Review* 24 (96), 1909, pp. 710–27; J. H. Clapham, 'The Spitalfields Acts, 1773–1824', *Economic Journal* 26 (104), 1916, pp. 459–71; Frank Warner, *The Silk Industry of the United Kingdom: Its Origin and Development* (London: Drane's, 1921). For silk spinning – the process of producing silk yarn from waste silk – see: J. A. Iredale and P. A. Townhill, 'An Early Silk Comb', *Textile History* 2 (1), 1971, pp. 57–64; J. A. Iredale and P. A. Townhill, 'Silk Spinning in England: The End of an Epoch', *Textile History* 4 (1), 1973, pp. 100–8. Silk spinning was also studied by Hollins Rayner earlier in the twentieth century. Hollins Rayner, *Silk Throwing and Waste Silk Spinning* (London: Scott, Greenwood & Co., 1908).

17   Gail Malmgreen, *Silk Town: Industry and Culture in Macclesfield 1750–1835* (Hull: Hull University

Donald C. Coleman studied the history of the Courtaulds – important producers of crape and later rayon.[18] Natalie Rothstein studied the designs and patterns of broad silk weaves made in Spitalfields in the eighteenth century, the only period when English broad weaving found international markets.[19]

The existing scholarship on the Indian and British silk industries, however, fails to address a series of key issues considered in this book, such as the attempts to alter the quality of Bengal raw silk to accommodate British requirements, and the profitability of the transfer of these technologies to Bengal. This absence is partly due to the fact that most scholarship only considers the silk industry through the adoption of national frameworks.

The English East India Company

The scholarship on the EEIC is vast and has been steadily growing over the past twenty years. The resurgence of interest in the Company's history is the result of developments in New Imperial History as well as interest in globalisation and in transnationalism.[20] The foundations for the study of the commercial and maritime history of the EEIC were laid most notably by K. N. Chaudhuri and Niels Steensgaard.[21] In the 1970s and 1980s, the Company came to be studied within the framework of the British political economy: particular attention was paid to the Company's role in state formation and in creating fiscal capacity.[22] A decade ago David Cannadine observed

Press, 1985); Jean-François Fava-Verde, *Silk and Innovation: The Jacquard Loom in the Age of the Industrial Revolution* (Ebook: Histancia, 2011); Paul Knight, 'The Macclesfield Silk Button Industry: The Probate Evidence', *Textile History* 35 (2), 2004, pp. 157–77; Natalie Rothstein, 'Canterbury and London: The Silk Industry in the Late Seventeenth Century', *Textile History* 20 (1), 1989, pp. 33–47; Stanley Chapman, 'Vanners in the English Silk Industry', *Textile History* 23 (1), 1992, pp. 71–86.

18 Donald C. Coleman, *Courtaulds: An Economic and Social History*, vol. 1: *The Nineteenth Century Silk and Crape* (Oxford: Clarendon Press, 1969); Donald C. Coleman, *Courtaulds: An Economic and Social History*, vol. 2: *Rayon* (Oxford: Clarendon Press, 1969). In addition to the history of the Courtaulds the history of another important silk producer was also mapped – for the Berisfords, see Charles Berisford Sebire and J. F. Sebire, *Berisfords: The Ribbon People; The Story of a Family Business* (London: William Sessions Ltd., 1966).

19 Natalie Rothstein, *Spitalfields Silks* (London: Stationery Office, 1975), pp. 1–2; Natalie Rothstein, *Silk Designs of the Eighteenth Century: In the Collection of the Victoria and Albert Museum, London* (London: Thames and Hudson Ltd., 1990).

20 Philip J. Stern, 'History and Historiography of the English East India Company: Past, Present, and Future!', *History Compass* 7 (4), 2009, p. 1146.

21 Chaudhuri, *Trading World of Asia*; Niels Steensgaard, *The Asian Trade Revolution of the Seventeenth Century: The East India Companies and the Decline of the Caravan Trade* (Chicago: University of Chicago Press, 1973).

22 For the influence of the EEIC on state formation in Britain see, for example: John Brewer, *Sinews of Power: War, Money, and the English State* (New York, NY: Alfred A. Knopf, 1989); Bruce G. Carruthers, *City of Capital: Politics and Markets in the English Financial Revolution* (Princeton: Princeton University Press, 1996), pp. 137–60; Michael Braddick, *State Formation*

how scholars had started to approach the EEIC not only from national or European perspectives, but also from imperial and global viewpoints.[23]

When the EEIC is discussed in economic and business history literature, it is usually with regard to the Company's trading activities, its organisation, and its role in British politics.[24] K. N. Chaudhuri, Om Prakash and Tirthankar Roy emphasise the Company's role in expanding intra-Asian and Eurasian trade.[25] As a joint-stock company, it altered the way business was carried out, 'pioneering the shareholder model of corporate ownership and building the foundation of modern business administration'.[26] As Roy observes, the Company acted as 'an agent of change in transforming the business and politics in South and East Asia'.[27] In the second part of the eighteenth century it conquered vast regions of South and East Asia.[28] Gradually, the Company started to rule the Indian subcontinent, establishing itself as a colonial power.[29] The requisite political and administrative power over the Indian subcontinent further expanded the possibilities of the Company to shape the region's development. Overall, the literature has focused on the Company as a power structure and considered the role of the EEIC in the conquest of

in Early Modern England, c.1550–1700 (Cambridge: Cambridge University Press, 2000); Steve Pincus, 'The Making of a Great Power? Universal Monarchy, Political Economy, and the Transformation of English Political Culture', *European Legacy* 5 (4), 2000, pp. 531–45; Steve Pincus, 'Whigs, Political Economy, and the Revolution of 1688–89', in David Womersley, Paddy Bullard and Abigail Williams (eds), *'Cultures of Whiggism': New Essays on English Literature and Culture in the Long Eighteenth Century* (Newark, DE: University of Delaware Press, 2005), pp. 62–82; Lucy Sutherland, *The East India Company in Eighteenth-Century Politics* (Oxford: Clarendon Press, 1952).

23   David Cannadine, '"Big Tent" Historiography: Transatlantic Obstacles and Opportunities in Writing the History of Empire', *Common Knowledge* 11 (3), 2005, pp. 379–80.

24   Bowen, *Business of Empire*; Bruce Buchan, 'The Emergence of the Technostructure: Lessons from the East India Company, 1713–1836', *Journal of Management History* 41 (1), 2003, pp. 105–16; Ann M. Carlos and Stephen Nicholas, 'Giants of an Earlier Capitalism: The Chartered Companies as Modern Multinationals', *Business History Review* 62 (3), 1988, pp. 398–419; Ann M. Carlos and Stephen Nicholas, 'Theory and History: Seventeenth-Century Joint-Stock Chartered Trading Companies', *Journal of Economic History* 56 (4), 1996, pp. 916–24; Santhi Hejeebu, 'Contract Enforcement in the English East India Company', *Journal of Economic History* 65 (2), 2005, pp. 496–523.

25   Tirthankar Roy, *The East India Company: The World's Most Powerful Corporation* (London: Allen Lane, 2012), p. 1.; Chaudhuri, *Trading World of Asia*, pp. 10–15; Om Prakash, *European Commercial Enterprise in Pre-Colonial India* (Cambridge: Cambridge University Press, 1998), pp. 268–315.

26   Nick Robins, *The Corporation that Changed the World: How the East India Company Shaped the Modern Multinational* (London: Pluto Press, 2012), p. xxii.

27   Roy, *East India Company*, p. 1; Chaudhuri, *Trading World of Asia*, pp. 131–45; Prakash, *European Commercial Enterprise in Pre-Colonial India*, pp. 315–37.

28   Anthony Wild, *The East India Company: Trade and Conquest* (London: HarperCollins Illustrated, 1999), pp. 130–41.

29   Roy, *East India Company*, p. 2.

South and East Asia.[30] Likewise the scholarship has discussed the Company's influence on the development of India.[31]

The role of the EEIC in manufacturing has been largely overlooked. In the late eighteenth century, while directly influencing political and economic development, in Bengal in particular the EEIC also assumed the role of a silk manufacturer. This book shows that the EEIC's involvement in production created new management and organisational challenges that necessitated different solutions from those adopted in the export trade.

British Political Economy

It needs to be highlighted that business activity takes place in the confines of political economy. Political economy facilitated, constrained or even precluded the formation of enterprises, shaped access to the goals and the strategies of business ventures, and provided legitimacy to economic activity.

In an essential way, political economy shaped the viability of the silk trade and the British silk industry as well as the policies of the East India Company. During the eighteenth and nineteenth centuries, market forces operated in the framework of mercantilist regulations and pressure group politics.[32] In the eighteenth century British industrial and trade policies were influenced by mercantilism. Silk weaving was considered a strategic industry in Britain and it was protected against competition by a ban on imports of finished silks, whereas the importation of raw silk from dependent territories was supported by low tariffs.[33] Colonial settlements played an important role as sources of raw materials and as markets for the export and/or re-export of finished

---

30 For a short overview of the EEIC's military activities in India see, for example: Wild, *East India Company: Trade and Conquest*, pp. 130–41. The scholarship also considers the role of the EEIC in establishing colonial rule in India as considered by: Douglas M. Peers, 'Gunpowder Empires and the Garrison State: Modernity, Hybridity, and the Political Economy of Colonial India circa 1750–1860', *Comparative Studies of South Asia, Africa, and the Middle East* 27 (2), 2007, pp. 245–7 and C. A. Bayly, *The Birth of the Modern World, 1780–1914* (Oxford: Blackwell, 2004), p. 259.

31 There are two strands in the debate considering the impact of the Company's rule and colonial rule in general on Indian development. The first contends that development of India was hampered during the Company's rule. It is maintained that economic prosperity was hindered by extractive institutions or, alternatively, by the creation of a fragmented multiclass state with a sluggish economy. The second strand argues that there were both positive and negative changes. Negative impacts were discussed by Acemoglu *et al.*, 'Reversal of Fortune', pp. 1256–69; Atul Kohli, *State-Directed Development: Political Power and Industrialization in the Global Periphery* (Cambridge: Cambridge University Press, 2004), pp. 221–57. For a more balanced view, see Roy, *East India Company*, pp. 188–222.

32 Patrick O'Brien, Trevor Griffiths, Philip Hunt, 'Political Components of the Industrial Revolution: Parliament and the English Cotton Textile Industry, 1660–1774', *Economic History Review* 44 (3), 1991, pp. 395–423, and especially p. 396.

33 Mercantilist approaches to economic policies were not static over the eighteenth century. However, mercantilist economic policies in respect of the British silk industry were fairly stable and followed the pattern described for manufacturing in general. British industry was

goods.[34] Textiles were often the target of import prohibition:[35] the import of finished silk textiles was banned by 1699, 1702 and 1720 legislation in order to support domestic production.[36] British silk production can be considered one of the major eighteenth-century import substitution projects, even though it eventually failed.[37] The switch from a mercantilist to a laissez-faire approach in the nineteenth century denoted a major change in British economic policies.[38] The effects on the silk industry and silk trade were nothing short of staggering. By 1860 the British market had opened up to imports of French silk textiles, which caused a major restructuring in British silk weaving. The exclusion of the East India Company from economic activity from 1833 onwards resulted in major changes in the trade and production of Bengal raw silk as the Company was replaced by private entrepreneurs in Indian trade and business.

The switch from mercantilism to laissez-faire policies represented an alteration in the perception of those business activities deemed beneficial for the national economy. For the East India Company, the rise of laissez-faire policies meant the loss of legitimacy for its economic role and activities. During the mercantilist era, the balance of payments and the promotion of employment were among the chief goals of economic policy. The Company was often criticised by seventeenth- and eighteenth-century pamphleteers and petitioners who argued that the EEIC's trade undermined precisely these two goals and posed a threat to national manufacturing interests. Yet, the Company could rely on two channels to legitimise its activities. First, the EEIC made a significant contribution to government spending by providing the British government with customs revenue.[39] Second, importation of raw silk enabled

---

supported by taxation, bans on imports, tariffs, etc. Peer Vries, *State, Economy and the Great Divergence: Great Britain and China, 1680s–1850s* (London: Bloomsbury, 2015), p. 431.

[34] Josiah Child, *A Supplement to a Former Treatise Concerning the East-India Trade* (London: n. p., 1689), p. 12; Thomas Papillon, *A Treatise Concerning the East-India Trade: Being a Most Profitable Trade to the Kingdom, and Best Secured and Improved by a Company and a Joint-Stock* (London: n.p., 1680), p. 3; Joshua Gee, *The Trade and Navigation of Great-Britain Considered: Shewing, that the Surest Way for a Nation to Increase in Riches, Is to Prevent the Importation of Such Foreign Commodities as May Be Raised at Home* (London: Sam Buckley, 1729), pp. 1–23.

[35] Lars Magnusson, *Mercantilism: The Shaping of an Economic Language* (London: Routledge, 1994), pp. 60–1.

[36] Chaudhuri, *Trading World of Asia*, p. 344.

[37] A different view of premodern import substitution policies is taken by Maxine Berg. She considers that encountering the superior production techniques in Asia encouraged learning, emulation and adaptation, and thus facilitated both market and product development as well as technological change. Berg, 'In Pursuit of Luxury'. From this point of view, the failure of the British silk industry to innovate is connected to the lack of competitive pressure.

[38] Although it has been proved recently that the extent of economic liberalisation was relatively modest, this book will use the term 'laissez-faire' policies as it reflects well the fact that trade policies became significantly less protectionist. Besides which, the term laissez-faire is particularly fitting for the changes experienced in the British silk industry.

[39] Huw Bowen emphasised that the government benefited more from customs revenue than

the EEIC to draw on the rhetoric of promotion of domestic manufacturing and employment. This was recognised by Edmund Burke, a political theorist as well as a politician, who maintained that the Company attempted to use its trade in raw silk to make its trading activities more appealing to the British mercantilist state and manufacturers by claiming it played an important role in supplying British manufacturers with raw materials.[40]

Many scholars challenged the perception that mercantilism was a 'closed' theory.[41] Yet this does not mean that the Company was unaware of the contents of the doctrine in spite of the fact that mercantilism was never a collection of precisely defined policies. Lars Magnusson argues that, for these reasons, mercantilism needs to be recognised as a discourse encompassing a range of perspectives as presented in contemporary pamphlets, tracts and books.[42] In spite of the wealth of arguments presented in mercantilist literature of the time, Magnusson observes that the majority emphasises the promotion of export-led growth as a key concept favoured by mercantilist governments.[43] This was achieved through measures to support domestic industry, principally the manufacturing sectors. This was also a perception shared by the Company as it argued that importation of raw silk from colonial settlements was of national interest to Britain. For the purposes of this study, the economic discourse is of most importance because it reflects the way in which the EEIC understood mercantilism and the way the Company applied the concept to both the British and Bengal silk industries.

Historiography interpreted mercantilism in several ways. One of the best accounts of the various interpretations was formulated by Rössner, who listed the possible approaches as:

from direct payments from the Company: in the 1820s, customs payments were more than £3 million annually. Bowen, *Business of Empire*, pp. 39–40.

40   Edmund Burke, *The Works of the Right Honourable Edmund Burke* (Boston: Wells and Lilly, 1826), vol. 4, p. 68.

41   Considering the debate about mercantilism as theory, Philipp Robinson Rössner observed that not even contemporary economic theories can be considered as closed ones. Philipp Robinson Rössner, 'Heckscher Reloaded? Mercantilism, the State, and Europe's Transition to Industrialization, 1600–1900', *Historical Journal* 58 (2), 2015, pp. 665 and 668. See also Alessandro Roncaglia, *The Wealth of Ideas: A History of Economic Thought* (Cambridge: Cambridge University Press, 2005). For criticism of the term 'mercantilism' see, for instance: Magnusson, *Mercantilism*.

42   Gerard Malynes, *A Treatise of the Canker of Englands Common Wealth* (London: Richard Field, 1601); Gerard Malynes, *The Maintenance of Free Trade, According to the Three Essential Parts of Traffique: Namely Commodities, Moneys and Exchange of Moneys, by Bills of Exchange for Other Countries* (London: William Shefford, 1622); Thomas Mun, *England's Treasure by Forraign Trade, or the Balance of our Forraign Trade is the Rule of our Treasure* (London: J. G., 1664); Josiah Child, *Brief Observations Concerning Trade and Interest of Money* (London: Henry Mortlock, 1668); James Steuart, *Inquiry into the Principles of Political Economy: Being an Essay on the Science of Domestic Policy in Free Nations* (London: A. Millax & T. Cadell, 1767).

43   Magnusson, *Mercantilism*, pp. 74, 96, 109 and 174.

the Midas fallacy (Adam Smith) meaning the confusion of money and wealth; the unifying state system (Eli Heckscher); mercantilism as state building (Gustav Schmoller); mercantilism as an economic discourse (Lars Magnusson); mercantilism as rent-seeking society (Robert B. Ekelund and Robert D. Tollison); mercantilism as development economics (Erich S. Reinert); finally the 'Jealousy of Trade' paradigm.[44]

Recently, interest in mercantilism was sparked by the works of Ha-Joon Chang, Erich S. Reinert, Prasannan Parthasarathi and others who point to import substitution policies and measures to promote domestic manufacturing as decisive for economic growth.[45] These various perceptions of mercantilism only confirm Julian Hoppit's point that heterogeneity was a characteristic of British political economies in the seventeenth and eighteenth centuries.[46]

The rise of laissez-faire policies in the nineteenth century in Britain had far-reaching effects on the Company's economic and political role in India. The push for liberalisation came from pamphleteers, economists and domestic government officials, as well as from merchants and industrial interests. It relied on a language of national prosperity and the idea of mutual benefit of unhindered commerce. For this book the most important issue concerns the changing perceptions of the institutional organisation of trade. During the eighteenth and nineteenth centuries we see a shift from one extreme position to another in Anglo-Indian trade – from favouring a monopoly trading company to favouring individual merchants.

[44]   Rössner, 'Heckscher Reloaded', p. 668; Adam Smith, *An Inquiry into the Wealth and Poverty of Nations* (State College, PA: University of Pennsylvania, 2005); Eli F. Heckscher, *Mercantilism* (London: George Allen and Unwin, 1955); Gustav Schmoller, *The Mercantile System and Its Historical Significance: Illustrated Chiefly from Prussian History: Being a Chapter from the Studien ueber die Wirtschaftliche Politik Friedrichs des Grossen* (New York: Macmillan, 1896); Robert B. Ekelund and Robert D. Tollison, *Mercantilism as a Rent-Seeking Society: Economic Regulation in Historical Perspective* (College Station, TX: Texas A&M University Press, 1981); Erich S. Reinert, *How Rich Countries Got Rich and Why Poor Countries Stay Poor* (London: Constable, 2007).

[45]   The authors favour heterodox approaches to economics rather than neo-liberal or neoclassical ones. They argue that developing countries need to practice import substitution policies and have generally active economic policies to counter underdevelopment. They support their argument by giving examples of European countries that followed such policies in the premodern era and/or during the first Industrial Revolution. Reinert, *How Rich Countries Got Rich*, pp. 21–100; Ha-Joon Chang, *Kicking Away the Ladder: Development Strategy in Historical Perspective* (London: Anthem, 2002), pp. 19–53; Prasannan Parthasarathi, 'Great Divergence: Article Review', *Past and Present* 176 (1), 2002, pp. 290–3; Justin Lin and Ha-Joon Chang, 'Should Industrial Policy in Developing Countries Conform to Comparative Advantage or Defy It? A Debate Between Justin Lin and Ha-Joon Chang', *Development Policy Review* 27 (5), 2009, pp. 482–502; Prasannan Parthasarathi, *Why Europe Grew Rich and Asia Did Not: Global Economic Divergence, 1600–1850* (Cambridge: Cambridge University Press, 2011), pp. 132–4; Joseph Inikori. *Africans and the Industrial Revolution* (Cambridge: Cambridge University Press, 2002), pp. 151, 449.

[46]   Julian Hoppit, *Britain's Political Economies: Parliament and Economic Life, 1660–1800* (Cambridge: Cambridge University Press, 2017), p. 325.

Although the monopolistic system was in retreat from the late seventeenth century onwards, as the largest and the most powerful organisation the EEIC was the last to be affected. Nonetheless, as 'monopoly privileges were surrendered, entry barriers into monopolistic companies were lowered, trading companies were dissolved, and overseas markets opened to individual merchants', the EEIC also forfeited its position.[47] The Company's critics, most importantly Adam Smith among them, considered the EEIC an inferior trade institution (solution) in comparison with individual merchants. By the first part of the nineteenth century this view was also adopted by policymakers. The effects on the organisation of trade were extensive and gave rise to agency houses: hybrid forms of ownership, in which English merchants relied on Indian managing agencies to reduce agency costs that arose due to the large geographical distance and imperfect communication channels.[48] Yet, due to the risks involved in trade, with limited time horizons – as business partnerships in England often dissolved with the death of one of the partners – preference in Anglo-Indian business was given to low-skilled and low-capital intensive ventures. Raw silk production did not fit into this picture.

Sources and Structure

This book draws from a variety of printed and manuscript sources at the British Library, Goldsmiths Library, the Library of the London School of Economics, and The National Archives. In particular, the EEIC archives deposited at the India Office Records proved essential in analysing the steps undertaken by the Company in the Bengal silk industry. Among the key sources are the Bengal Despatches, being the documents sent by the Court of Directors in London to the Board of Trade in Bengal (IOR/E/4), and the letters sent from Bengal to the Court in London (IOR/E/1). For the time period 1757–59, the records of the factory in Kasimbazar are an important source for understanding the procurement and trade of raw silk (IOR/G/23/13). Data on the silk trade comes mainly from the India Office Parliamentary Branch Records, especially the Reports from the Select Committee on the Affairs of The East India Company, which offers a wealth of information on silk (L/PARL/2/55).

Relying on the archives in the India Office Records is beneficial because of the number of documents by the Court of Directors in London sent to Bengal. The Court of Directors in London was the principal managerial

---

47   Ron Harris, *Industrializing English Law: Entrepreneurship and Business Organization, 1720–1844* (Cambridge: Cambridge University Press, 2000), p. 204.
48   Michael Aldous, 'Avoiding Negligence and Profusion: The Failure of the Joint-Stock Form in the Anglo-Indian Tea Trade, 1840–1870', *Enterprise & Society* 16 (3), 2015, pp. 654–9.

body of the EEIC and its archives contain a wealth of information on the filature silk production and silk trade. Moreover, the IOR/E/4 and IOR/E/1 documents also contain reports from the Company's silk specialists, the importance of which is heightened by the fact that reports sent by EEIC servants in India to London were not always reliable.[49] Several members of the Board of Trade in Bengal – the principal administrative and managerial body of the EEIC in Bengal – misinformed the Court and overcharged the Company for the silk they procured and/or produced on behalf of the EEIC, and thus their reports are misleading.[50] The potential limitation of the documents in the India Office Records is their narrow focus on the Company's filature silk production and lack of interest in information about silk production for local markets. However, since this book also focuses on the Company's activities, this should not have a negative impact. The documents might also be negatively biased against the Company's servants, and especially Bengalese reelers and peasants. However, the alleged cases of misconduct can often be supported by quantitative evidence, as in the case of fraud on the part of the Board of Trade. Furthermore, in order to lessen the EEIC bias, I use the Chancery Proceedings held by the National Archives when my research focuses on the principal–agent problems affecting the success of the filature silk production in Bengal.[51] These documents are a way to assess the trustworthiness of the information recorded by the Court of Directors.

My study of the political and economic environment of eighteenth- and nineteenth-century Britain is based on analysis of contemporary treatises and pamphlets. A collection of such resources is held at the Goldsmiths Library and the database 'Making of the Modern World' has enabled me to access items held by the Kress Library, Harvard. The most valuable information about the EEIC's silk production in Bengal can be found in the *Reports of the Committee of Warehouses of the East-India Company Relative to Extending the Trade on Bengal Raw-Silk*.[52] These reports were prepared by the EEIC and contain extensive data on the silk trade. One of these reports is to be found at the

---

49   The Board of Trade in Bengal was often not supplying appropriate information about silk production. For instance, the Board was deliberately keeping information on the costs of filature silk production from the Court of Directors, and in the period from the 1770s to 1780s it was buying silk from private filatures on behalf of the EEIC for prices at almost double the real production costs. IOR/E/4/630, 12 April 1786, pp. 390–1.

50   Davini relies in much of his dissertation on reports from servants such as William Aldersey or Simeon Droz. See for instance, Davini. 'Una Conquista Incerta', pp. 234–58. However, Droz and Aldersey were among the members of the Board of Trade sued by the EEIC in the Court of Chancery for fraud concerning the silk trade. The National Archives (hereafter TNA), TNA C 12/175/27, East India Company v. Aldersey, 24 March 1789 to 11 November 1789.

51   TNA C 12/175/27, 24 March 1789 to 11 November 1789.

52   Goldsmiths' Library (hereafter GL), 1795 fol. 16280, *Reports of the Committee of Warehouses of the East-India Company Relative to Extending the Trade on Bengal Raw-Silk* (London: n.p., 1795); Royal Society of Arts (hereafter RSA), RSA/SC/EL/2/31, *Third Report of the Committee of*

Goldsmiths' Library, while a second is in the Archives of the Royal Society of Arts. The most comprehensive report on the Company's silk production in Bengal is *Reports and Documents Connected with the Proceedings of the East-India Company in Regard to the Culture and Manufacture of Cotton-wool, Raw Silk, and Indigo in India* published by the EEIC in 1836.[53] For studying the English silk industry in the nineteenth century, the *Report from Select Committee on the Silk Trade with Minutes of Evidence, Appendix and Index* proved to be valuable.[54] Quantitative data comes from Reports by the Factory Commissioners: *Return of the Number of Power Looms used in Factories, in the Manufacture of Woollen, Cotton, Silk and Linen*, *Return of the Number of Persons Employed in Cotton, Woollen, Worsted, Flax and Silk Factories* and *Return of the Number of Cotton, Woollen, Worsted, Flax, and Silk Factories*.[55] Hansard's Historical Parliamentary Debates were valuable for studying the political economy of the silk industry and trade liberalisation in the nineteenth century.

Similar limitations as in the case of the documents in the India Office Records apply also to the above-mentioned documents. However, the reports contain quantitative data in particular which should not have biases. Moreover, to gain a different perspective on contemporary views of the Company's silk manufacturing activities, I rely on pamphlets and in particular on the *Considerations on the Attempt of the East-India Company to Become Manufacturers in Great Britain*.[56] The limitation of this source is its negative bias against the EEIC; however, many of the arguments of the pamphlet are supported by either the qualitative or quantitative evidence that it puts forward.

The book opens with an analysis of the early modern silk industry from the point of technology formation, organisation of production and competitiveness. Chapter 2 analyses the importance attributed to silk weaving in Britain and the mercantilist measures that were designed to protect this sector in the eighteenth century. Chapter 3 shows that the quality of the Bengal raw silk was low and that it could not easily be used in British weaving. Chapter 4 focuses on the transfer of the Piedmontese technologies to Bengal and the

Warehouses of the East-India Company Relative to Extending the Trade on Bengal Raw-Silk (London: n.p., 1795).

53   LSE Archives, W7204, East India Company, *Reports and Documents Connected with the Proceedings of the East-India Company in regard to the Culture and Manufacture of Cotton-wool, Raw Silk, and Indigo in India* (London: J. L. Cox, 1836).

54   House of Commons, *Report from Select Committee on the Silk Trade with Minutes of Evidence, Appendix and Index* (London: n.p., 1832).

55   House of Commons, *Return of the Number of Power Looms used in Factories, in the Manufacture of Woollen, Cotton, Silk and Linen* (London: n.p., 1836); House of Commons, *Return of the Number of Persons Employed in Cotton, Woollen, Worsted, Flax and Silk Factories* (London: n.p., 1836); House of Commons, *Return of the Number of Cotton, Woollen, Worsted, Flax, and Silk Factories* (London: n.p., 1857).

56   GL, 1796 fol. 16654, *Considerations on the Attempt of the East-India Company to Become Manufacturers in Great Britain* (London: n.p., 1796).

effects of the new technologies on the quantity and quality of Bengal raw silk imported into the British market. Chapter 5 examines the business and trading model set up by the Company in silk manufacturing and examines its profitability. Chapter 6 analyses the impact of selling the EEIC's silk factories to private entrepreneurs on Bengal raw silk production and exports. Finally, Chapter 7 investigates the effect of the implementation of laissez-faire policies on the British silk industry and the repercussions on the demand for Bengal raw silk.

Chapter 1

THE EARLY MODERN SILK INDUSTRY, TRADE AND MERCANTILISM

Silk has long been considered the queen of fabrics and has been associated with luxury consumption. It never achieved a high share of the global fibre market and yet the economic, social and cultural role of silk in premodern societies far outweighed its quantitative importance. As a labour-intensive industry, silk manufacturing produced goods of high value and brought revenues through taxation. Domestic production of silk prevented the outflow of bullion – something abhorred by mercantilists.[1] Due to its high value and low volume, silk became one of the first globally traded commodities. Thanks to its potential for employing the poor, silk was also considered a strategic industry in the early modern period.[2]

Scholarship has asserted the role of the silk industry in fostering economic development in the early modern and modern periods.[3] The contribution of

---

[1]   Debin Ma, 'The Great Silk Exchange: How the World Was Connected and Developed', in Debin Ma (ed.), *Textiles in the Pacific, 1500–1900. The Pacific World: Lands, Peoples and History of the Pacific, 1500–1900* (Aldershot: Variorum, 2005), pp. 4 and 25; Mary Schoeser, *Silk* (New Haven: Yale University Press, 2007), pp. 13–14. It is difficult to estimate the number of workers employed in the sector in the early modern period, especially as the tasks of sericulture and reeling were not the only ones that household members undertook. Although silk throwing, weaving and dyeing were centralised trades, it is equally difficult to estimate the number of workers employed in each of them. For discussion of these issues see Giovanni Federico, *An Economic History of the Silk Industry, 1830–1930* (Cambridge: Cambridge University Press, 1997), pp. 14–15.

[2]   See, for instance, Luca Molà, *The Silk Industry of Renaissance Venice* (Baltimore: Johns Hopkins University Press, 2000), pp. 34–6.

[3]   The role of the silk industry in economic development was in particular stressed by Debin Ma in a study explaining the differing paths of industrialisation and development of Japan and China in the early nineteenth century. Debin Ma, 'Why Japan, Not China, Was the First to Develop in East Asia: Lessons from Sericulture, 1850–1937', *Economic Development and Cultural Change* 52 (2), 2004, pp. 369–94. In the nineteenth century, the silk industry contributed to the development of other East Asian countries, as noted in Kazuko Furuta, 'Silk-Reeling in Modern East Asia: Internationalization and Ramifications of Local Adaptation: In the Late 19th Century', in Ma (ed.), *Textiles in the Pacific*, pp. 191 and 195–206. Sanjay Sinha draws attention to the development potential of the silk industry in labour-abundant and agro-based

the silk industry to development was, however, reliant on the adoption of up-to-date technologies. Technology leadership in the early modern silk industry was achieved by China, Italy and France.[4] In Europe, adoption of new technologies in the silk industry was endorsed by governments through support for migration of those persons skilled in silk production, tariff protection of domestic silk production, preferential tariffs on raw silk imports, and endorsement of industrial espionage.[5] Such economic policies had their grounding in the mercantilism of the early modern period. The nineteenth-century rise of classical economics and the implementation of laissez-faire policies led to the disbanding of the measures protecting the silk industry in Europe. This in turn led to the decline and restructuring of the less competitive silk industries such as that in Britain. Similarly, as in other industries, the nineteenth century brought innovations in silk technologies and organisation, and the shift of technology leadership to Europe. In the late nineteenth century, great progress was achieved by the Japanese silk industry which successfully adopted and adapted European silk technologies, supported by the Meiji government and entrepreneurs.

Development of the Bengal silk industry was strongly influenced by the British political economy and its connection to the British silk industry. Studying it only with reference to Britain, however, would be inconclusive as the industry was also shaped by global trends in silk production and consumption. To consider the Bengal silk industry from a broader perspective, this chapter first summarises the stages of silk production. Second, it outlines the development of the silk industry from a global perspective and then third, it gives an overview of silk production in India. Fourth, the chapter identifies the global leaders of raw silk production in the early modern period, and finally discusses the changes experienced by the silk industry in the nineteenth century.

economies. Sinha argues that the silk industry should have been promoted in rural parts of India even in the twentieth century because of its employment potential – especially for women – and because it encourages the upgrading of technology. Currently both the United Nations and the World Bank are promoting the silk industry as a sector with high potential for poverty alleviation. Sanjay Sinha. 'Development Impact of Silk Production: A Wealth of Opportunities', *Economic and Political Weekly* 24 (3), 1989, pp. 157–63.

4   Sanjay Sinha, *The Development of Indian Silk: A Wealth of Opportunities* (London: Intermediate Technology Publications, 1990), pp. 4–5. For the origins of sericulture in India see: Lotika Varadajan, 'Silk in Northeastern and Eastern India: The Indigenous Tradition', *Modern Asian Studies* 22 (3), 1988, pp. 565–70.

5   For discussion of these issues see: Ratan Chand Rawlley, *Economics of the Silk Industry* (London: P. S. King and Son Ltd., 1919), pp. 16–19; Lesley Miller, 'Material Marketing: How Lyonnais Silk Manufacturers Sold Silks, 1660–1789', in Jon Stobart and Bruno Blondé (eds), *Selling Textiles in the Long Eighteenth Century: Comparative Perspectives from Western Europe* (Basingstoke: Palgrave Macmillan, 2014), pp. 85–98; Lesley Miller, 'La Cultura de la Manufacture: Les Marchands Fabricants', in Maria-Anne Privat-Savigny (ed.), *Lyon au XVIIIe Siècle: Un Siècle Surprenant!* (Lyon: Musée Gadagne/Sogomy, 2012), pp. 109–21; Paola Bertucci, 'Enlightened Secrets: Silk, Intelligent Travel, and Industrial Espionage in Eighteenth-Century France', *Technology and Culture* 54 (4), 2013, pp. 820–52.

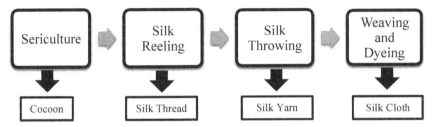

Figure 1.1   Phases of silk production

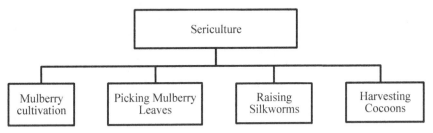

Figure 1.2   Phases of sericulture

Stages of Silk Production

Although this book focuses primarily on the process of silk reeling, as it also discusses British silk weaving, I will briefly outline the key stages of silk production. Silk is a natural fibre which originates as a filament. In order to be used in the textile industry it has to be first processed into raw silk or, in other words, silk thread (Figure 1.1). Only after obtaining raw silk, can the thread be woven. The main stages of silk textile production are therefore: sericulture, silk reeling, throwing, weaving, dyeing and finishing.

Sericulture covers the cultivation of mulberry trees, picking mulberry leaves, raising silkworms, and the harvesting of cocoons (Figure 1.2). The quantity of leaves produced by a mulberry tree depends on the species, on the system of cultivation and manuring, and on climate.[6] The cultivation of mulberry trees can accompany the cultivation of other crops. In Europe, sericulture used to be combined with domestic horticulture, tobacco and fruit cultivation.[7] Silk filaments are produced by silkworms — the larvae of the domesticated moth *Bombyx mori* — when forming a cocoon.[8] In Europe *Bombyx*

6   Pruning, manuring and disease control are essential for a good harvest of high-quality mulberry leaves. Joseph Schober, *Silk and the Silk Industry* (London: Constable & Co. Ltd., 1930), pp. 17, 19.

7   Ibid., p. 17.

8   The majority of silk filaments used in the silk industry are produced by *Bombyx mori* larvae. Smaller quantities of silk are also produced from filaments secreted by non-domesticated

mori is 'monovoltine', meaning that it creates only one generation of larvae per year; in Bengal, by contrast, there can be between five and seven crops of silkworms annually. After hatching, the larvae spends the next thirty-five days feeding on mulberry leaves and so an abundant supply of fresh leaves is therefore crucial for this first stage. The silkworms also need to be fed continuously with fresh leaves in order to prevent them from contracting diseases and have to be kept in hygienic conditions.[9] This is achieved by placing the leaves on trays that are regularly changed. Mature silkworms form cocoons which are made from a single silk filament.[10] The worm then turns into a chrysalis and after few weeks into a moth. As the moth can destroy the cocoon, the chrysalis has to be killed before the metamorphosis is completed.[11]

The next step is reeling: the unwinding of cocoons and the preparation of the silk thread.[12] Cocoons are placed in a basin of water heated to a high temperature.[13] Water softens sericin – the substance that binds the cocoons together – and the cocoons unwind into single long filaments. Five to twenty of these filaments are then drawn together with the use of a reeling machine or hand reel. The reeled silk thread is then dried and the sericin binds the filaments together again.[14] These principles of silk thread production had practically not altered since the early modern period. The key technological change of the nineteenth century was the adoption of a steam boiler for heating water in the basins and the adoption of croissure – a mechanism of crossing or intertwining two threads or even one thread with itself. Croissure enabled production of a rounder, smoother and more compact thread by squeezing out excess water and firmly attaching the filaments. The two types of croissure developed were the less-advanced French chambon system and the more efficient Italian tavellette croissure, which produced a thread of a higher cohesion.[15]

Although the EEIC only got involved in sericulture and silk reeling in Bengal, the process of silk throwing is important because in the late 1790s the Company started throwing Bengal silk in Britain. Throwing is a term used

---

moths. This silk is called wild silk and its principal types are *tussah* or *tasar* (native to Southern India and China, an uneven, stiff silk with a glass lustre), yama-mai (from Japan, the most similar to mulberry silk), *eri* or *eria* and *fogara* (from Eastern India, which can only be spun, not thrown). Schober, *Silk and the Silk Industry*, pp. 20–1.

9   Richard Hills, 'From Cocoon to Cloth: The Technology of Silk Production', in Simonetta Cavaciocchi (ed.), *La Seta in Europa Secc. XIII–XX* (Prato: Istituto Internazionale di Storia Economica, 1993), pp. 61–2.

10   Schober, *Silk and the Silk Industry*, pp. 14–15.

11   Hills, 'From Cocoon to Cloth', p. 62.

12   Ibid., p. 65.

13   The temperature to which water was heated in the early modern period varied. The current recommendation is 75–80°C.

14   A single cocoon would not give a thread of sufficient strength. Ibid., pp. 65, 67–9.

15   Tammanna N. Sonwalkar, *Hand Book of Silk Technology* (New Delhi: New Age International Ltd. Publishers, 1993), pp. 53–5.

for the operations of twisting and doubling by which fine raw silk threads are turned into more substantial silk yarns. This process is often necessary because silk thread is typically too fine for weaving. The number of threads that are doubled together and the amount of twist applied is determined by the type of fabric to be produced from the yarn.[16] The main types of thrown silk used in weaving are tram, crêpe yarn and organzine. Trams are used as wefts and are formed of two or more threads twisted with five to ten twists per inch. Crêpe yarn has a heavier twist with fifty to eighty turns per inch, while organzine has a very high twist and is mostly used for warps. The thread is first twisted, then doubled two-, three- or fourfold, and then twisted again in the opposite direction of the first twisting.[17] Organzine is considered the highest-quality silk yarn and has the highest twist.[18]

The process that follows throwing is weaving. Silk weaving was an important sector of the British economy and the importation of Bengal raw silk was supposed to support it. At this stage silk yarn is made into silk textiles – broad cloths or small-wares such as ribbons. The most common weaves are plain weave, twill weave – creating a pattern of diagonal parallel ribs – and satin weave, which is particularly popular for silk. Due to its strength, elasticity and durability, silk is suitable for pattern weave, especially figured fabrics. A number of silk figured weaves were created since antiquity, and their improvement and supply relied on technical advancement of the weaving technology as pattern weaving is technically demanding as well as labour-intensive, time-consuming and expensive. The first figured fabrics were produced in China and later in Persia, the Byzantine Empire and Europe. Although nearly identical in weave, the Chinese fabrics were of warp effect while the western ones are of weft effect. Among the most well known in Europe are plain weaves also known as tabby weaves, twill-ground tissues, satin-ground tissues: among these two subgroups are satin and twill damasks, and plain and figured velvets.[19]

The key milestones in pattern weaving in Europe were the introduction of the horizontal loom around the thirteenth century, and the twelfth-century introduction of the draw-loom, which enabled pattern repetition, increased the speed of weaving and did not impose limits on the width of the cloth.[20]

16   Silk and Rayon Users' Association, *The Silk Book* (London: Silk and Rayon Users' Association, 1951), p. 28; Hills, 'From Cocoon to Cloth', p. 67.

17   William S. Murphy, *The Textile Industries: A Practical Guide to Fibres, Yarns, and Fabrics in Every Branch of Textile Manufacture, Including Preparation of Fibres, Spinning, Doubling, Designing, Weaving, Bleaching, Printing, Dyeing and Finishing* (London: Gresham, 1912), pp. 174–5; Silk and Rayon Users' Association, *The Silk Book*, p. 28; Hills, 'From Cocoon to Cloth', p. 67–9.

18   Murphy, *Textile Industries*, p. 175.

19   J. F. Flanagan, 'Figured Fabrics', in Charles Singer (ed.), *A History of Technology III: From the Renaissance to the Industrial Revolution, c.1500–c.1750* (Oxford: Clarendon Press, 1957), pp. 194–205.

20   Hills, 'From Cocoon to Cloth', pp, 73, 82.

Besides a weaver to operate it, a draw-loom needed a drawboy who was seated on the top of the loom and worked the cords used for raising the warp threads to create a pattern.[21] The introduction of the Jacquard mechanism in the 1800s led to the mechanisation of the drawboy's task by enabling the weaver to operate the cords with a foot lever.[22] The next step was the introduction of the power loom – an automatic weaving loom invented in 1784 – that led to the increased mechanisation of weaving in the nineteenth century.

To enhance the beauty of the produced fabric, the silk is subjected to processes of dyeing, printing and finishing.[23] There are two methods of dyeing: yarn-dyeing, which precedes weaving, and piece-dyeing, which follows weaving. Yarn-dyeing is more expensive but the characteristics that result cannot be produced otherwise. In order for dyeing to be successful the natural gum that is a component of the silk fibre has to be removed. The yarn or woven textile is thus first boiled in soapy water, then rinsed in clear water and hung up to dry. Afterwards it is bleached in the fumes of burning sulphur. The yarn or fabric is then placed on metal frames and immersed in the dye-bath. Once in the dye-bath the fabric is continually lowered and raised to complete the penetration. Washing and drying as well as finishing follows afterwards.[24]

Global Overview of the Development of Silk Industry

By the eighteenth century, the silk industry had undergone several centuries of development. Knowledge and the technologies of silk production varied among regions. International trade made the silk industry a competitive sector in which constant technological innovation as well as improvements in the organisation of labour and raising of skill levels were essential in remaining competitive.[25]

According to legend, sericulture and silk manufacturing originated in China where *Bombyx mori* was first domesticated around 3000 BC.[26] From China the production of silk spread east, south and south-west.[27] It is supposed that silk manufacturing techniques were brought to Europe in the sixth century AD.[28]

---

21 Hills, 'From Cocoon to Cloth', p. 85; Robert Patterson, 'Spinning and Weaving', in Charles Singer (ed.), *A History of Technology II: The Mediterranean Civilizations and the Middle Ages, 700 BC – 1500 AD* (Oxford: Clarendon Press, 1956), p. 166.

22 Patterson, 'Spinning and Weaving', pp. 166–7.

23 Silk and Rayon Users' Association, *The Silk Book*.

24 Ibid.

25 Claudio Zanier, 'Pre-Modern European Silk Technology and East Asia: Who Imported What?', in Ma (ed.) *Textiles in the Pacific*, p. 113.

26 Schober, *Silk and the Silk Industry*, pp. 1–2.

27 Linus Pierpont Brockett, *The Silk Industry in America: A History* (New York: George F. Nesbitt & Co., 1876), p. 16.

28 Ibid., pp. 15–17.

By the seventeenth century the silk industry was already established in most of Asia as well as in Europe.[29] The production areas were, however, concentrated in only a few regions. Among the most important of the seventeenth and eighteenth centuries were Jiangning, Suszhou and Hangzhou in China; Bengal, Kashmir and Gujarat in India; Levant and Transcaucasia in Persia; Florence, Piedmont, and Lucca in Italy; Lyon and Tours in France; and Spitalfields, Macclesfield and Coventry in England.[30] The fact that the list of significant producers did not alter substantially does not mean that the leaders in the market remained unchanged. Ernest Pariset distinguished the history of the silk industry up to the twentieth century into the ages of Chinese, Arab, Italian and French producers, according to how they were able to adapt to competitive pressures.[31]

Not all producers manufactured the same silk fabrics or achieved the same quality. In the seventeenth and eighteenth centuries Italy and France were at the technological cutting edge of silk production in Europe.[32] Their expertise in the silk production was based on the formation of human capital and on technological innovation. Since the thirteenth century Italy had been the market leader in finished silks as well as in the production of the highest quality raw silk.[33] Italy pioneered new techniques of silk throwing using the flyer-wheel and bobbin as well as water-powered twisting mills.[34] Moreover, a new system of silk reeling was established in Piedmont in the middle of the seventeenth century and it became the leading region for the production of the high-quality silk yarn known as organzine.[35] France established its silk industry in the fifteenth century and due to technological innovations overtook its competitors by the beginning of the nineteenth century.[36] Lyon became known as the silk-weaving capital and set the fashion in Europe.[37]

29 Federico. *Economic History of the Silk Industry*, p. 4.
30 Shelagh Vainker, *Chinese Silk: A Cultural History* (New Brunswick: The British Museum Press, 2004), p. 172; Mark Steele, 'The Comparative Economics of Government and Guild Regulation in the European Silk Industry in the Early Modern Period', in Cavaciocchi (ed.), *La Seta in Europa*, p. 201.
31 Ernest Pariset, *Les Industries de la Soie* (Lyon: Imprimerie Pitrat Aîné, 1890), pp. 299–357.
32 Ibid., pp. 323–48.
33 Zanier, 'Pre-Modern European Silk Technology and East Asia', p. 114.
34 Hills, 'From Cocoon to Cloth', pp. 69, Patterson, 'Spinning and Weaving', p. 207.
35 Zanier, 'Pre-Modern European Silk Technology and East Asia', pp. 142, 146–9; Roberto Davini, 'The History of Bengali Raw Silk as Interplay between the Company Bahadur, the Bengali Local Economy and Society, and the Universal Italian Model, c.1750–c.1830', *Commodities of Empire Working Paper* 6 (2008), pp. 5–7.
36 Mau Chuan-Hui, 'Silk Industry: Technology and Human Capital Formation in France and China' (paper presented at the 'Epstein Memorial Conference: Technology and Human Capital Formation', London, June 2008), pp. 1–2.
37 Luce Boulnois, *The Silk Road* (London: George Allen & Unwin Ltd., 1963), pp. 212–13; Zanier. 'Pre-Modern European Silk Technology and East Asia', p. 118.

France excelled particularly in weaving techniques for figured fabrics, leading to the 1801 invention of the Jacquard loom that revolutionised silk weaving.[38]

In Asia the market leader was China, the cradle of silk culture. China produced silk fabrics primarily for its domestic market but also traded in silk fabrics and raw silk in exchange for metals.[39] The finished silks it produced were highly praised and Chinese silk thread was as valued as that from Piedmont. Up until the seventeenth century China was the leader in technological innovation in the silk industry, which itself acted as a stimulus to European manufacturers to improve their processes.[40] The reeling technology invented as early as during the Song period (960–1127) made China the producer of the finest and thinnest silk thread until the 'Piedmontese revolution' of the seventeenth century.[41] China remained the leader in sericulture close to the eighteenth century and only then did the European silk industry get ahead due to its incorporation of new scientific methods.[42]

Neither India nor Britain had a silk industry at a similar level of development as that in France, Italy or China in the seventeenth and eighteenth centuries. They lagged behind not only in terms of the technologies used but also with regards to the formation of human capital.[43] However, both countries were producing silks for their respective domestic markets. England focused on smaller wares such as ribbons and lower-quality goods. The British silk industry benefited from the immigration of French Protestant silk weavers seeking refuge following the revocation of the Edict of Nantes by Louis XIV in 1685.[44] Nevertheless, during the eighteenth century the industry was not able to keep pace with the technological development of its competitors and had to be sustained by state protection.[45]

This account of producing regions draws attention to two distinctive features of the premodern silk industry. First, in the premodern era Europe did not lag behind Asia in the production of silk textiles and second, Europe achieved this without a sufficient domestic supply of raw silk. Asia, meanwhile,

---

[38] W. English, 'The Textile Industry: Silk Production and Manufacture, 1750–1900', in Charles Singer (ed.), *A History of Technology IV: The Industrial Revolution, c.1750–c.1850* (Oxford: Clarendon Press, 1958), pp. 318–19.

[39] Dennis O. Flynn and Arturo Giráldez, 'Silk for Silver: Manila, Macao-Nagasaki Trade in the 17th Century', in Ma (ed.), *Textiles in the Pacific*, pp. 33–6.

[40] Zanier. 'Pre-Modern European Silk Technology and East Asia', pp. 114–15, 142.

[41] Ibid., pp. 142–7.

[42] Ibid., pp. 110, 142.

[43] Mulberry sericulture was introduced by the Mughals to India only in the fourteenth or fifteenth centuries. D. C. Johnson, 'Silk in Mughal India' (unpublished paper presented at the conference 'Historical Systems of Innovation: The Culture of Silk in the Early Modern World (14th–18th Centuries)', Berlin, December 2010). The fact that the English silk industry lacked human capital can be illustrated by the boost that it experienced thanks to the immigration of French Protestant silk weavers in the late seventeenth century. Frank Warner, *The Silk Industry of the United Kingdom: Its Origin and Development* (London: Drane's, 1921), pp. 35–43; Natalie Rothstein, *Spitalfields Silks* (London: Stationery Office, 1975).

[44] Warner, *Silk Industry of the United Kingdom*, pp. 35–43; Rothstein, *Spitalfields Silks*.

[45] Moira Thunder, *V&A Pattern: Spitalfields Silks:* (London: V&A Publishing, 2011), p. 4.

did possess a significant natural comparative advantage in terms of its climatic conditions as sericulture benefits from a warm temperate climate and also the availability of cheap labour skilled in silkworm rearing. Moreover, as pointed out by Giovanni Federico, the need to feed silkworms fresh mulberry leaves renders the location of sericulture crucial.[46] This allows the expense of transportation, an important part of production costs, to be minimised, while securing a fresh supply of leaves for the worms. Since silkworms are highly susceptible to epidemics, rearing them in scattered peasant houses is advantageous. The best environment is thus a 'densely populated area with dispersed dwellings and few opportunities for non-agricultural work'.[47]

As the techniques for preserving cocoons were unknown prior to the nineteenth century, the next stage of silk production, reeling, was located in the same place as sericulture.[48] Nonetheless, determining factors would be similar. Due to the low value added, both labour and transport costs were decisive.[49] Labout not only has to be cheap, but the workers have to possess manual skills and be attentive in order to produce a high-quality thread.[50]

Trade became an important feature of the global silk industry earlier than in other sectors. Due to the qualities of silks that gave them the title 'queen of fabrics', they were items for which there was a great demand. Their high value and low volume made their transport possible as well as economically viable.[51] These factors made silks one of the first goods to overcome what Fernand Braudel calls the 'tyranny of distance' and become items of long-distance trade.[52] The labelling of the trans-Asian trade route as the Silk Road can be taken as a confirmation of the importance of silks for trade. The combination of a high price and a high demand for silks became an incentive for establishing a silk industry domestically. However, since many regions did not have the climatic conditions favourable for sericulture, the trade in raw silk started to grow.[53] Thus, due to the spread of the silk industry, the market began to be twofold: a demand for raw silk and demand for silk fabrics. Moreover, the establishment of silk industries stimulated a regional trade in silk.

China monopolised the Eurasian trade in silk from the consolidation of

---

46 Federico, *Economic History of the Silk Industry*, pp. 13–15.

47 Ibid., p. 15.

48 The method of drying cocoons developed in the nineteenth century enabled them to be transported long distances; without drying the cocoons are easily spoilt. Claudio Zanier, 'Silk and Weavers of Silk in Medieval Peninsular India' (unpublished paper presented at the conference 'Historical Systems of Innovation', Berlin, December 2010).

49 Federico, *Economic History of the Silk Industry*, pp. 16–18.

50 In this respect the situation was the same in Asia and in Europe. Ibid., p. 20.

51 Ma, 'Great Silk Exchange', p. 1.

52 Fernand Braudel, *Civilization and Capitalism, 15th–18th Century*, vol. 1: *The Structures of Everyday Life* (Los Angeles: University of California Press, 1992), p. 429; Ma, 'The Great Silk Exchange', p. 1.

53 Ibid., p. 4.

the Silk Road up to the rise of silk production in Persia and Byzantium.[54] The development of the latter, in the era of Tang China and Abassaid Persia, marked the partition of the silk trade 'into two rather self-contained trading circuits. While Chinese raw silk or silk fabrics largely went to Japan, Southeast Asia, parts of Central and South Asia, Persian silk (mostly raw silk) became the major supply source for the Middle East, Europe and North Africa.'[55]

Silk and India

The Indian silk industry has a long history; it is supposed that silk culture spread to India from Khotan.[56] The knowledge of mulberry sericulture was later lost and in the pre-medieval period mainly wild or Tussor varieties of silk were used for fabric production.[57] The real boost to the industry came from the Mughals who brought with them the knowledge of silk culture as practised along the Silk Road in Central Asia.[58] Mulberry sericulture was introduced to India in the fourteenth or fifteenth centuries.[59] In the medieval period the centre of sericulture was in Kashmir, but by the seventeenth century the industry was in decline there and Bengal became the new centre. From the middle of the seventeenth century Bengal supplied the whole Mughal Empire from Kabul to Lahore. The silk was, however, of a less fine quality that that produced in Persia, Syria, Sayd or Beirut.[60] The main production regions were found in the Bengal districts of Rungpore, Dinagepore, Purneah and Howrah.[61] Several varieties of wild silk such as atlas, eri, muga and tusser continued to be produced.[62] However, these wild varieties were not suitable for export due to their colour. Tusser silk, for example, is typically a light gold to brown colour but in Europe such a colour was not fashionable. A method of dyeing tussar silk was only developed by Thomas Wardle in the nineteenth century, but until then it was impossible to dye and there was, therefore, no demand for tusser silk in Europe.[63]

---

[54] Ibid., pp. 7–8.

[55] Ibid., p. 8.

[56] Khotan is today the Chinese province of Xinjiang. Federico, *Economic History of the Silk Industry*, p. 3.

[57] Warner, *Silk Industry of the United Kingdom*, p. 378. Throughout this paper, I use the Indian periodisation of the history of the subcontinent where medieval is defined as the pre-Colonial period ending in the mid eighteenth century.

[58] Johnson, 'Silk in Mughal India'.

[59] Sinha, *Development of Indian Silk*, pp. 4–5.

[60] François Bernier, *Travels in the Mogul Empire* (London: W. Pickering, 1826), vol. 1. p. 439.

[61] J. Geoghegan, *Some Account of Silk in India, Especially of the Various Attempts to Encourage and Extend Sericulture in that Country* (Calcutta: Department of Revenue and Agriculture, 1872), p. 2.

[62] Tusser silk can sometimes be referred to also as tasar silk. Brenda King, *Silk and Empire: Studies in Imperialism* (Manchester: Manchester University Press, 2005), p. 70.

[63] Brenda M. King, 'The Transformation of Tusser Silk' (paper presented at the conference: 'Textile History of America Symposium', Lincoln, Nebraska, January 2004), pp. 285–6.

India was also an important producer of woven silk fabrics. Among the famous Indian silk products were carpets, velvet pavilions, satins, taffetas and patolas.[64] The main centre for silk weaving during the seventeenth and eighteenth centuries was Gujarat but it was also practised in Kasimbazar and Benares.[65] Although some woven silks were exported, such as those from Gujarat to Southeast Asia through the entrepôt of Malacca, silk textiles were produced primarily for the domestic market.[66] Indian goods, silks among them, were brought by the Moors to Europe in the fourteenth and fifteenth centuries.[67] Fresh interest in Indian silk came with the rise of the European trading companies and in particular the Dutch and English East India companies who soon recognised trade in silks as a viable commercial opportunity. When the European trading companies arrived in India, the market for Kasimbazar silk was already well developed and its silk was traded within the Mughal Empire and across Asia. The Dutch East India Company (VOC) was the first among the trading companies to import raw silk to Europe.[68] With the growth of the English silk industry in the seventeenth century the English East India Company (EEIC) increased its efforts in obtaining supplies of raw silk from India, and by the end of the century drove the VOC out of the market.

The EEIC had been interested in silk since the start of trading in the Indian Ocean, but 'the Company did not at first estimate Bengal silk so much as those of Persia, China, Japan, Siam, and Cochin-China'.[69] The Company's commercial interest in Bengal raw silk dated back to the breakdown of the negotiations between Sir Thomas Roe and the Sophy of Persia in 1617, which had aimed to secure for the EEIC the monopoly in the trade of Persian silk.[70] The trade in Bengal raw silk was promoted from 1675 when the well-known Company servant Streynsham Master was sent to India with the specific task of obtaining information about the ideal variety of raw silk to be bought in the Bay of Bengal, the best season and method for buying silk, and the weight

64   Sinha, *Development of Indian Silk*, p. 5.
65   Ibid., pp. 5–7; K. N. Chaudhuri, *The Trading World of Asia and the English East India Company, 1660–1760* (Cambridge: Cambridge University Press, 1978), p. 345.
66   King, *Silk and Empire*, pp. 66–7.
67   Rawlley, *Economics of the Silk Industry*, p. 23.
68   Ibid., p. 25. The quality of Bengal silk did not match the standard demanded in Europe. Thus, to improve the quality of Bengal raw silk, over 80 per cent of the imported silk had to be reeled in the Company's own reeling workshop. Irfan Habib, *The Agrarian System of Mughal India 1556–1707* (New Delhi: Asia Publishing House, 1963), p. 57; Om Prakash, *The Dutch East India Company and the Economy of Bengal, 1630–1720* (Princeton: Princeton University Press, 1985), pp. 55–7, 219; Roberto Davini, 'Una Conquista Incerta. La Compagnia Inglese delle Indie e la Seta del Bengala, 1769–1833' (unpublished Ph.D. thesis, European University Institute, 2004), p. 15.
69   L. Liotard, *Memorandum on Silk in India, Part 1* (Calcutta: Superintendent of Government Printing, 1883), p. 18.
70   Geoghegan, *Some Account of Silk in India*, p. 1.

of raw silk and its price.[71] The legislation of 1699 prohibiting the importation of Indian silks into England and the Acts of 1700 and 1720 prohibiting the wearing of finished silks imported from Asia, all curtailed the Company's opportunities for legally importing finished silk fabrics into Britain.[72] The EEIC continued trading in silk fabrics though most of them were legally re-exported, particularly to the North American colonies.[73] However, the Company did not seem to ascribe such importance to the trade in silk fabrics as it did to the trade in raw silk.[74]

Trading raw silk had its specific characteristics as it is not a raw material but a semi-manufactured commodity. Until the nineteenth century, cocoons could not be stored or transported without becoming spoiled.[75] The most basic method of processing cocoons is to reel them into a silk thread which is also referred to as raw silk. Silk thread is too fine to be used for weaving and it has to be first thrown into silk yarn.[76] Therefore, when the EEIC was exporting raw silk that was to be used by the English silk-weaving sector, it was exporting a processed product. It was this stage of production that made the trade in Bengal silk so challenging as the sericultural and silk-reeling methods used in India rendered the silk thread too coarse and uneven, and thereby limited its use by European silk weavers to the production of small articles of haberdashery.[77]

Global Leaders in the Raw Silk Market in the Early Modern Period

Since this book focuses on the attempts of the English East India Company to improve the quality of Bengal raw silk to match the best-quality silks on the market – raw silk from Italy and China – it is necessary to emphasise the

---

[71] Streynsham Master, *The Diaries of Streynsham Master, 1675–1680*, ed. Richard Temple (London: J. Murray, 1911), p. 204.

[72] Chaudhuri, *Trading World of Asia*, p. 344. Prior to 1757 the Company was interested in both wrought and raw silk, and only after that date did it start to focus mainly on raw silk. Indrajit Ray, 'The Silk Industry in Bengal during Colonial Rule: The "De-industrialisation" Thesis Revisited', *Indian Economic Social History Review* 42 (3), 2005, p. 340.

[73] Rothstein, *Spitalfields Silks*, pp. 1–2. In theory, all the imported silk fabrics were re-exported. However, evidence shows that in some periods there was a large amount of smuggling and illegal sales of silk. Ray, 'Silk Industry in Bengal during Colonial Rule', pp. 344–5, 359–64.

[74] Initially the aim of the EEIC's policy was to maintain a balance between the imports of finished silks and raw silk. Among the silk textiles exported from the Bengal district of Kasimbazar were taffetas and coloured silks such as banhus, printed handkerchiefs, phulikats, dharies, etc. Chaudhuri, *Trading World of Asia*, p. 344.

[75] It was not until the nineteenth century that a technique for the preservation of cocoons was developed. Zanier, 'Silk and Weavers of Silk'.

[76] Hills, 'From Cocoon to Cloth', p. 67.

[77] Goldsmiths' Library (hereafter GL), 1796 fol. 16654, *Considerations on the Attempt of the East-India Company to Become Manufacturers in Great Britain* (London: n.p., 1796), p. 21; GL, 1795 fol. 16280, *Reports of the Committee of Warehouses of the East-India Company relative to Extending the Trade on Bengal Raw-Silk* (London: n.p., 1795), p. 13; Chaudhuri, *Trading World of Asia*, p. 346.

factors that gave these regions their competitive edge. Advanced technology, a long tradition of sericulture and institutions that encouraged the production of high-quality raw silk were the elements that underpinned their leadership.

In China, silk culture had a long tradition: silk was already being produced some five or six thousand years ago and China retained its technological leadership in silk production until the nineteenth century.[78] The development of Chinese silk-reeling methods as well as the development of sericulture was encapsulated in the voluminous work of Dieter Kuhn. What Kuhn's and other works on the Chinese silk industry show is that China benefited from a long-term familiarity with raw silk production techniques. It can be argued that these benefits were similar to those that gave India its advantage in producing cottons. As in the Indian cotton industry, the technical knowledge of Chinese artisans and peasants lay at the heart of the production of high-quality silk threads and fabrics. However, the Chinese silk industry did not rely solely on the tacit intergenerational diffusion of knowledge, as contemporary 'best practice' was repeatedly codified. It was argued by Gaines K. C. Liu that 'the Chinese have developed a set of nomenclature which is definite and specific as in any modern science'.[79]

From early on the knowledge of the best methods of sericulture was codified with the aim of putting it into practice. The first books on the technology of sericulture and on other stages of silk production, as compiled by official authorities as well as by private individuals, were published in the thirteenth and fourteenth centuries. Records show that some of these books were widely distributed, which implies that the knowledge of 'best practice' was disseminated.[80]

Gaines K. C. Liu emphasised the importance of the codification for creation and dissemination of the knowledge of production techniques. In particular, codification ensured that the processes of sericulture and silk reeling were performed with great precision in spite of being carried out by peasants in rural areas. Chinese peasants and artisans thus benefited from knowledge gleaned from centuries of sericulture and, although living 'by traditions and experiences, they know when their work should be started, how it should be done, and what to expect under normal conditions'.[81]

Among the most important works was the *Book of Agriculture* which includes

---

[78] Peng Hao, 'Sericulture and Silk Weaving from Antiquity to the Zhou Dynasty', in Dieter Kuhn (ed.), *Chinese Silks* (New York: Yale University Press, 2012), p. 66.

[79] Gaines K. C. Liu, 'The Silkworm and Chinese Culture', *Osiris* 10, 1952, p. 165. The knowledge was codified in several treatises, among which the most important are the classical references: the *Fu on Silkworm* by Sun Ching; the *Tsan Ching* by Liu An; the *Chi Ming Yao Shu* by Chia Sheh; the *Tsan Sa* by Ch'in Kuan; the *Keng Chi Tu* by Lou Shou; the *Nung Sang Chi Yao* by the Ministry of Agriculture of the Yuan Dynasty; the *Tsan Sang Hoh Pien* by Wan Chi. Ibid., p. 185.

[80] Zhao Feng, 'Silk Artistry of the Yuan Dynasty', in Kuhn (ed.), *Chinese Silks*, pp. 330–1.

[81] Liu, 'Silkworm and Chinese Culture', p. 177.

an explanation of grafting techniques. The application of grafting enabled the cultivation of new varieties of mulberries with a greater yield of leaves.[82] The *Compilation on Agriculture and Sericulture* describes methods of silkworm cultivation: the way to determine the quantity of mulberry leaves the worm necessitates, the time the worm needs to grow in different environments, and the maximum density at which silkworms could be kept, and also identifies the factors that could negatively affect the silkworms. *Exploitation of the Works of Nature* presents guidelines on how to 'select breeds of silkworms, cure silkworm disease, raise mulberry trees and silkworms and collect cocoons'.[83]

The accumulated knowledge about sericulture was very specific about the practices of silkworm egg selection and the treatment of eggs and silkworms. It contained methods of feeding, regulating the transformation of silkworms into moths and methods securing the uniform development of caterpillars. Feeding was especially emphasised as 'caterpillars will not pupate unless they have consumed the necessary amount of leaves they need and the longer the period of feeding, the less silk will be produced'.[84] The Chinese also developed methods of crossbreeding silkworms and of force-cropping. To summarise, the knowledge the Chinese accumulated about sericulture enabled peasants to produce the high-quality cocoons necessary to produce high-quality silk thread.

Apart from setting the best practices in sericulture, the Chinese were at the cutting edge of silk-reeling technologies. The methods of silk reeling were also codified: both Dieter Kuhn and Zhao Feng mention *The Farmer's Essentials* published during the Yuan period (1271–1368). This book emphasises that the aim of reeling is the production of a 'silk thread fine, round, even, and of proper tension, so that it is without contractions, remissness, knots, and lumps'.[85] According to Kuhn this quotation also characterised the objective for which the various silk-reeling devices were constructed, that is to achieve the most efficient production of high-quality silk thread.[86] From the technological point of view, Chinese reeling methods were the most advanced on the market until the Piedmontese revolution in the seventeenth century. Among the most significant inventions was a reeling frame invented in the Song period (960–1127), which allowed the Chinese to produce a silk thread thinner and finer than anywhere else in the world.[87]

[82]   Zhao Feng, 'Silk Artistry of the Yuan Dynasty', p. 331.
[83]   Chen Juanjuan and Huang Nengfu, 'Silk Fabrics of the Ming Dynasty', in Kuhn (ed.), *Chinese Silks*, p. 374.
[84]   Liu, 'Silkworm and Chinese Culture', p. 182.
[85]   As cited in Dieter Kuhn, 'Textile Technology: Spinning and Reeling', in Joseph Needham (ed.), *Science and Civilization in China: Chemistry and Chemical Technology* (Cambridge: Cambridge University Press, 1988), vol. 5, part 9, pp. 339–40.
[86]   Ibid., pp. 354–5.
[87]   Zanier, 'Pre-Modern European Silk Technology and East Asia', p. 144.

Not all raw silk was reeled using the Song reeling frame: local practices and economic necessity gave rise to a plenitude of silk-reeling frames.[88] The development of highly sophisticated silk-reeling frames represents evidence of the advancement of Chinese reeling technologies. However, these frames were not accessible to all: according to Kuhn 'only the well-to-do [silkworm breeders] could afford highly mechanised silk-reeling frames'.[89] Most silk was produced in peasant families as it was a typical cottage-industry item. Peasants without access to reeling frames used hand-driven reels to produce lower-quality tsatlees and natives, or they stored or sold their cocoons.[90] Kuhn pointed out that peasants could also have hired reeling frames from their landlords. According to Kuhn, many of the small-scale producers, incentivised by the higher price they could get for reeled silk, preferred to hire high-quality reeling devices than to produce tsatlees or sell cocoons.

Peasants in China had strong incentives for producing silk. It was a significant item of tax payment throughout Chinese history: payment in silk was one of the most important means of making a payment in kind.[91] Second, China had a flourishing commercial market in silk, which promised high potential earnings.[92] Moreover, silk was the most important Chinese export item in the premodern period and the Ming dynasty (1368–1644) promoted silk production through tax reform. Dennis O. Flynn and Arturo Giráldez have argued that 'by commuting tax payments exclusively to payment in silver the Ming "Single Whip" tax reform indirectly mandated the production of export items which were acceptable in exchange for silver on the international markets'.[93] For Chinese peasants, silk was the most easily produced export item and government fiscal policy thus provided a 'powerful driving force' for silk production. In general, a better grade of silk attracted a higher price and it can be inferred, therefore, that peasants were incentivised to favour quality in production.

Overall, Chinese sericulture and silk reeling differed markedly from the Italian silk industry. Whereas the Chinese silk industry achieved its pre-eminence without the stringent organisation of production and the emergence of institutions focused on the enforcement of quality, it was precisely these factors that secured Italy its superiority in the European silk industry. Although both China and Italy relied on silk production to accumulate tax revenues and bullion, in China silk production was promoted indirectly. Raw silk as well as silk fabrics were produced mostly by peasants and techniques were applied due to the widespread knowledge of 'best

---

88   Kuhn, 'Textile Technology', p. 351.
89   Ibid.
90   Tsatlees or natives were uneven and elliptical silk threads. Ibid., p. 337.
91   Ibid., pp. 285–9.
92   Ibid., pp. 288–9.
93   Flynn and Giráldez, 'Silk for Silver', p. 36.

practice', which was transferred from generation to generation as much as it was formally codified.

Silk culture spread to Italy in around the twelfth century. The methods of sericulture and silk reeling developed largely independently from China.[94] Unlike in China, sericulture became a rural venture only in the seventeenth century, while silk reeling remained an urban activity.[95] The growth of the Italian silk-weaving industry was the main impetus for developing sericulture and silk-reeling technologies from the twelfth to the sixteenth century.[96] For several centuries Italy was at the forefront of high-quality silk fabric production, and the development of sericulture and silk reeling was essential to provide a silk thread of a suitable quality for weaving.

The technologies developed and knowledge accumulated led Pariset to label the fifteenth and sixteenth centuries as the age of Italy in silk production.[97] Italy's pre-eminence continued until the late eighteenth century when it was overtaken by France, with the exception of the production of raw silk. Its leadership of the industry can be attributed to climatic conditions, the stringent organisation of production and the quality control that was characteristic for all stages of Italian silk production. The works of Luca Molà, Carlo Poni, Claudio Zanier and Mauro Ambrosoli on the Italian silk industry all illustrate the influence of guilds over silk production.[98] The guild's power was typically enforced by the Italian city-states, which relied on silk exports to generate customs revenue.[99] Moreover, special institutional arrangements emerged to protect trade secrets and to enforce quality standards.

Italian states competed with each other in silk production and 'secrets of technical practices were jealously guarded'.[100] The extent of the protection went so far that in Bologna, for instance, revelation of Bolognese technological secrets could be penalised by death.[101] Institutional arrangements were created in an attempt to regulate the creation and diffusion of knowledge. Carlo Belfanti, in his discussion of the laws and regulations that were created by Italian states and guilds in order to reward and safeguard invention,

---

[94]   There is evidence that silk reeling developed independently from at least the seventeenth century, Zanier, 'Pre-Modern European Silk Technology and East Asia', p. 153.

[95]   Davini, 'History of Bengali Raw Silk', p. 6; Carlo Poni, 'Comparing Two Urban Industrial Districts: Bologna and Lyon in the Early Modern Period', in Pier Luigi Porta, Roberto Scazzieri and Andrew S. Skinner, *Knowledge, Social Institutions and the Division of Labour* (Cheltenham: Edward Elgar, 2001).

[96]   Davini, 'History of Bengali Raw Silk', p. 6.

[97]   Pariset, *Les Industries de la Soie*, p. 422.

[98]   Molà, *Silk Industry of Renaissance Venice*; Poni, 'Comparing Two Urban Industrial Districts'; Mauro Ambrosoli, 'The Market for Textile Industry in Eighteenth Century Piedmont: Quality Control and Economic Policy, *Rivista di Storia Economica* 16 (3), 2000, pp. 343–64.

[99]   For instance: ibid., p. 344.

[100] Poni, 'Comparing Two Urban Industrial Districts', p. 204.

[101] Ibid., p. 204.

mentions in several instances the arrangements adopted in the Italian silk industry.[102] Among these were guild rules binding its members to secrecy, bureaucratic processes to evaluate innovations, recruitment of specialised labour, or the granting of patents.[103] Various institutional innovations also emerged to regulate the quality of the product, whether raw silk or silk fabric.

Regulation of production was a characteristic of the Italian silk industry: Carlo Poni, for example, argues that in Bologna silk production was organised in industrial districts and the whole 'network of production was controlled and coordinated by a few merchant-manufacturers'.[104] In Bologna, quality enforcement became central to the whole process of silk production. Not only were weaving, dyeing and finishing regulated, but even the trade in cocoons.[105] Although they were were produced in the countryside, cocoons had to be sold exclusively in the city market which was controlled by guild rules and the city authorities, as well as by the pope.[106] In order to enforce quality standards, reeling became an urban activity in Bologna.[107] Thanks to these institutional arrangements Bologna was producing the high-quality raw silk necessary for the Bolognese silk-throwing mills.

In the case of Bologna in the 1780s and 1790s the institutional regulation of the processes of silk production became the source of the decline in competitiveness. In some centres of the Italian silk industry, for instance in Piedmont, reeling became a rural proto-industrial activity in the seventeenth and eighteenth centuries.[108] Reallocation of reeling to rural areas reduced the labour costs but in Bologna, however, such a development was constrained by guild and city regulations, and Bologna's competitiveness decreased. However, this should not be seen simply as a case of undercutting competition by resorting to the use of cheap proto-industrial labour. As pointed out by Carlo Poni, the key to the declining competitiveness of the Bolognese silk industry was not regulation per se but rather the lack of institutional innovation, which would have enabled the industry to adapt.[109] After all, the highest level of institutional control of silk production processes was most probably achieved in Piedmont, the producer of the most sought-after raw and thrown silk in Europe.[110]

---

102 Carlo Belfanti, 'Guilds, Patents, and the Circulation of Technical Knowledge: Northern Italy during the Early Modern Age', *Technology and Culture* 45 (3), 2004, pp. 570–2.

103 Ibid., pp. 574, 576–8.

104 Poni, 'Comparing Two Urban Industrial Districts', p. 201.

105 Guild regulation of weaving, dyeing and finishing processes was common in most European industries. Production of thread was typically less regulated.

106 Poni, 'Comparing Two Urban Industrial Districts', p. 204.

107 Ibid., pp. 204–5.

108 Davini, 'History of Bengali Raw Silk', p. 6; Poni, 'Comparing Two Urban Industrial Districts', p. 211.

109 Ibid.

110 Ambrosoli, 'Market for Textile Industry', pp. 344, 346; William Aglionby, 'Of the Nature

Raw and thrown silk from Piedmont in the Kingdom of Savoy gradually gained such a reputation for its high quality that the state began to focus solely on their production. The Kingdom of Savoy oriented its economic policy on silk exports and developed a system in support of silk production. Contemporary traders, technicians, politicians and writers on economics from all over Europe attributed Piedmontese success to superior reeling technology. However, as Claudio Zanier recently pointed out, Piedmontese leadership in raw and thrown silk production would be impossible without the host of changes in sericulture, in the training of labour, and in the organisation of production, which were implemented following the innovation of reeling machinery in the seventeenth century – the so-called Piedmontese reeling revolution.[111] In Piedmont, technological and institutional competition went hand in hand and in this way it managed to draw on what Carlo Poni calls the 'key to successful competition'.[112]

The Silk Industry in the Nineteenth Century

To obtain a full understanding of the nineteenth-century Bengal raw silk industry, it is also necessary to consider developments in raw silk production and export markets. The nineteenth century marked a new wave of intensive technological changes in all stages of the silk industry, the spread of silk weaving to new regions (most notably to the USA), the growth of new markets for raw silk and an increase in exports of raw silk as well as finished silks. Giovanni Federico has shown that between 1820 and 1920 the quantity of silk traded grew twentyfold.[113] The main silk-weaving and raw silk-importing countries were Britain, France, Germany, Switzerland and the USA. The leading regions for raw silk production were Italy, China and Japan, accounting for about two-thirds of raw silk production and exports in the period 1850–1930.[114] The silk industry spearheaded industrialisation in both Europe and Asia as factory production techniques and inanimate power (water or steam) were applied on a large scale, especially in silk reeling, from the second part of the nineteenth century.[115] The Bengal raw silk industry was sidelined in this period as it was unable to respond to the technological

of Silk, as It is Made in Piedmont', *Philosophical Transactions* 21 (1699), p. 184.; Zanier, 'Pre-Modern European Silk Technology', p. 114; Davini, 'History of Bengali Raw Silk', pp. 4–5.

[111] Zanier, 'Pre-Modern European Silk Technology and East Asia', p. 139.

[112] Poni, 'Comparing Two Urban Industrial Districts', p. 211.

[113] Federico, *Economic History of the Silk Industry*, p. 4.

[114] Debin Ma, 'The Modern Silk Road: The Global Raw-Silk Market, 1850–1930', *Journal of Economic History* 56 (2), 1996, p. 331.

[115] Ibid., pp. 334–5.

changes, capture new export opportunities or even retain its European markets.[116]

The technological and organisational changes in the system of silk production and trade occurred within the framework of a transportation and communication revolution, which facilitated an unprecedented level of market integration in the global raw silk market. Although transportation costs constituted only a small percentage of the value of raw silk, the spread of steam-powered shipping, the opening of the Suez Canal and the development of telegraph communications, all decreased the transaction costs of international trade.[117] In the case of the raw silk trade, the reduction in information costs enabled the characteristics of raw silk to be matched to the demands of weavers in the importing countries. Moreover, besides the flow of goods and information about export markets, the flow of knowledge and technology facilitated the modernisation of raw silk production in East Asia.

The nineteenth-century silk industry was characterised by a remarkable level of mutual adaptation and technological complementarity among both raw silk production and silk-weaving regions. The most notable is the case of the mutual adaptation in sericulture and silk reeling in Japan and silk weaving in the USA. As pointed out by Debin Ma, it was a case of market integration of commodities, technologies and institutions.[118] The main US centre of silk weaving was in Paterson, New Jersey, whose expansion had been facilitated by the migration of English silk weavers.[119] Economic history literature has shown that high wages in the USA incentivised the adoption of labour-saving technologies, which in the case of silk weaving meant the use of power looms.[120] This made possible the employment of women and children as unskilled labour, as power looms relied on operator skills to a much lesser extent than was the case with handlooms. Even though silk woven by power looms was of a lower quality, this was not a problem in a market such as the USA, with a ready demand for cheaper, standardised silk textiles. The key issue was to acquire raw silk of a standardised quality – a coarser thread of high strength and flexibility – which was able to withstand the pressure of power loom weaving. This was exactly what the Japanese raw silk producers

---

[116] This becomes apparent from the quantitative data on imports of Bengal raw silk as well as the description of production techniques. See for instance: *East India Products, Part II: Reports on the Silk Industry in India and on the Supply of Timber in the Burmah Markets* (London: George Edward Eyre and William Spottiswoode, 1874).

[117] Ma, 'Modern Silk Road', pp. 337–9.

[118] Ibid., p. 342.

[119] Richard D. Margrave, 'Technology Diffusion and the Transfer of Skills: Nineteenth-Century English Silk Migration to Paterson', in Philip B. Scranton (ed.), *Silk City: Studies in the Paterson Silk Industry, 1860–1940* (Newark: New Jersey Historical Society, 1985), pp. 9–34.

[120] For a discussion of the role of factor endowments for technology paths in the US see: John Habakkuk, *American and British Technology in the Nineteenth Century: The Search for Labour-Saving Inventions* (London: Cambridge University Press, 1962).

were able to supply. Japan was a newcomer to the raw silk export trade, entering the market in the 1850s, starting to export machine-reeled silk from the 1870s and expanding the production of machine-reeled silk from the 1890s.[121] Its success was based on the adoption and adaptation of European silk-reeling technologies. The competitiveness of the Japanese silk industry was also boosted by the outbreak of the pebrine disease which wiped out European raw silk production in the 1840s and 1850s.[122]

Until the late 1870s most of the raw silk produced in Japan was hand-reeled, although a small number of Western-style filatures existed, reeling silk according to the Italian method.[123] The first steam filature – the Tomioka Model filature – was established in 1870 by French experts on behalf of the Japanese government which was concerned by the poor quality of Japanese silk.[124] The filature was set up according to French standards, machinery was imported from France and neither the machinery nor management of the filature was adapted to the Japanese environment. Due to a lack of modification the success of the technology transfer was initially marred by the unprofitability of the Tomioka filature.[125] Filatures built subsequently introduced several alterations: for example they were smaller and equipped with wooden machines made in Japan, operated by water instead of steam power and which produced thicker silk; they also introduced longer working hours and night shifts, as well as a wage-incentive system.[126] The diffusion of the filature system was not instantaneous and hand-reeled rivalled machine-reeled silk until 1890, but declined dramatically after 1900.[127] The switch to machine reeling helped to enforce standardisation of the quality of the reeled silk, a feature of key importance for utilisation in US machine weaving. Experimentation in sericulture was a further factor that was key to the rise of Japanese raw silk production. Japan developed a summer–fall rearing technology that made it possible to rear silk outside of instead of during the

---

[121] By 1900 the share of hand-reeled silk was below 10 per cent of total exports. Debin Ma, 'Between Cottage and Factory: The Evolution of Chinese and Japanese Silk-Reeling Industries in the Latter Half of the Nineteenth Century', *Journal of the Asia Pacific Economy* 10 (2), 2005, p. 198.

[122] Pierre Cayez, *L'industrialisation Lyonnaise au XIXe siècle: du grand commerce à la grande industrie* (Lille: Universite de Lyon II, 1977), pp. 558–9; Ma, 'Modern Silk Road', p. 332. Claudio Zanier, 'Japan and the "Pébrine" Crisis of European Sericulture during the 1860s', *Bonner Zeitschrift für Japanologie* 8, 1986, pp. 51–63.

[123] Yukihiko Kiyokawa, 'Transplantation of the European Factory System and Adaptations in Japan: The Experience of the Tomioka Model Filature', *Hitotsubashi Journal of Economics* 28 (1), 1987, p. 30.

[124] Ibid., p. 27.

[125] Lillian M. Li, 'Silks by Sea: Trade, Technology, and Enterprise in China and Japan, *Business History Review* 56 (2), 1982, p. 206.

[126] Kiyokawa, 'Transplantation of the European Factory System', pp. 32–3.

[127] Ma, 'Between Cottage and Factory', p. 198.

main agricultural harvest season, which facilitated the spread of sericulture.[128] The key breakthrough was the adoption of the F1 hybrid silkworm, as this meant a standardisation of the silkworm variety and therefore also of the raw silk. In addition, the introduction of the F1 hybrid led to an increase in sericultural productivity. Furthermore, the fact that all farmers were rearing the same variety of silkworm facilitated the spread of best practice in sericulture and created an environment conducive for an efficient inspection network.[129] The shift towards standardisation in sericulture and silk-reeling practices in Japan were of great importance for the development of the American silk-weaving industry.

The position of China as the leader in innovations in sericulture and silk reeling was eroded in the nineteenth century when pre-eminence switched to Europe, namely to France and Italy. The advances of the Italian tavelle and French Chambon systems included the shift of silk reeling into silk mills, the use of silk-reeling machines and the adoption of steam power for heating water in basins.[130] China did not keep pace with these innovations: only after the Opium Wars, and the forceful opening of the Chinese market, were European technologies adopted. Modernisation in silk reeling started only in the 1860s and the diffusion of European silk-reeling technologies was slow. Silk reeling thus remained a cottage industry producing hand-reeled silk until the 1900s. Yet the silk industry still became one of the first sectors to adopt modern industrial technologies and approaches. Chinese hand-reeled silk was not suitable for US machine weaving and the vast majority of Chinese raw silk was exported to France, where the French silk-weaving industry could make use of it thanks to the continued use of hand-looms. This was due to the fact that the French silk industry continued to focus on the manufacture of luxury items of high quality and sumptuous patterns, which could not be produced with power looms. At the same time the use of hand-looms made it possible to weave Chinese raw silk that was not of a uniform quality but whose grades and characteristics reflected the non-standardised process of hand-reeling.[131]

The ascendency of China and Japan in the global raw silk market was facilitated also by the outbreak of the pebrine disease in the first part of the nineteenth century. The pebrine disease was first recorded in 1845 in France,

[128] Li, 'Silks by Sea', p. 201.

[129] Ma, 'Why Japan, Not China', pp. 375–7.

[130] It should not be assumed that the silk-reeling machines were very sophisticated. In comparison with other industries, silk manufacture was less capital intensive. The main reasons for the mechanisation and centralisation of silk reeling continued to be quality enforcement and the need to minimise reeling costs, as cocoons were expensive and represented 85–75 per cent of the final price of raw silk. Federico, *Economic History of the Silk Industry*, pp. 18–20 and 112–20.

[131] Ma, 'Modern Silk Road', pp. 333–5; Li, 'Silks by Sea', p. 196.

and by 1865 affected all the raw silk producing regions of Europe with the effect that total annual cocoon production was reduced from 21,000 tonnes during 1846–52 to 7,500 tonnes in 1856.[132] Such a silk famine in Europe made the importation of raw silk from Asia, which was as yet unaffected, become a matter of survival for the European silk-weaving industry. Moreover, as the pebrine disease devastated the European stock of silkworms it also became necessary to import silkworms from Asia in order to revive sericulture in Europe. The spread of the disease was checked only in 1870 when Louis Pasteur suggested a mother moth examination method to stop the spread of the protozoan microsporidian parasites causing the disease.[133] Pasteur's discovery reinforced the use of scientific methods in sericulture in Europe and in Asia. The subsequent recovery of European sericulture was slow, while French raw silk production never resumed its leading position, making French silk weaving dependent on imports. In Italy the process of recovery was much more successful, such that in the period 1873 to 1875 Italian raw silk constituted over 30 per cent of the world total of raw silk exports.[134]

Conclusion

In the early modern period the undisputed leaders in the production of raw silk were Italy and China. Indian production methods lagged behind those of China and Italy. Both the Chinese and Italian silk technologies were highly advanced and allowed for the production of very high-quality thread that was round, fine, smooth and of a high strength, with each skein containing only threads made of the same number of filaments. Early-modern silk technologies were among the most advanced in respect of mechanisation and organisation of production. Water-powered silk-throwing mills had been used in Italy since the sixteenth century and factory production methods took root in silk reeling in the seventeenth century. By the nineteenth century, Italian and now also French silk technologies shifted manufacture even further towards the use of inanimate power and centralisation of production. By the late nineteenth century similar technologies were also adopted in China and Japan, and at the same time sericulture started to employ scientific methods. The goal of such innovative technologies was to produce raw silk of a standardised quality which could be easily utilisable in power loom weaving.

By the late nineteenth century the raw silk export market was dominated by China, Italy and Japan. Since dried cocoons are bulky and heavy, raw silk

---

[132] R. Govindan, T. K. Narayanaswamy and M. C. Devaiah, *Pebrine Disease of Silkworm* (Bangalore: University of Agricultural Sciences Bangalore, 1997), pp. 1–4.

[133] Ibid., pp. 35–6.

[134] Federico, *Economic History of the Silk Industry*, p. 36.

continued to be exported in reeled form in the nineteenth century.[135] The differing technological demands of silk weaving in the major silk-weaving regions of the nineteenth century indicates that, despite the transportation and communication revolutions that enabled a high level of integration of the global raw silk market, the degree of substitutability and complementarity of raw silk was limited.[136] Therefore, matching the quality and price of the raw silk to the demand from silk-weaving regions was the key to success in the global raw silk market, and the adoption of technologies matching both the factor endowments at home and the quality requirements of export markets was necessary. In Japan this was achieved thanks to the modernising efforts of the Meiji government and the active role of merchant networks in facilitating change.[137] In China, raw silk production and the procurement of hand-reeled raw silk were organised by Western entrepreneurs.[138] Italy retained its leadership in raw silk production and continued to produce the highest-quality silk. Moreover, Italian raw silk production was also the most productive in the world, carried out by small companies financed by foreign, and especially British, capital.[139]

[135] Ibid., p. 11.

[136] Ma, 'Modern Silk Road', pp. 345–7.

[137] This was shown by the Yokohama wholesalers in particular, who acted as agents of change in the Japanese silk industry providing credit, managing the co-operatives of small-scale producers and imposing standardisation measures. Li, 'Silks by Sea', pp. 214–16.

[138] Ma, 'Between Cottage and Factory', pp. 201–2.

[139] Federico, *Economic History of the Silk Industry*, pp. 130–1, 166–7.

Chapter 2

EMPIRE, THE ENGLISH EAST INDIA COMPANY, AND BENGAL RAW SILK

> [A]ccording to the most considerable Traders and Manufacturers; it appears that the staple of the Bengal Silk is in quality equal to, and would answer all the purposes of, the Italian or Spanish sorts, if reeled in the same manner, so as to render it easier to wind, and to work with less waste; and that, with such advantages, it would sell at a much higher price than at present [...], but if it would wind and Reel as fast as the Piedmont and Italian Sorts, 500 Bales would not be too much for this market, and fetch from 25 to 30 per cent more than it sells for at present, and the lower letters proportionably; even those of D and E might be so perfectly manufactured for answering the uses of the Spanish and Calabria Silk, as to increase 20 per cent on the present price; and no quantity would be too large for sale here.[1]

The history of the British silk industry is inextricably linked with the importation of raw silk. Climatic conditions in Britain do not allow for the rearing of silkworms, thus the rise of silk weaving in the seventeenth century gave an impetus to raw silk imports. Before the late nineteenth century, raw silk came primarily from the Mediterranean, Turkey and Persia. The fact that domestic production prevented the outflow of bullion and gave employment opportunities to the poor, guaranteed silk weaving a privileged position and support from government. The steady demand for raw silk and government backing for the importation of raw silk from the colonies underpinned the English East India Company's interest in Bengal raw silk. Furthermore, the Company needed to expand Indian exports to Britain in order to transfer its Indian Diwani revenues and meet its financial obligations in London.

This combination of factors underlaid the EEIC's perception that Bengal raw silk was one of 'the choicest goods', and induced the Company to become a silk manufacturer in Bengal.[2] This chapter argues that the interest in Bengal

---

1   India Office Records and Private Papers (hereafter IOR) IOR/E/4/619, 31 January 1770, pp. 653–5.
2   IOR/E/4/621: 'Bengal Despatches, 24 November 1772', p. 380.

raw silk was aided by changes to the EEIC's finances in the aftermath of the Battle of Plassey (1757) and the acquisition of the Diwani of Bengal, Bihar, and Orissa (1765). It also argues that the promotion of silk was informed by the British government's support of its domestic silk industry: the government was keen to secure supplies of raw silk from colonial settlements and promoted various initiatives in this respect.

The creation of the Company's 'Bengal Silk Enterprise' can be placed among the 'attempts to improve the quantity and quality of goods in order to transfer the Diwani revenues to Britain'.[3] Following Huw Boven's argument, this book asserts that the EEIC's Bengal silk industry venture was part of a strategy directed at remitting revenues from territorial acquisitions through an increase in the volume of goods imported into Britain.[4] The importance that was attributed to the expansion of the silk trade is conveyed in the East India Company's correspondence and documents in which raw silk was ascribed the status of one of the 'choicest' piece goods with potentially large returns for the Company.[5]

In order to bring the attempts of the EEIC into a broader perspective this chapter first considers the British market for raw silk and second, the initiatives to introduce silk processing in other parts of the British Empire. Third, it examines the changes to the Company's finances after 1765 when the EEIC gained the rights to tax Bengal, and fourth, it considers the factors that facilitated the Company's interest in expanding the trade in Bengal raw silk. The chapter concludes by exploring the role of mercantilism in facilitating the Company's commitment to its Bengal silk venture.

The British Market for Raw Silk

The British silk industry is often equated with Spitalfields silk weaving. In spite of the fame that the Spitalfields industry attained between 1730 and 1760 and the scholarly attention it has received over the past two generations of historians, the majority of British silk production was of a lower quality in comparison with other world producers and was mostly focused on small items rather than high-quality cloth.[6] Nonetheless, silk yarn and manufactures

---

3   Huw V. Bowen, *Revenue and Reform: The Indian Problem in British Politics, 1757–1813* (Cambridge: Cambridge University Press, 1991), p. 21.

4   Huw Bowen, 'Investment and Empire in the Later Eighteenth Century: East India Stockholding, 1756–1791', *Economic History Review* 42 (2), 1989, p. 189; The importance of the import trade for repatriating wealth from India is also recognized by Anthony Webster, 'The Political Economy of Trade Liberalization: The East India Company Charter Act of 1813', *Economic History Review* 43 (3), 1990, p. 408.

5   For instance IOR/E/4/621: 'Mr Wiss, Superintendent of Silk Trade, in Bengal Despatches, 24 November 1772', pp. 379–80.

6   Spitalfields' reputation was made by the accomplished work of designers such as Joseph

were among the seven principal British exports in the second half of the seventeenth century.[7]

The typology of the wares produced underpinned the demand for raw silk in the British market. Whereas broad weaving called for silk thread of the highest quality (in most cases the threads needed to be thrown into organzine before they could be used), most of the British silk-weaving industry only needed medium-quality raw silk.[8] The silk required was to be neither too fine nor too coarse and had to be easily workable – that is, without the need to re-reel it prior to use. This is also reflected in the quotation at the start of the chapter, in which the Company considers the production of silk of all varieties. The most basic division of raw silk on the British market was made according to its fineness, with A being the most fine and E the most coarse.[9] The Company's orders for raw silk consignments in the late eighteenth century reveal that only 11 to 17 per cent of silk sent to London from Bengal was to be of the highest grade, and show a robust demand for raw silk of B and C fineness.[10] Thus, the EEIC did not necessarily need to produce the finest raw silk in Bengal, but that of a quality good enough to produce small wares.

The British silk industry was primarily a producer of medium- to low-quality silks and specialised in smaller wares of haberdashery such as ribbons, trimmings, buttons, handkerchiefs, gloves, hosiery, stockings, galloons, and bandannas; fabrics such as bombazines, crapes and gauzes; and sewing silk.[11] In the eighteenth century, the principal silk-manufacturing

Dandridge, John Vansommer, Christopher Baudouin, James Leman and Anna Maria Garthwaite. Natalie Rothstein, *Spitalfields Silks* (London: Stationery Office, 1975), pp. 1–2. See also: Frank Warner, *The Silk Industry of the United Kingdom: Its Origin and Development* (London: Drane's, 1921), p. 42; Natalie Rothstein, 'The Silk Industry in London, 1702–6' (unpublished M.A. thesis, University College London, 1961); Natalie Rothstein, *Silk Designs of the Eighteenth Century: In the Collection of the Victoria and Albert Museum, London* (London: Thames and Hudson, 1990); and Gail Malmgreen, *Silk Town: Industry and Culture in Macclesfield 1750–1835* (Hull: Hull University Press, 1985), p. 8.

7   B. R. Mitchell, *British Historical Statistics* (Cambridge: Cambridge University Press, 1988), pp. 469–70.

8   The quality of raw silk was extremely important in determining the quality of the final product – silk cloth or smaller wares such as ribbon. Luca Molà has mapped out the variety of different types of raw silk used in the Italian silk industry in the early modern period. Molà also points to the fact that raw silk was divided into several classes according to the region it came from, as well as according to its quality. Luca Molà, *The Silk Industry of Renaissance Venice* (Baltimore: Johns Hopkins University Press, 2000), pp. 55–6.

9   The literature on the European silk industry mentions different systems of categorising the quality of silk so this classification was probably not the only one. Luca Molà for instance points to the fact that silk was divided into categories according to the region of origin and several other characteristics. Ibid.

10   IOR/E/4/640, 25 June 1793, p. 518; IOR/E/4/645A, p. 339.

11   Warner, *Silk Industry of the United Kingdom*, p. 42; Malmgreen, *Silk Town*, p. 8; D. C. Coleman, *Courtaulds: An Economic and Social History*, vol. 1: *The Nineteenth Century Silk and Crape* (Oxford: Clarendon Press, 1969), p. 23.

regions were London, Norfolk, Dorset, the Midlands, Cheshire, Lancashire and Staffordshire. In London, Spitalfields was a major centre of manufacture focusing principally on the production of broad textiles. The West Midlands region, and Coventry especially, focused instead on the production of ribbons, Cheshire on mixed fabrics and Norwich on the production of bombazines and crapes. Moreover, Macclesfield was a centre of silk throwing, while Lancashire produced ribbons.[12]

The climatic conditions of the British Isles would not allow the cultivation of mulberry trees and silkworm rearing. The British silk industry was therefore totally dependent on imports of raw silk. In the early eighteenth century most of the lower-quality raw silk was procured from Turkey, Spain and Portugal and used in the manufacture of smaller wares. Silk from Turkey, for instance, was used in the production of damasks, galloons and stockings.[13] The best-quality raw silk was imported from Italy, from where Britain also imported thrown silk as only Italian raw or thrown silk was used in broad weaving.[14] High-quality Chinese silk was also imported as it was appreciated for its whiteness and was used principally in the production of hosiery and gloves.[15] Bengal raw silk, by contrast, was considered to be of the lowest quality to be found on the market and its use prior to the 1770s was limited.[16]

Despite the fact that the consumption of silk textiles had already spread beyond the elites in the late Middle Ages, and silk started to be consumed by wider social strata, the quality of silk thread still played a key role.[17] The quality of the thread was regulated by market demand, not by a state-imposed institutional framework or by guilds.[18] Silk thread necessary for dress accessories such as bonnets, hats, gloves, belts, stockings and shoes – items also in common use among the less wealthy – did not need to be made of

[12] Gerald B. Hertz, 'The English Silk Industry in the Eighteenth Century', *English Historical Review* 24 (96), 1909, p. 714; Jean-François Fava-Verde, *Silk and Innovation: The Jacquard Loom in the Age of the Industrial Revolution* (Ebook: Histancia, 2011), p. 6.

[13] Hertz, 'English Silk Industry', p. 711.

[14] Goldsmiths' Library (hereafter GL), 1796 fol. 16654, *Considerations on the Attempt of the East-India Company to Become Manufacturers in Great Britain* (London: n.p., 1796), pp. 12, 18, 31. The best-quality thrown silk came from the region of Piedmont and was called organzine. Hertz, 'English Silk Industry', p. 711, Coleman, *Courtaulds: An Economic and Social History*, pp. 16–17.

[15] Dionysius Lardner, *A Treatise on the Origin, Progressive Improvement, and Present State of the Silk Manufacture* (Philadelphia: Carey & Lea, 1832), p. 68.

[16] Ibid., p. 67.

[17] For the changing pattern in consumption of finished silks see: Beverly Lemire and Giorgio Riello, 'East & West: Textiles and Fashion in Early Modern Europe', *Journal of Social History* 41 (4), pp. 890–2.

[18] Such an approach was taken by the French and English governments in the eighteenth century, but only with regards to finished products. Philippe Minard, Pierre Gervais and Judith Le Goff, 'Colbertism Continued? The Inspectorate of Manufactures and Strategies of Exchange in Eighteenth-Century France', *French Historical Studies* 23 (3), 2000, p. 479; William J. Ashworth, 'Quality and the Roots of Manufacturing "Expertise" in Eighteenth-Century Britain', *Osiris* 25 (1), 2010, pp. 238–44.

such high-quality thread as that required for broad weaving.[19] Yet, in spite of the specialisation of the eighteenth-century British silk industry in the production of smaller wares rather than on the highest-quality broad silks, the Company's focus on increasing the quality of the Bengal thread was well reasoned. Without quality improvements, the Company-imported silk could not gain a higher market share because its use remained limited. Even in the production of haberdashery, a certain standard of silk quality was necessary such that it was ready to be used without needing to be reworked prior to throwing and reeling.[20]

Both thrown and raw silk were imported into Britain. Raw silk was cheaper and its importation was favoured by tariffs lower than those levied on thrown silk, but it needed to be thrown into yarn before it could be used.[21] British weavers either bought thrown silk directly on the foreign market or imported raw silk and had it thrown into yarn in mills outside London.[22] According to Gerald B. Hertz, some 947,000 lbs. of raw silk were thrown per annum in Britain in the period from 1785 to 1812.[23] In spite of the increasing quantity of raw silk thrown in Britain, the manufacture of silk cloth and other products was not without problems. First, there were issues with the quality of raw silk available for throwing. Second, the sector often experienced fluctuations in the demand for thrown silk. In the 1720s, Britain lost access to the best-quality raw silk available on the market – Piedmontese raw silk, which

19 John Styles has shown that haberdashery made of silk was commonly worn by the lower social classes in eighteenth-century England. See John Styles, *The Dress of the People: Everyday Fashion in Eighteenth-Century England* (New Haven: Yale University Press, 2007), pp. 30–2; John Styles, 'Clothing the North: The Supply of Non-Élite Clothing in the Eighteenth-Century North of England', *Textile History* 25 (2), 1994, pp. 155–6. Apart from haberdashery, the production of mixed textiles also used silk thread of a lower quality. For instance, the Italian silk industry had started producing waste and second-choice silks from the fifteenth century despite the practice being treated unfavourably by guild officials. Molà, *Silk Industry of Renaissance Venice*, pp. 90, 163–7.

20 RSA/SC/EL/2/31. *Third Report of the Committee of Warehouses of the East-India Company relative to Extending the Trade on Bengal Raw-Silk* (London: n.p., 1795), pp. 6–7, 11–14. Although a switch to the production of lower-quality and more affordable silk occurred in broad weaving as the competition from printed cotton textiles negatively affected demand for silk textiles, the major shift came only in the second part of the nineteenth century. At the same time, demand for a comparatively lower-quality silk thread to be used in broad weaving increased in conjunction with the rise of the American silk manufacturing sector. The US-made silk textiles were not of as high a quality as European silks and were intended for consumption by the middle classes. Lemire and Riello, 'East & West', pp. 890–2; Debin Ma, 'The Great Silk Exchange: How the World was Connected and Developed', in Debin Ma (ed.), *Textiles in the Pacific, 1500–1900. The Pacific World: Lands, Peoples and History of the Pacific, 1500–1900* (Aldershot: Variorum, 2005), pp. 24, 26; Kazuko Furuta, 'Silk-Reeling in Modern East Asia: Internationalization and Ramifications of Local Adaptation: In the Late 19th Century', in Ma (ed.), *Textiles in the Pacific*, pp. 207, 210–11.

21 Coleman, *Courtaulds: An Economic and Social History*, pp. 18–19.

22 Fava-Verde, *Silk and Innovation*, p. 6.

23 Hertz, 'English Silk Industry', p. 721.

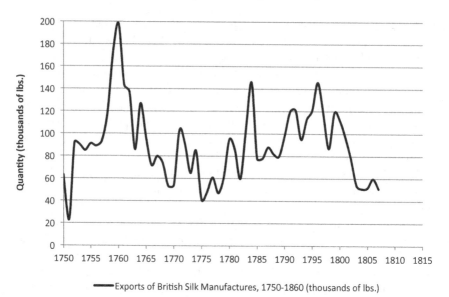

Figure 2.1   Exports of British silk manufactures, 1750–1808

Source: Data adapted from B. R. Mitchell, *British Historical Statistics* (Cambridge: Cambridge University Press, 1988), p. 364.

had the highest fineness and strength, lustre and uniformity of threads.[24] Without access to Piedmontese raw silk, the silk yarn thrown in British mills could never compete with thrown silk produced in Italy. Since British broad weaving – which required the highest-quality silk – was only a small part of the entire British production this might not seem to be such a setback. The real problem was that mechanised throwing necessitated the input of a raw silk of a standardised quality; although lower-quality silk, e.g. silk of a lesser fineness, was sufficient for weaving ribbons and smaller wares, silk threads of uneven strength frequently broke when being thrown in mechanised mills. The issue with lower-quality silk was the lack of standardisation of the quality of silk threads: for instance, threads made of a different number of filaments

---

[24] The decision of the King of Savoy to ban exports of Piedmontese raw silk to Britain was in retaliation for the setting up of a hydraulic silk-throwing mill in Derby by the Lombe brothers in 1718. John Lombe obtained the designs of the technology in Italy illegally and his story became one of the best-known cases of premodern industrial espionage. GL, 1795 fol. 16280, *Reports of the Committee of Warehouses of the East-India Company relative to Extending the Trade on Bengal Raw-Silk* (London: n.p., 1795), p. 2; Lardner, *Treatise on the Origin*, p. 62; S. R. H. Jones, 'Technology, Transaction Costs, and the Transition to Factory Production in the British Silk Industry, 1700–1870', *Journal of Economic History* 47 (1), 1987, pp. 75–7; Giuseppe Chicco, *La Seta in Piemonte 1650–1800: Un Sistema Industriale d'Ancien Régime* (Milan: Franco Angeli, 1995), pp. 71–96.

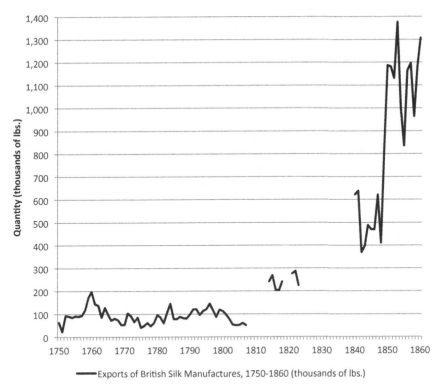

Figure 2.2   Exports of British silk manufactures, 1750–1860

Source: Data adapted from B. R. Mitchell, *British Historical Statistics* (Cambridge: Cambridge University Press, 1988), pp. 364–5.

were mixed in one bale of silk or the threads were of a low strength.[25] These factors made throwing such silk in mills built according to the Piedmontese model difficult, and had a negative impact overall on the quality of thrown silk as well as on the efficiency of mill throwing. Complaints about the quality of silk threads and their frequent breakages were common, especially for Bengal raw silk.[26]

Silk throwing was also negatively affected by periods of stagnation in silk weaving. Figure 2.1 shows the fluctuation in exports of British silk manufactures. After a stagnation period lasting from the 1720s to the 1750s, the industry went through a phase of expansion in the 1760s as the British silk industry captured most of the French trade in silk during the Seven Years War (1756–63). The slump that occurred once peace was established could only be overcome by a prohibition of the import of all foreign silks and

---

25   This was due to poor-quality cocoons or ineffective reeling methods.
26   IOR/E/4/627, 12 July 1782, p. 351; IOR/E/4/625, 9 April 1777, p. 175.

velvets.[27] Unfortunately, the stagnation of the industry could not be reversed and low levels of production and exports continued until the 1810s.[28] Figure 2.2 shows the considerable growth of the industry after the 1810s, and most particularily in the 1850s.

The stagnation of the British silk-weaving industry obviously also had negative consequences for the demand for raw silk. However, this was not the sole factor that negatively affected the demand for Bengal raw silk. The quality of Bengal silk remained the main issue throughout the eighteenth and nineteenth centuries. First, in the beginning of the eighteenth century not all of the Bengal raw silk was of a quality high enough to be used even in the production of small wares. Moreover, some of the Bengal silk was not easily workable because it needed to be re-reeled before use. The ease with which Italian silk could be used was one of the reasons for its popularity.[29] For the Company this signified that, without changes to production methods, Bengal raw silk would not gain a higher market share in Britain.

Initiatives to Introduce Silk-Processing Technologies in the British Empire

The attempt to introduce new methods of silk reeling into Bengal was not an isolated experiment. Trading companies and settler organisations such as the Trustees for the Establishment of the Colony of Georgia and the Virginia Company were keen to adopt sericulture and silk-processing technologies in other parts of the British Empire, especially in North America. All such attempts were supported by the British government through exemption on tariffs etc. – thus attesting its interest in securing imports of raw silk from overseas dependent territories. It is important to perceive the English East India Company's attempts to expand imports of Bengal raw silk to Britain in the framework of other initiatives because the Company's plan was guided by a similar logic. At the same time, however, the attempt to introduce new silk-processing technologies to Bengal has a special role in the history of silk technology transfers to the British colonies. In comparison with attempts to adopt sericulture and silk reeling in North America, silk production in Bengal was successful. Moreover, it was the only project that was carried out in a country already producing raw silk.

The first attempt to promote the overseas production of raw silk for the market took place in the seventeenth century and was initiated by James I in 1623.[30] The plan and the king's involvement in it was described by L. P.

---

[27]   Coleman, *Courtaulds: An Economic and Social History*, p. 18.
[28]   Ibid., p. 20.
[29]   GL, 1796 fol. 16654, *Considerations*, pp. 3, 12–13.
[30]   Hertz, 'The English Silk Industry, p. 716. Attempts to produce raw silk in England and its colonies were among the 'new agricultural projects' initiated in the sixteenth and seventeenth

Brockett: 'he [James I] sent over the mulberry trees and the silk-worm eggs, and directed the company who were managing the colony to follow up his order by suitable legislation'.[31] In spite of encouragement in the form of financial rewards for planters producing silk and fines for those failing to cultivate mulberry trees, the project was unsuccessful. In comparison with tobacco production, silk was less profitable and the project of promoting raw silk production in Virginia was abandoned.[32]

Georgia was another of the several North American colonies that introduced raw silk production. According to Ben Marsh, the trustees advertised their keen interest in cultivating silk (together with wine) in order to appeal to the British Parliament and public, and gain support and funding for the setting up of the colony.[33] Marsh contends that in the first few years after the Georgia colony was established, the trustees devoted considerable effort and funding to the implementation of silk production. The biggest challenge they faced was to secure a labour force not only willing to take up silk production but skilled enough for the task.[34] To attract workers, the trustees offered financial, technological and educational support as well as salaries, bounties and bonuses.[35] They also imported equipment and specialist literature, and institutionalised apprenticeship.[36] In spite of these efforts, the experiment turned out to be unsuccessful in the long term. Georgia lacked labour sufficiently skilled in silk production to succeed and by the 1780s sericulture was practically extinct. Growing mulberry trees proved to be in competition for land with rice and corn cultivation. Furthermore, knowledge of sericulture and silk reeling never became widespread in Georgia.[37]

Attempts to adopt silk production were also made in South Carolina and Connecticut in the eighteenth century. The silk produced in South Carolina was supposed to be of a very high quality: Brockett argued in the nineteenth century that its raw silk was 'said by Thomas Lombe ... to have been equal

---

centuries. Joan Thirsk, *Economic Policy and Projects: The Development of a Consumer Society in Early Modern England* (Oxford: Oxford University Press, 1978), p. 7; Charles E. Hatch Jr, 'Mulberry Trees and Silkworms: Sericulture in Early Virginia', *Virginia Magazine of History and Biography* 65 (1), 1957, p. 3.

31   Linus Pierpont Brockett, *The Silk Industry in America: A History* (New York: George F. Nesbitt & Co., 1876), p. 26.

32   Hatch, 'Mulberry Trees and Silkworms', pp. 4–5, 9, 50–61.

33   Ben Marsh, *Georgia's Frontier Women: Female Fortunes in a Southern Colony* (Athens and London: University of Georgia Press, 2007), p. 53.

34   James C. Bonner pointed to the fact that labour was generally scarce in Georgia and that sericulture could rely on the cheaper labour of women and children was considered an advantage. However, the workforce in Georgia lacked a knowledge of sericulture. James C. Bonner, 'Silk Growing in the Georgia Colony', *Agricultural History* 43 (1), 1969, pp. 143–4.

35   Ibid., p. 144.

36   Marsh, *Georgia's Frontier Women*, p. 55.

37   Ibid., pp. 56, 59–61; Bonner, 'Silk Growing in the Georgia Colony', p. 144.

or superior to any of the Italian'.[38] In Connecticut, silk production was taken up in the 1750s and was supported by bounties towards mulberry cultivation. Silk production was attempted in various other places in North America, such as New Jersey, New York, Delaware and Maryland. However, none of these places became important producers of raw silk.[39] These attempts either failed altogether or, at best, silk production was carried out on a small scale as a domestic manufacture until it finally disappeared in the middle of the nineteenth century.[40]

According to Hertz, attempts to establish raw silk production in the American colonies failed because of high wages. Hertz points to the fact that both nominal and real wages were higher than in Italy – the main European producer of reeled and thrown silk.[41] Slave labour could not be used because of the skills required. Ben Marsh argues that the high costs of labour combined with a lack of knowledge of sericulture and silk reeling were the prime reasons for the failure of raw silk production in Georgia.[42] Similar explanations for the lack of success were also given by Brockett, yet he also draws attention to the competitive pressures to which silk production was subject in the colonies. In Virginia, silk had to compete with tobacco cultivation, and in Georgia with cotton and agricultural crops.[43] Moreover, both Brockett and James C. Bonner observed that the export trade was badly affected by the War of Independence, which left the American silk producers without a market.[44]

Another factor that undermined silk processing in North America was 'imperfect reeling'. Problems with the quality of reeled silk were experienced in most areas of silk production in the world, perhaps with the exception of Italy and China. This was the result of technological issues, principal–agent problems, and the low quality of cocoons. Often two or more of these factors were present simultaneously, as for example in Bengal. It has been argued that in North America the problem lay principally in reeling, as noted by Brockett when he observed that the cocoons were excellent but that the reeling was

---

38 Brockett, *Silk Industry in America*, p. 29.
39 Nelson Klose, 'Sericulture of the United States', *Agricultural History* 37 (4), 1963, pp. 225–34.
40 Brockett, *Silk Industry in America*, pp. 34–5.
41 Hertz, 'English Silk Industry', p. 718. He agrees with John Habakkuk's thesis that the high wages and labour scarcity induced the adoption of labour-saving technologies in antebellum America. John Habakkuk, *American and British Technology in the Nineteenth Century: The Search for Labor-Saving Inventions* (London: Cambridge University Press, 1962), pp. 4–11.
42 Marsh, *Georgia's Frontier Women*, pp. 56–61. The importance of having access to cheap labour in order to succeed in raw silk production was also pointed out by Giovanni Federico, *An Economic History of the Silk Industry, 1830–1930* (Cambridge: Cambridge University Press, 1997), pp. 14–15.
43 Brockett, *Silk Industry in America*, pp. 28–9; Marsh, *Georgia's Frontier Women*, p. 56.
44 Brockett, *Silk Industry in America*, pp. 28–9; Bonner, 'Silk Growing in the Georgia Colony', p. 147.

very poor.[45] The inferior standard of reeled silk had a damaging effect on the quality of woven textiles and was thus frequently addressed as a matter of priority. In most of North America, reeling was carried out using a hand-reel. In Georgia, attempts were made to introduce innovations in silk reeling and the trustees there relied mostly on acquiring the necessary knowledge of silk processing from Italian immigrants. Among the people entrusted to promote silk production in Georgia was Pickering Robinson, a silk specialist who was later commissioned by the EEIC to supervise the adoption of Piedmontese silk-reeling technology in Bengal.[46] In spite of the support, attempts to innovate silk-reeling technologies ultimately failed. The failure attests to the difficulties presented by setting up silk production in areas of the New World. All these attempts to adopt silk-processing technologies in the American colonies also attest to the importance given to supplying the British silk-weaving sector with raw silk produced in areas either directly or indirectly dependent on the British Crown. Both the trading and settler companies followed mercantilist reasoning and made silk production one of the goals of their policies. The British government supported these efforts directly by supplying mulberry trees and silkworms, and more frequently indirectly by exempting raw silk from duties.[47]

The English East India Company's Finance and Bengal Raw Silk after Plassey

The key factor that influenced the EEIC's decision to invest in silk manufacturing was the need to transfer revenues from Bengal through the export of goods. When Lord Clive won the Battle of Plassey (1757) and secured control over Bengal and later the Diwani of Bengal, Bihar and Orissa (1765), everyone expected new fortunes to be made by the Company.[48] However, the transfer of bullion back to England was logistically difficult and bills of exchange could only be used in a limited way. Therefore the export trade became the major vehicle for transferring revenues to Europe.[49] In order to achieve this, the Company relied on the expansion in the trade of items called 'the choicest goods': raw silk, raw cotton, textiles, and indigo.

The acquisition of the Diwani, or in other words the right to collect land rents, customs duties, exclusive privileges, fines and forfeits, presented

45   Brockett, *The Silk Industry in America*, p. 32.
46   Marsh, *Georgia's Frontier Women*, p. 60.
47   In 1749 an Act was passed through Parliament which exempted raw silk from Carolina and Georgia from export duties. Ibid., p. 28.
48   The assumption of the Diwani presented the Company with the right to collect land rents, customs duties, farms of exclusive privileges, fines and forfeits. House of Commons, 'Fourth Report of the Secret Committee', *Reports from Committees of the House of Commons*, 1715–1801 (1) IV, 1803, p. 95.
49   Huw Bowen, 'Lord Clive and Speculation in East India Company Stock, 1766', *Historical Journal* 30 (4), 1987, p. 909.

the Company with a new source of revenue.[50] It thus altered the financial structure of the Company. It is difficult to assert the extent to which the Company financed its investment in the procurement of export goods from its territorial revenues. However, bullion shipments might be taken as an indicator of the change that took place. The Company traditionally relied on bullion shipments to finance the purchase of goods in Asia, and in the period 1708–60 bullion made up to 75 per cent of the value of all of the Company's exports to Asia.[51] By contrast, in the decade from 1762 to 1772, it amounted to only 23 per cent on average.[52] According to Om Prakash, in the post-1760 period the purchase of piece goods in India and China was financed primarily from the Diwani revenues and with bills of exchange.[53] Bills of exchange were 'rupee receipts obtained against bills of exchange payable in London or elsewhere' and were used by the Company employees in India to transmit to Europe the fortunes made in private trade.[54] As for the Diwani revenues, Om Prakash contends that 'it would seem impossible to work out on a systematic basis what proportion of the total exports of the English East India Company in the post-1765 era would have been financed from the Bengal revenues', though he concludes that 'it would have been substantial'.[55]

The major change in the system of EEIC finance was that the Bengal territorial revenues were used for the purchase of export goods. However, it needs to be pointed out that the Company remained dependent on profits from the export trade because the Diwani revenues could not be used as ready money. Huw Bowen and others have argued that expanding the Company's exports to Europe became an essential instrument for transferring the territorial revenue surplus to Britain.[56] The Company workers in India were repeatedly ordered to increase the purchase of exportable goods, particularly raw silk, indigo and textiles, as it was claimed that 'the Company through this Channel may have the benefit of receiving as a large a proportion of the Bengal Revenues as circumstances will possibly admit of'.[57] Huw Bowen goes further by arguing that after 1765 'the financial wellbeing of the Company was balanced on a knife-edge'.[58] At home the liabilities to the stockholders were rising due to

---

[50]   House of Commons, 'Fourth Report of the Secret Committee', p. 95.
[51]   Bowen, *Revenue and Reform*, p. 111.
[52]   Ibid.
[53]   Om Prakash, 'The English East India Company and India', in Huw V. Bowen, Margarette Lincoln and Nigel Rigby (eds), *The Worlds of the English East India Company* (Rochester, NY: Boydell Press, 2002), pp. 10–12.
[54]   Ibid., p. 10.
[55]   Ibid., p. 12.
[56]   Bowen, 'Investment and Empire', p. 189; Webster, 'Political Economy of Trade Liberalization', p. 408.
[57]   'The Directors to the President and Council of Bengal, 20 November 1767', as cited in Bowen, 'Lord Clive and Speculation', p. 909.
[58]   Bowen, 'Investment and Empire', p. 189.

an increase in dividend payments. Moreover, among the home charges were also interests on home bond debt, charges on East India House and Board of Control, and payments on the account of Her Majesty's Troops and establishments, and the Company also had liabilities to the government in the form of customs and duty payments.[59] These liabilities served as a powerful incentive for the EEIC to expand the export trade from Asia to Europe.

The precarious balance of the Company's finances became apparent in 1772. Since 1757, when the Company had come into possession of the Diwani, it had paid the British government £400,000 annually and also paid high dividends to its stockholders. These sums were paid on the understanding that the Company's Indian territorial revenues would surpass its costs. Not only were the estimates 'unduly optimistic', but the Company also encountered a series of unforeseeable circumstances.[60] Lucy S. Sutherland names among these the higher military costs due to French aggression and the trade depression in Bengal that was exacerbated by the 1769–70 famine, and increases in administrative costs.[61] Among the Company's Indian expenses were charges incurred in collecting tax revenue, military and naval charges, civil, judicial and police charges, investment in public works and interest on bond debt in India.[62] In 1771, over £1 million in bills of exchange were drawn in London by the Company's employees.[63] Moreover, in the same year it lost another £1 million in the tea trade.[64] Combined with a general credit crisis, the Company suddenly became unable to meet its short-term liabilities and defaulted.

In response to this crisis, the Company decided to focus on expanding the trade in goods and to decrease its Bengal expenditures:

> However, bad and disagreeable as our situation is, it behoves us to take the most eligible Methods to yield the future Supplies and those appear to us to be a reduction of our Civil and Military Experience in India, and the procuring

---

[59]   Bhimrao R. Ambedkar, 'Administration and Finance of the East India Company' (unpublished M.A. thesis, Columbia University, 1915), p. 16; Bowen, 'Investment and Empire', p. 190.

[60]   Lucy Sutherland, *The East India Company in Eighteenth-Century Politics* (Oxford: Clarendon Press, 1952), p. 225.

[61]   Ibid.

[62]   Ambedkar, 'Administration and Finance of the East India Company', p. 15; John F. Richards, 'The Finances of the East India Company in India, c. 1766–1859', *London School of Economics Working Papers* 153 (11), 2011, p. 19. See also: John F. Richards, 'Fiscal States in Mughal and British India', in Bartolomé Yun-Casalilla and Patrick O'Brien (eds), *The Rise of Fiscal States: A Global History, 1500–1914* (Cambridge: Cambridge University Press, 2012), pp. 410–42.

[63]   IOR/E/4/621: 'Mr Wiss, Superintendent of Silk Trade, in Bengal Despatches, 24 November 1772', p. 379.

[64]   Ibid. The Company's tea trade in the 1760s and 1770s was negatively affected by competition with Dutch East India tea smuggled into Britain and by the political changes in the North American colonies, mainly the boycott of tea imports.

a large and ample Investment in the choicest Piece Goods that the Country of Bengal can produce that are proper for the Europe market, with the largest returns in raw silk that are possible.[65]

Among the items in which investment was promoted were indigo, raw cotton, cotton textiles and raw silk. The focus on each of these commodities was underpinned by specific factors. Indigo production was encouraged in response to the market opportunity represented by the loss of colonial supplies from South Carolina in the 1780s and by the later interruption of supplies from Saint Domingue in 1791 due to the slave rebellion.[66] Cotton textiles were important for the re-export trade and were exported to the Atlantic and African markets.[67] Raw cotton and opium were used to buy tea in China. The importance of China trade increased and it became an essential source of profits.[68]

What connects the attempts at enlarging exports of the aforementioned goods is the Company's effort to match their quality to the demands of the export markets. Such steps were often essential, as Huw Bowen observes: 'there was no point in importing commodities into Britain if nobody wished to buy them'.[69] In this respect, the most thorough attempt to match quality to international demand was undertaken in the silk industry.

Bengal Raw Silk as One of the 'Choicest Goods'

The EEIC had high expectations about its venture into the production of raw silk in Bengal. The importance ascribed to the silk industry is summed up by George Williamson, a former employee of the EEIC in Bengal, when he observed that: 'the possession of the Dewanny making the company anxious to increase the silk investment in order to get home the surplus revenue'.[70] It was thought that the new method of reeling would bring quality improvements to the Bengal silk thread which would result in a 25 per cent increase

---

[65] Ibid., pp. 379–80.

[66] J. R. Ward, 'The Industrial Revolution and British Imperialism, 1750–1850', *Economic History Review* 47 (1), 1994, p. 49.

[67] Huw Bowen, *Business of Empire: The East India Company and Imperial Britain, 1756–1833* (Cambridge: Cambridge University Press, 2006), p. 238. The Company's re-export trade in textiles suffered a blow during the American War of Independence.

[68] Ashin Das Gupta, 'India and the Indian Ocean in the Eighteenth Century', in Uma Das Gupta (ed.), *The World of the Indian Ocean Merchant, 1500–1800: Collected Essays of Ashin Das Gupta* (Oxford: Oxford University Press, 2001), p. 214; Michael Greenberg, *British Trade and the Opening of China, 1800–1842* (Cambridge: Cambridge University Press, 1951), pp. 5–17.

[69] Bowen, *Business of Empire*, p. 236.

[70] GL, 1775 fol.: George Williamson, *Proposals Humbly Submitted to the Consideration of the Court of Directors, for Affairs of the United Company of Merchants of England, Trading to the East-Indies: For Improving and Increasing the Manufactures of Silk in Bengal* (London: n.p., 1775), p. 13.

Table 2.1   Sale value and freight cost of the English East India Company's
commodities traded to Britain, March 1804 to September 1808

Goods	Sale value (£)	Freight cost (£)	Proportion of freight-to-sale value (%)
Bengal raw silk	1,603,663	59,411	3.7
Piece goods	4,073,587	508,400	14.2
Spice	185,279	33,326	18.0
Cinnamon	381,822	69,893	18.0
Drugs, etc.	665,877	315,913	47.4
Sugar	937,648	669,123	71.4
Saltpetre	900,092	650,697	72.3
Total	8,747,968	2,306,823	26.4

Source: IOR/L/PARL/2/55, 'Supplement to the Fourth Report on the Affairs of the
East India Company, Appendix No. 47, 1808–12', p. 138.

in its price on the British market.[71] Such anticipation was fuelled by the
outstanding reputation of the Italian methods of reeling that had made the
Piedmontese silk the most sought-after and the most expensive raw silk on the
European markets.

This chapter argues that the EEIC's decision to become a silk manufacturer was influenced by several factors. The Company's expectation for silk to
be one of the 'choicest goods' was supported by the value of the freight-to-
sale ratio (percentage of the cost of freight of raw silk). Table 2.1 shows that
with a mere 3.7 per cent freight-to-sale cost, raw silk was the most profitable
commodity per freight unit.[72] Extending the trade in raw silk also seemed
a reasonable move because this commodity was already an important part
of Bengal's exports. K. N. Chaudhuri's data for the 1750s shows that raw
silk represented 9.4 per cent of the value of the EEIC's Bengal exports and
was the second most important item in the Bengal export trade after cotton
cloth.[73] Moreover, the Company's interest was facilitated by the British
government's support of the domestic silk-weaving industry. As the British
silk industry lacked a source of domestic raw silk and faced competition from

71 IOR/E/1/61, fols 486–487v: 'Letter 240 James Wiss in London to the Court Outlining the
    Advantages of the Italian Method of Spinning Silk in Bengal, 18 November 1777', p. 487.
72 Although, the data refers to the 1800s there is no reason to believe that the proportions were
    significantly different in the previous decades.
73 The export of textiles from Bengal accounted for more than 85 per cent of the total on
    average. K. N. Chaudhuri, *The Trading World of Asia and the English East India Company,*
    1660–1760 (Cambridge: Cambridge University Press, 1978), pp. 510, 534.

the superior silk production of France, it could only be sustained through protective legislation.[74]

The British silk industry was supported by three of the key mercantilist measures identified by Adam Smith: the import of silk fabrics was curtailed by prohibitions or duties; the importation of raw silk was encouraged through reductions in import duties; and measures encouraging the export of British silk fabrics were put in place.[75] Never a leader in international markets from the seventeenth to the beginning of the nineteenth century, British silk products were, however, among the principal export goods of the British Isles. The weaving sector was dependent on imports of raw silk and its consumption was far from trivial. Mitchell's historical statistics show that in the 1750s and 1760s, raw silk was quantitatively the most important raw material imported into Britain.[76] This explains why the British government was keen to secure supplies of raw silk from colonial settlements by differentiating import duties. As Table 2.2 shows, import duties on Bengal raw silk were lower than those imposed on Chinese or Italian raw silk in the periods 1750–65 and 1801–23.

A further factor that incentivised the Company to invest in silk was the growth of intra-Indian trade. Huw Bowen has pointed to the fact that the second half of the eighteenth century saw a significant expansion of the intra-Asian trade.[77] The expansion of the so-called 'country trade' served the financial and commercial needs of the Company. Instead of importing bullion in order to pay for goods destined for the European market, the EEIC procured those export goods in exchange for Asian goods demanded in particular Asian markets. The best-known example of the intra-Asian trade is the imports of opium and raw cotton from India into China in exchange for tea.[78] The EEIC therefore used Bengal raw silk in the intra-Indian trade in

---

[74]   Moira Thunder, *V&A Pattern: Spitalfields Silks* (London: V&A Publishing, 2011), p. 4; Coleman, *Courtaulds: An Economic and Social History*, p. 14; Malmgreen, *Silk Town*, pp. 8–9.

[75]   Adam Smith, *An Inquiry into the Wealth and Poverty of Nations* (State College, PA: University of Pennsylvania, 2005); Raymond L. Sickinger, 'Regulation or Ruination: Parliament's Consistent Pattern of Mercantilist Regulation of the English Textile Trade, 1660–1800', *Parliamentary History* 19 (2), 2000, pp. 225–8.

[76]   Mitchell, *British Historical Statistics*, p. 463.

[77]   Huw V. Bowen, 'British Exports of Raw Cotton from India to China during the Late Eighteenth and Early Nineteenth Centuries', in Giorgio Riello and Tirthankar Roy (eds), *How India Clothed the World: The World of South Asian Textiles, 1500–1850* (Leiden: Brill, 2009), pp. 115–17.

[78]   Bengal raw silk was exported mainly to the Malabar and Coromandel coasts. The value of Bengal raw silk traded there in 1805 was 2,055,594 sicca rupees (£222,689). When compared with data from Figure 2.1, it means that less than 10 per cent of the whole production of raw silk in Bengal was exported to Malabar and Coromandel coasts. However, data by William Milburn might not be totally reliable as in many cases it does not match the Company's statistics. The important information produced by Milburn is the geographical distribution of trade rather than its quantities. William Milburn, *Oriental Commerce* (London: Black, Perry & Co., 1813), vol. 2, pp. 138–9. For country trade see: Das Gupta, 'India and the Indian

Table 2.2   Import duties on raw and thrown silk imported into Britain, 1704–1823

	Raw silk				Thrown silk
	China	**Bengal**	**Italy**		
1704–47	2s. 6d.	1s. 3d.	11d.	1704–47	3s. 2d.
1747–50	3s. 2d.	1s. 7d.	1s. 3d.	1747–65	4s. 0d.
1750–65	3s. 2d.	1s. 3d.	1s. 7d.	1765–79	4s. 6d.
1765–79	10d.	10d.	10d.	1779–81	4s. 9d.
1779–84	11d.	11d.	11d.	1781	4s. 11d.
1784	3s. 0d.	3s. 0d.	3s. 0d.	1782–84	5s. 2d.
1797	3s. 3d.	3s. 3d.	3s. 3d.	1784	7s. 4d.
1801	5s. 1d.	3s. 9d.	5s. 1d.	1797	8s. 0d.
1807	5s. 5d.	4s. 9d.	5s. 5d.	1805	11. 5d.
1817–23	5s. 6d.	3s. 6d.	5s. 6d.	1807	12s. 2d.

Source: D. C. Coleman, *Courtaulds: An Economic and Social History*, vol. 1: *The Nineteenth Century Silk and Crape* (Oxford: Clarendon Press, 1969), pp. 18–19.

order to supply Bengal with raw cotton; 'a sufficient quantity remain to supply the trade in India, and thereby to procure cotton for the province of Bengal, without exporting your specie for that Raw material'.[79] However, it was not only the quantity of raw material that the Company needed to increase. In 1778 James Wiss reported to London that since imports of Chinese raw silk had been allowed into the Bombay market three years earlier, Bengal raw silk lost ground 'on Account of their bad quality and of the difficulty of winding them'.[80] He encouraged the Company to prohibit the trade in raw silk between China and Bombay. He added that only Bengal raw silk sent to Bombay and reeled in the Italian method would have found a market there. Thus, improvements in the quality of Bengal raw silk were also important for the Company's intra-Asian trade. This is apparent when the value of the exports of raw silk from Bengal is compared with the value of the exports of Bengal raw silk to Britain (Figure 2.3).

Ocean in the Eighteenth Century', pp. 188–224; Greenberg, *British Trade and the Opening of China*, pp. 75–103.

[79]   IOR/E/4/623: 'Silk, Growth of Mulberry Plantations Encouraged, 24 December 1776', p. 284.

[80]   IOR/E/1/63, fols 19–20v: 'Letter 8 Report of James Wiss to the Committee of Correspondence on the Silk Trade in India, London, 14 July 1778', p. 19. James Wiss was one of the silk specialists contracted by the EEIC to implement the Piedmontese system of reeling in Bengal. LSE Archives, W7204, East India Company. *Reports and Documents Connected with the Proceedings of the East-India Company in regard to the Culture and Manufacture of Cotton-wool, Raw Silk, and Indigo in India* (London: J. L. Cox, 1836), p. xvii; IOR/E/4/625, 9 April 1777, p. 171.

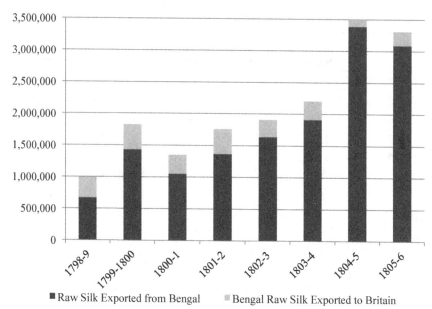

■ Raw Silk Exported from Bengal   ▨ Bengal Raw Silk Exported to Britain

Figure 2.3   Value of raw silk exported from Bengal, 1798–1806

Source: Compiled from L/PARL/2/55: 'Appendix to the First Report of the Select Committee on the Affairs of the East India Company', p. 60, 'Appendix to the Fourth Report of the Select Committee on the Affairs of the East India Company', p. 230.

These factors show that the Company's interest in producing raw silk had a strong footing. The question that arises is whether the trade data for the 1770s to the 1810s confirms the Company's expectations. For this purpose, I consider the role of the trade in Bengal raw silk in the Company's Eurasian trade. The EEIC trade data for the period 1793 to 1812 shows that raw silk accounted on average for 6.8 per cent of the Company's total sales of Indian and Chinese goods in Europe. For Bengal raw silk, the Company's data is available only for the period 1793–1807, when it accounted on average for 4.7 per cent of total sales. However, this figure is not necessarily representative of the actual importance of raw silk, as it needs to be understood in connection with the emergence of tea as a key trade commodity. In the late eighteenth century, the China tea trade became an essential source of profit as well as a tool for remitting Indian revenues. The growth of this trade was driven by two factors: first, it was facilitated by an increase in the demand for tea in Britain. Imports of tea from China were boosted by Pitt's Commutation Act of 1784, which reduced the import duty on tea from 119 per cent to a mere 12.5 per cent.[81] Second, demand for tea also increased in other parts of Europe and

---

[81]   Moreover, the increase in demand was associated with the expansion of British manufacturing, as the growth of the tea trade was facilitated by the increased consumption of tea

Table 2.3 Value of the London sales of the English East India Company's goods, 1793–1810

Goods	Total sales (£)	Average annual sales (£)	Share (%) of goods on average annual sales
Tea	55,160,230	3,064,457	53.5
Piece goods	26,054,301	1,447,461	25.3
Raw silk	7,014,986	389,721	6.8
Pepper	3,322,835	184,602	3.2
Saltpetre	3,060,956	170,053	3.0
Spices	1,974,099	109,672	1.9
Drugs, sugar, indigo, etc.	5,031,516	279,529	4.9
Other goods	8,415,292	467,516	8.2
Total	110,034,215	6,113,011	100.0

Source: Compiled from L/PARL/2/55: 'Appendix, No. 24 to the Fourth Report of the Select Committee on the Affairs of the East India Company', pp. 492–3.

the Atlantic world.[82] For these reasons, the share of tea exceeded 50 per cent of the Company's sales in this period. However, when silk is compared with the sales of other items, its role becomes more apparent. Table 2.3 shows that raw silk was the third most important export product on the London market. According to data from the Select Committee on the Affairs of the East India Company, 81 per cent of the value of raw silk imported to London in the period 1799–1806 came from Bengal.[83]

Drugs, especially opium, as well as sugar and indigo were the only other items besides raw silk that the EEIC attempted to manufacture under its direct control in India. However, its venture into the manufacturing of these goods

by the urban working class. Huw Bowen, 'Sinews of Trade and Empire: The Study of Commodity Exports to the East India Company during the Late Eighteenth Century', *Economic History Review* 55 (3), 2002, p. 469; Ward, 'The Industrial Revolution and British Imperialism', pp. 53–5. Amanda Vickery shows that servants were also consuming tea and were given an allowance of tea in the eighteenth century. Amanda Vickery, *The Gentleman's Daughter: Women's Lives in Georgian England* (London: Yale University Press, 1998), pp. 27, 142, 222, 207–8.

82 Bowen, 'British Exports of Raw Cotton', p. 118.

83 The average annual value of the Company's exports of raw silk to London in the period 1799–1806 amounted to £406,560, with approximately £329,635 from Bengal. L/PARL/2/55: 'Appendix to the First Report of the Select Committee on the Affairs of the East India Company', p. 60; L/PARL/2/55: 'Appendix to the Fourth Report of the Select Committee on the Affairs of the East India Company', p. 230; L/PARL/2/55: 'Appendix, No. 24 to the Fourth Report of the Select Committee on the Affairs of the East India Company', pp. 492–3.

was never as extensive as its involvement in the silk industry. The Company referred to sugar, indigo, and coffee as 'new articles' of trade and attempted to expand the market for such goods as it had done with Bengal raw silk. Its engagement in the 'new articles' however, was mostly limited to experimentation and the Company's efforts never translated 'into extensive sales of [such] new commodities in London'.[84] On the other hand, the officially sanctioned private trade in these articles was extensive.[85] This leads to the conclusion that private traders were more successful than the Company in procuring new trade items such as sugar, indigo or coffee, but failed to procure raw silk.

Mercantilism and the English East India Company's Commitment to Raw Silk Production in Bengal

It is indisputable that the EEIC's engagement in the Bengal silk industry was principally motivated by profit. However, mercantilist principles played an important part in driving the Company's commitment to invest in raw silk production. During its rule over India, the EEIC was involved in several projects entailing production processes and a number of reports survive, detailing the efforts undertaken by the Company in cultivating raw silk, raw cotton, indigo, sugar and opium.[86] Similarly, the Company ventured into the production of cotton textiles.[87] Claudio Zanier has argued that these ventures were a mere extension of the Company's commercial activities, guided by short-term financial gains. My aim is to show that the EEIC's investment in Bengal raw silk production was in fact guided by factors other than just short-term returns.

Mercantilism was a 'practical political economy policy' of the seventeenth and eighteenth centuries, which focused on solving the question of 'how to achieve national wealth and power'.[88] Mercantilism never became a doctrine with strictly defined principles.[89] Nevertheless, it is usually stated

---

[84] Bowen, *Business of Empire*, p. 245.

[85] Ibid.

[86] Another attempt to promote silk production was carried out on the Coromandel Coast but this project did not succeed. Maxine Berg, 'Passionate Projectors: Savants and Silk on the Coromandel Coast 1780–1798', *Journal of Colonialism and Colonial History* 14 (3), 2013, pp. 18–19.

[87] LSE Archives, W7204, East India Company, *Reports and Documents*; East India Company, *Debate on the Expediency of Cultivating Sugar in the Territories of the East India Company* (London: Reporter, 1793); East India Company, *Report of the Select Committee of the Court of Directors upon the Cotton of This Country: With Appendixes* (London: n.p., 1793).

[88] Lars Magnusson, 'Introduction', in Lars Magnusson (ed.), *Mercantilism: Critical Concepts in the History of Economics*, 4 vols (London: Routledge, 1995), vol. 1, p. 4.

[89] Ibid., p. 6; Donald C. Coleman, 'Mercantilism Revisited', *Historical Journal* 23 (4), 1980, pp. 773–91.

that the prevention of an outflow of bullion, a positive balance of payments and the promotion of employment were among the prime concerns of mercantilist theories. Similar conclusions can be reached through the analysis of contemporary pamphlets and treatises. Most of the texts published by seventeenth- and eighteenth-century economic writers deal with the practical questions of how to expand trade, improve the balance of trade, increase production and the employment of the poor.[90] Ideas differ significantly, especially about the level of trade protectionism to be applied and to the role of the East India Company. However, when we look at mercantilist writings concerning the British silk industry, a certain level of consensus emerges. First, there was general agreement that the silk industry should be protected by the government through an import ban on finished silk textiles. Second, raw silk should be imported from colonies rather than from other European countries because the latter were considered trade competitors.[91] From this point of view, the EEIC's plan to import silk from Bengal was considered favourably.

J. Thorp, a contemporary writer, even considered the Company's efforts in improving the quality of Bengal raw silk as insufficient and urged for more attention to be given to the issue.[92] Mercantilist principles therefore illustrate contemporary thought about the production of raw materials in non-territorial settlements for their use in British manufacturing. In the case of the silk industry, mercantilist principles are usually assumed to correspond with import substitution policies. In Britain, the import of finished silks was restricted with the aim of substituting these imported textiles with domestic production. In general the rationales of import substitution policies in pre-industrial Europe included the prevention of outflow of bullion and mitigation of the threat of riots and idleness of workers.[93] Josiah Child had already argued in 1689 that through the importation of inputs for the domestic industry, foreign trade stimulated the national growth of employment and manufacturing.[94] In the eighteenth century, Joshua Gee claimed that it was of national importance to

---

90 For a collection of significant mercantilist writers see: Magnusson (ed.), *Mercantilism: Critical Concepts*.

91 See for instance: J. Thorp, *Considerations on the Present State of the Cotton and Silk Manufactories of Great Britain: And the Impropriety of Continuing to Draw the Supply of Materials for the Latter from France and Italy* (London: Lane, Darling & Co., 1807), pp. 10–13, 15–17; Joshua Gee, *The Trade and Navigation of Great-Britain Considered: Shewing, that the Surest Way for a Nation to Increase in Riches, Is to Prevent the Importation of Such Foreign Commodities as May Be Raised at Home* (London: Sam Buckley, 1729), pp. 1–23.

92 Thorp, *Considerations*, pp. 16–17.

93 David Omrod, *The Rise of Empires: England and the Netherlands in the Age of Mercantilism, 1650–1770* (Cambridge: Cambridge University Press, 2003), p. 168; Harky G. Johnson, 'Mercantilism: Past, Present and Future', *The Manchester School* 42 (1), 1974, p. 3.

94 Josiah Child, *A Supplement to a Former Treatise Concerning the East-India Trade* (London: n.p., 1689), p. 12; Thomas Papillon, *A Treatise Concerning the East-India Trade: Being a Most Profitable Trade to the Kingdom, and Best Secured and Improved by a Company and a Joint-Stock* (London: n.p., 1680), p. 3.

engage in plantation cultivation due to the 'Profits our Plantations may yield us, by raising Hemp, Flax, Silk, Iron, Pot-ash, &c.'.[95] Gee also argued that the promotion of trade, manufactures and colonies was essential for increasing the wealth of the nation.[96] He dedicated several pages of his treatise to the trade in raw silk and argued for the necessity of importing cheap raw silk from Asia and promoting the cultivation of silk in British colonies.[97]

The perception that extraterritorial settlements should be used as a source of raw materials for British manufacturers was also widely accepted by the EEIC. Such thinking seems to permeate its policies in Bengal, especially in respect of the silk industry. The Company's correspondence in the 1770s and 1780s shows a great deal of commitment to the implementation of the Italian method of reeling. EEIC records illustrate its faith in the success of the venture and the possible returns on this investment. Raw silk was labelled as a 'valuable item of trade' and employees were ordered to keep investing in raw silk even during the Company's financial difficulties in 1772.[98] This attitude was underpinned by the expectation that the production of 'Bengal Italian raw silk' would generate profits. Furthermore, mercantilist principles played a key role: the Company considered the export of Bengal raw silk to be to be of benefit to British manufacturers and the investment returns in general:

> It is in the increase of this Article of Our Investment that we chiefly depend for the bringing home our Revenues; the Importation being a national benefit and the Consumption more unlimited than that of the Manufactured Goods. You must therefore continue to bestow the greatest attention to it.[99]

It was the trade in raw silk that the Company attempted to use to make its trading activities more appealing to the mercantilist state.[100] It drew especially on the mercantilist objective of securing raw material imports without the necessity of depending on foreign countries. The EEIC emphasised that the production of 'Bengal Italian raw silk' would allow the British silk industry to reduce its dependence on imports of Italian raw silk. This is why the Company stressed the import substitution policy as underpinning the strategic importance of its Bengal project. The same argument was present also in letters sent from London to Bengal, in which it was pointed out that the

95   Gee, *The Trade and Navigation of Great-Britain*, p. v.
96   Ibid., pp. 2–23.
97   Ibid., pp. 43–4, 87–92.
98   IOR/E/4/621: 'Bengal Despatches, 24 November 1772', p. 380; IOR/E/4/619: 'Cultivation of Mulberry, 17 March 1769', p. 333; IOR/E/4/625: 'Silk, Italian Method of Spinning and Winding Introduced into India by Mr Wiss, 9 April 1779', p. 133; IOR/E/4/621: 'Mr Wiss, Superintendent of Silk Trade, 24 November 1772', p. 379.
99   IOR/E/4/618, 16 March 1768, p. 919.
100 Edmund Burke, *The Works of the Right Honourable Edmund Burke* (Boston: Wells and Lilly, 1826), vol. 6, p. 68.

Company was 'desirous to promote by all possible means the increase and improvement of your Investment of Raw Silk as an object equally beneficial to the Nation and the Company'.[101] The pressure from London to increase the number of mulberry trees was apparent: 'your attention to their cultivation will most essentially promote the Interest of the Company, and of the Nation, Raw Silk, and especially Filature Silk being a very beneficial article of our imports, and of great consequence to our manufactures of Britain'.[102] The Company considered Bengal raw silk 'an article of such national consequence' and assigned its improvement great importance.[103]

If the Company drew on mercantilist ideas with the aim of achieving independence from having to import raw materials, it also applied mercantilist thinking in the administration of Bengal. The Court of Directors claimed that it was necessary for the Company to change its policies after the Battle of Plassey and that 'it became necessary to adopt measures more consonant with the improved situation of their affairs. The Company were now become the rulers of a valuable, extensive and fertile country, producing, in ordinary periods, revenues more than equal to the current expenses of its management.'[104] In relying on mercantilist principles in administering Bengal, the Company principally sought efficient use of Bengal resources and promoted employment. Silk was deemed by the Company as the item of trade most suitable for expansion due 'first, as affording to the means for extended cultivation, and next, by creating additional employment for the natives: two objects that ought never be lost sight of in all well-regulated states'.[105] The Company sought to prevent the workers' idleness, a condition typically despised by mercantilists.

Yet the EEIC never lost sight of any opportunity for profits. The Company went into Bengal silk production because it expected that once Piedmontese methods of reeling were implemented, the trade in Bengal raw silk would be profitable. The Company's goal was not to promote the industry for the sake of the development of Bengal. Hence, in the periods when raw silk production proved to be an unprofitable venture, the Company scaled down its investment and focused on recovering the costs incurred. Such a situation occurred in the 1790s when the British market became overstocked.

I argue that it was this combination of factors that made Bengal raw silk a potentially profitable item of trade. Mercantilist thinking made the EEIC

---

101 IOR/E/4/619: 'Richard Wilder, Bengal Raw Silk, 17 March 1769', p. 339.
102 IOR/E/4/623: 'Silk, Growth of Mulberry Plantations Encouraged', p. 286.
103 IOR/E/4/621: 'Bengal Despatches, 7 April 1773', p. 471.
104 GL, 1795 fol. 16280, *Reports of the Committee of Warehouses of the East-India Company*, pp. 13–14.
105 Ibid. This was a view also taken by William Milburn at the beginning of the nineteenth century. Milburn maintained that raw silk 'appeared the most eligible for the interests of that country [Bengal]; first, as affording the means for extending cultivation; and, secondly, by creating additional employment for the natives'. Milburn, *Oriental Commerce*, p. 252.

support the venture for much longer than an investment policy based only on short-term decisions would suggest. It is true that after 1785 the EEIC did not embark on any new projects of technology transfer, but neither did the Company cease its investment, and it also adopted several innovations. The EEIC continued to produce raw silk in its several filatures until the 1830s when the filatures were sold to private manufacturers in accordance with the 1833 Charter which revoked the Company's right to carry out any economic activities.[106] The Company's understanding that further improvement to the quality of Bengal raw silk was essential to retrieve 'the heavy sums which have been sunk in bringing this article to its present state of perfection', suggests that the 'sunk' costs compelled the Company to continue with this venture until the 1830s.[107]

Conclusion

In the eighteenth and early nineteenth centuries, silk weaving held the position of a strategic industry in Britain. Climatic conditions in Britain made importation of raw silk a necessity. The EEIC's venture into Bengal silk manufacturing was not an isolated experiment but needs to be considered along with the other initiatives focused on extending raw silk production in British colonial settlements. Besides Bengal, attempts were made to produce raw silk in several North American colonies. Such plans were guided by the mercantilist objective of securing supplies of raw materials from dependent territories. However, with the exception of Bengal, none of these initiatives was successful in bringing raw silk to the British market.

The Company's venture into silk manufacturing in Bengal was under-pinned by five factors. First, the importation of Bengal raw silk was supported by low duties. Second, raw silk was quantitatively the most important raw material imported into Britain in the 1750s and 1760s.[108] Third, Bengal raw silk was the Company's second most important Bengal export item. Fourth, compared with other commodities, raw silk had the lowest proportion of freight-to-sale cost. Finally, Bengal raw silk was used in the intra-Indian trade to procure raw cotton and other items for Bengal. All these factors made the plan to extend the trade in raw silk a rational decision on the part of the Company.

Apart from these factors, investment in raw silk production was also facilitated by the mercantilist principles of the EEIC. The rhetoric of the

---

[106] Claudio Zanier, 'Silk Culture in Western India: The 'Mutti Experiment' (1830–47)', *Indian Economic and Social History Review* 21 (4), 1984, pp. 463–4.

[107] L/PARL/2/55: 'Appendix to the Fourth Report', p. 217.

[108] Mitchell, *British Historical Statistics*, p. 463.

promotion of national interest was used not only in communicating with British manufacturers but also in correspondence with the Company's Bengal factors. The Company perceived the venture into the Bengal silk industry as a project of national importance – which was meant to support silk manufacturing in Britain – as much as an investment project supposed to generate profits.

Chapter 3

BENGAL, PIEDMONT AND THE ENGLISH EAST INDIA COMPANY

> The silks are not certainly so fine as those of Persia, Syria, Sayd, Bairut, but they are of a much lower price, and I know from indisputable authority that if they were well selected and wrought with care, they might be manufactured into most beautiful stuffs.[1]

So ran François Bernier's comments on the silk production of Mughal India in the late seventeenth century. The methods of silk production used in India were not at the forefront of technological innovation but Bernier's view also indicates the potential ascribed to Indian silk production by Europeans. This chapter explores the methods of sericulture and silk reeling used in Bengal before the EEIC started to be directly involved in the region's silk industry. The chapter first considers how Indian raw silk was perceived on the European market and then focuses on the organisation of Bengal silk production, comparing it to that in China and Europe. It shows that the quality of raw silk produced by the Bengalese methods did not match the quality requirements of British silk weavers. The chapter then discusses the initial approach taken by the EEIC to improve quality, and explores the problems in achieving these aims as posed by the system of procurement. Finally, it suggests reasons why the EEIC considered it feasible to increase the quality of raw silk by altering production methods.

Bengal Raw Silk Production in Comparative Perspective

India and China constituted the main industrial areas of the world in premodern times.[2] India attained a pre-eminent position particularly in

---

1 François Bernier, *Travels in the Mogul Empire* (London: W. Pickering, 1826), vol. 1, p. 439.
2 Maxine Berg, 'Useful Knowledge, 'Industrial Enlightenment', and the Place of India', *Journal of Global History* 8 (1), 2013, p. 117.

cotton textile production, a sector in which the subcontinent developed superior knowledge and exceptional productive skills.[3] This chapter asks whether that superior knowledge of production processes also characterised raw silk production. Should the phrase 'textile factory of the world' include India's silk industry in the eighteenth century?

Indian cotton production was exported to other regions in Asia as well as to Africa, the Americas and Europe, fostering long-distance trade and conquering global markets. The distinctive aesthetic qualities, designs and colours created a strong international demand for Indian cottons. India's pre-eminent position in the production of cotton textiles in the premodern period was underpinned by its superior knowledge of dyeing and printing, and the precision of its weavers and other textile artisans.[4] However, the success of the cotton industry was achieved mainly thanks to the high quality of Indian finishing processes.[5] In the case of cotton textiles, India's 'comparative advantage' rested upon knowledge stemming from long-term familiarity with production techniques and practices by Indian artisans.[6]

As this chapter shows, superior knowledge and/or sophisticated production technologies did not characterise the Bengal silk industry. Some contemporary travelogues create a misleading impression that Bengal was a region renowned for the production of silks suitable for European markets, often confusing the demand for finished and raw silk.[7] Moreover, the story of raw silk production needs to be disentangled from that of silk weaving, even if these two stages

---

[3]   See Giorgio Riello and Tirthankar Roy (eds), *How India Clothed the World: The World of South Asian Textiles, 1500–1850* (Leiden: Brill, 2009); Prasannan Parthasarathi, 'Cotton Textiles in the Indian Subcontinent, 1200–1800', in Giorgio Riello and Prasannan Parthasarathi (eds), *The Spinning World: A Global History of Cotton Textiles, 1200–1800* (Oxford: Oxford University Press, 2009), pp. 17–41.

[4]   Giorgio Riello, 'Asian Knowledge and the Development of Calico Printing in Europe in the Seventeenth and Eighteenth Century', *Journal of Global History* 5 (1), 2010, pp. 1, 6; Parthasarathi, 'Cotton Textiles', pp. 18–21.

[5]   Giorgio Riello, *Cotton: The Fabric that Made the Modern World* (Cambridge: Cambridge University Press, 2013), p. 83.

[6]   Ibid., p. 362. In particular, it was knowledge of the finishing processes that rendered Indian cotton textiles a highly sought-after item on the global market. Ibid., p. 80.

[7]   Bengal, and in particular the region of Kasimbazar, was the only centre of commercial production of raw silk in seventeenth- and eighteenth-century India. When the European trading companies arrived in India, the trade in Kasimbazar silk was already well developed and its silk was traded within the Mughal Empire and across Asia. The Dutch East India Company was the first among the trading companies to import raw silk to Europe. However, to improve the quality of Bengal raw silk, over 80 per cent of the imported silk had to be reeled under the Company's control in its own reeling workshop. Irfan Habib, *The Agrarian System of Mughal India 1556–1707* (New Delhi: Asia Publishing House, 1963), p. 57; Om Prakash, *The Dutch East India Company and the Economy of Bengal, 1630–1720* (Princeton: Princeton University Press, 1985), pp. 55–7, 219; Roberto Davini, 'Una Conquista Incerta. La Compagnia Inglese delle Indie e la Seta del Bengala, 1769–1833' (unpublished Ph.D. thesis, European University Institute, 2004), p. 15.

of production are intimately related. Prior to the standardisation of the nineteenth century, silk was not a homogeneous product and woven silks from different countries or those using different methods of production could be easily distinguished.[8] Giovanni Federico contends that specific production methods resulted in particular physical characteristics, which made a 'certain type of silk comparatively more suited for producing a specific type of silkware and/or for being processed with some type of equipment'.[9] The types of silk product demanded by European and Indian consumers varied, and so different qualities of raw silk were needed. Eighteenth-century Indian consumers valued silk fabrics for the reputation of the place where the fabric was woven or for their colours; by contrast, Europeans demanded high-quality silk fabrics with fashionable designs.[10] Europeans also valued lightness and a uniformity of texture, characteristics which could only be achieved if high-quality raw materials were used. This in turn required advanced reeling technology and high-quality cocoons.

Positive views of the Indian silk industry relate to the superior quality of the finished silk fabrics, not raw silk. Brenda M. King, for instance, claims that 'the silk textiles of India were and still are, some of the most widely admired and skilfully produced in the world'.[11] This view of Indian silks can be traced back to premodern sources. Travel accounts by Europeans show a certain degree of admiration for Indian silk products. The seventeenth-century French traveller François Bernier, for example, observed that in Bengal there were 'such a quantity of cotton and silks that the Kingdom may be called the common storehouse for the two kinds of merchandise, not of Hindustan or the Empire of the Great Mughal only, but of all the neighbouring kingdoms, and even of Europe'.[12] This and other positive views are, however, in stark

---

8   Giovanni Federico, *An Economic History of the Silk Industry, 1830–1930* (Cambridge: Cambridge University Press, 1997), p. 53.

9   Ibid.

10 C. A. Bayly, 'The Origins of Swadeshi (Home Industry): Cloth and Indian Society 1700–1930', in Arjun Appadurai (ed.), *The Social Life of Things. Commodities in Cultural Perspective* (Cambridge: Cambridge University Press, 1986), p. 286; Roberto Davini, 'A Global Supremacy: The Worldwide Hegemony of the Piedmontese Reeling Technologies, 1720s–1830s', in Anna Guagnini and Luca Molà (eds), *History of Technology*, vol. 32 (London: Bloomsbury Publishing, 2014), p. 99; Debin Ma, 'The Great Silk Exchange: How the World was Connected and Developed', in Debin Ma (ed.), *Textiles in the Pacific, 1500–1900. The Pacific World: Lands, Peoples and History of the Pacific, 1500–1900* (Aldershot: Variorum, 2005), pp. 24, 26.

11 Brenda M. King mostly focuses on the weaving skills of Indian artisans and on the finishing processes that enabled the production of high-quality silk fabrics. She does not address the issue of raw materials used for the production of such silk products. The use of imported raw silk of a finer quality might reconcile the evidence on the production of low-quality silk thread and high-quality silks being woven in India. Brenda M. King, *Silk and Empire: Studies in Imperialism* (Manchester: Manchester University Press, 2005), pp. 55–6.

12 Bernier, *Travels in the Mogul Empire*, p. 439. Jean-Baptiste Tavernier also shows admiration

contrast to the situation the EEIC encountered when exporting raw silk. Bengal raw silk was repeatedly described as being of inadequate quality by British silk manufacturers and weavers, and was criticised for the coarseness and unevenness which allowed it to be used only in the production of haberdashery.[13]

Mulberry silk culture was introduced to India in the fifteenth century. Three hundred years later, Indian production methods lagged behind other world areas, particularly China, Italy and France, the leaders in silk manufacturing.[14] There was no apparent pressure from the domestic weaving sector to upgrade the available technologies. The principal regions of raw silk production in Bengal in the eighteenth century were Rungpore, Malda, Bauleah, Jungypore, Kasimbazar, Gonatea, Commercolly and Radanagore (Figure 3.1).

The organisational, technical and gender divisions of labour in the Bengal silk industry in the eighteenth century show several similarities to that in China and Europe. In all these places, silkworm rearing and mulberry cultivation were carried out in rural areas or in close proximity to sericulture.[15] This was due to the technological limitations of eighteenth-century silk production: there was no method of preserving cocoons for long periods of time, and without timely reeling the quality of cocoons deteriorated.[16] The gender division of labour in sericulture in Bengal was similar to that in Europe and China: women reared silkworms, while mulberry cultivation was a male task.[17] However, there were several differences in the gendered

Indian silks. Jean-Baptiste Tavernier, *Travels in India* (London: Macmillan & Co., 1889), vol. 2, pp. 2–4.

[13]   All the contemporary materials called the silk 'unequal in skeins', meaning that the skeins contained silk threads of different colours and were made of a different number of filaments. Goldsmiths' Library (hereafter GL), 1796 fol. 16654, *Considerations on the Attempt of the East-India Company to Become Manufacturers in Great Britain* (London: n.p., 1796), p. 21; GL, 1795 fol. 16280, *Reports of the Committee of Warehouses of the East-India Company relative to Extending the Trade on Bengal Raw-Silk* (London: n.p., 1795), pp. 13; K. N. Chaudhuri, *The Trading World of Asia and the English East India Company, 1660–1760* (Cambridge: Cambridge University Press, 1978), p. 346.

[14]   Sanjay Sinha, *The Development of Indian Silk: A Wealth of Opportunities* (London: Intermediate Technology Publications, 1990), pp. 4–5. For the origins of sericulture in India see: Lotika Varadajan, 'Silk in Northeastern and Eastern India: The Indigenous Tradition', *Modern Asian Studies* 22 (3), 1988, pp. 565–70.

[15]   Roberto Davini, 'The History of Bengali Raw Silk as Interplay between the Company Bahadur, the Bengali Local Economy and Society, and the Universal Italian Model, c.1750–c.1830', *Commodities of Empire Working Paper* 6 (2008), p. 6.

[16]   The long-distance transportation of cocoons was not possible until a method of drying them was developed in the nineteenth century. Without drying, cocoons easily became spoilt. Claudio Zanier, 'Silk and Weavers of Silk in Medieval Peninsular India' (unpublished paper presented at the conference 'Historical Systems of Innovation: The Culture of Silk in the Early Modern World (14th–18th Centuries)', Berlin, December 2010).

[17]   Jordan Goodman, 'Cloth, Gender and Industrial Organization towards an Anthropology of Silkworkers in Early Modern Europe', in Simonetta Cavaciocchi (ed.), *La Seta in Europa Secc. XIII–XX* (Prato: Istituto Internazionale di Storia Economica, 1993), p. 231.

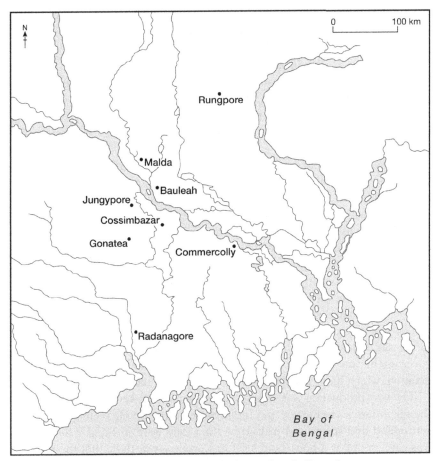

Figure 3.1   Map of the principal silk-producing regions in Bengal

Note: Cossimbazar is also spelt variously Cossimbuzar and Kasimbazar, and Malda is also spelt Mauldah.

Source: Adapted from Roberto Davini, 'Una Conquista Incerta. La Compagnia Inglese delle Indie e la Seta del Bengala, 1769–1833' (unpublished Ph.D. thesis, European University Institute, 2004), p. 221.

divisions of labour in silk reeling. In Europe and China silk reeling was a female occupation; in India, however, it was undertaken by both men and women.[18] In India, men were involved if reeling was carried out by cuttanies, male reelers who travelled from village to village, or if it was done

18   Dieter Kuhn, 'Textile Technology': Spinning and Reeling', in J. Needham (ed.), *Science and Civilization in China: Chemistry and Chemical Technology* (Cambridge: Cambridge University Press, 1988), vol. 5, part 9, p. 204; Goodman, 'Cloth, Gender and Industrial Organization', p. 231.

in households it was undertaken by women.[19] In Europe, reeling was carried out by women, with the exception of Sardinia where it was done by men. Throwing and weaving were male occupations. Thus, as argued by Jordan Goodman, the gender division of labour in the silk industry was different compared with other European textile industries. The first part at least of the proverb 'women spin and men weave' was inaccurate for the European silk industry.[20] In India men were involved in the production of silk even more heavily. Moreover, the Company's requirement for raw silk created a new demand for male re-reelers.[21]

The system of organisation of production in Bengal showed many similarities to China as silk production relied predominantly on small-scale, peasant households. Several imperial workshops were established in China but large-scale production was not widespread.[22] Sericulture was a labour-intensive activity and, as argued by Dennis O. Flynn and Arturo Giráldez, the supervision of sericulture (the processes of mulberry cultivation and silkworm rearing) would have been expensive and therefore, they argue, 'decentralized production evolved as the cost-effective choice'.[23] In addition, reeling was done mostly at the household level although Chinese peasants used better technology, particularly with the adoption of inexpensive hand-reeling machines.[24] The most significant difference between India and China in the silk industry was the involvement of the government. In China the government was active in promoting silk production, particularly through taxation, which indirectly favoured an increase in quality.[25]

The way production was organised represented the key difference between the silk industries in Europe and India. Sericulture and silk reeling were more centralised and specialised in Europe than they were in India.[26] Sericulture was carried out at a household level in Europe, as in India, but the requirements on labour varied due to the different number of harvests. In Europe there was one crop per year and peasants therefore did not need to focus

19   This is illustrated in GL, 1775 fol.: George Williamson, *Proposals Humbly Submitted to the Consideration of the Court of Directors, for Affairs of the United Company of Merchants of England, Trading to the East-Indies: For Improving and Increasing the Manufactures of Silk in Bengal* (London: n.p., 1775), pp. 17–18, it can also be observed from Figure 3.2.

20   Goodman, 'Cloth, Gender and Industrial Organization', pp. 231–4.

21   Although this is not explicitly stated in any document, the sources make no allusion to re-reelers being female.

22   The number of imperial workshops expanded particularly during the seventeenth century. It is said that the workshops in Hangchow, Nanking and Soochow employed some 7,000 artisans and 1,863 looms in 1685. Dennis O. Flynn and Arturo Giráldez, 'Silk for Silver: Manila, Macao-Nagasaki Trade in the 17th Century', in Debin Ma (ed.), *Textiles in the Pacific*, p. 35.

23   Ibid., p. 36.

24   Kuhn, 'Textile Technology', p. 337.

25   Flynn and Giráldez, 'Silk for Silver', p. 36.

26   Davini, 'History of Bengali Raw Silk', pp. 7–9.

exclusively on sericulture. In Italy, the major European producer of raw silk, mulberries were grown on the edges of fields or intermixed with other crops, and their cultivation did not require large amounts of labour.[27] In Bengal, by contrast, there were three to six harvests a year and mulberry trees were grown as shrubs, which meant that their cultivation required more labour and land.[28] If a peasant family decided to engage in sericulture in Bengal, the whole family had to be involved: the men in mulberry planting; the women in silkworm rearing and silk reeling. As a result sericulture was a 'marginal, and low-intensity activity' in Italy, but comparatively more land- and labour-intensive in Bengal.[29]

In Europe sericulture became a highly centralised sector under the influence of merchant-entrepreneurs and guilds.[30] Silk reeling was also highly centralised. Master artisans retained control over specialised knowledge and possession of their tools but they also came under the control of the merchant-entrepreneurs and the jurisdiction of guild regulations.[31] In those cases where silk was produced through a putting-out system, merchants owned the material throughout the whole production cycle and artisans were paid on a piecework basis.[32] The most advanced systems of raw silk production in Europe were rather different. Several new features in the organisation of production, such as reeling in factory-like establishments and time wages, were developed in Piedmont in order to ensure high-quality reeling and efficient production.[33]

In comparison with Europe, the system of organisation of production in India allowed the producers more independence.[34] Raw silk was produced under an arrangement similar to the European putting-out system.[35] However, as the towns and villages that cultivated mulberries and reared silkworms were

27   Ibid., p. 8.

28   Ibid., p. 8, IOR, Bombay (Misc. Public Documents, etc.), 1793.m.17: 'Letter from Giuseppe Mutti to John Bell Esquire on 20th October 1838'.

29   Davini, 'History of Bengali Raw Silk', p. 8.

30   Luce Boulnois, *The Silk Road* (London: Allen and Unwin, 1966), p. 214; Luca Molà, *The Silk Industry of Renaissance Venice* (Baltimore: Johns Hopkins University Press, 2000), p. xiv; Franco Franceschi, *Florence and Silk in the Fifteenth Century: The Origins of a Long and Felicitous Union* (Fiesole: Edizioni Cadmo, 1995), pp. 5, 7–9.

31   Molà, *Silk Industry*, p. xiv. Spinners, weavers and dyers in Florence were forbidden to establish their own organisations and had to follow the regulations of the silk guild. In Lyon, the sector was regulated by La Fabrique Lyonnais. Franceschi, *Florence and Silk*, pp. 9, 16.

32   Ibid., pp. 8–9.

33   Davini, 'History of Bengali Raw Silk', p. 15.

34   Riello, *Cotton*, pp. 62–4; Bishnupriya Gupta, 'Competition and Control in the Market for Textiles: Indian Silk Weavers and the English East India Company in the Eighteenth Century', in Riello and Roy (eds), *How India Clothed the World*, pp. 292–7.

35   The putting-out system varied in different parts of Europe. Thus, it is no surprise that it is still disputed whether the concept can also be applied to premodern Asia. In the case of the silk industry it is possible to argue along the lines of Frank Perlin, who contended that the system of organisation of production in pre-colonial South Asia was similar to that of the

scattered, this meant that the production of silk thread became increasingly fragmented and middlemen played an important role in procurement.[36]

Methods of Raw Silk Production in Eighteenth-Century Bengal

The reports and letters from silk specialists employed by the EEIC contain a wealth of information about the methods employed to produce silk thread in Bengal. Their reports for London frequently referred to the inefficiency of the sericultural and silk-reeling practices used in Bengal. None of these processes were close to the methods practised in either Italy or China.

George Williamson – a former employee of the EEIC – wrote one of the best descriptions of the methods used in the production of raw silk in Bengal in 1775, and Figure 3.2 shows drawings that accompanied his descriptions of rearing and feeding the worms, and of reeling and winding the silk. There were three main stages, each being carried out by a different producer: mulberry planting and silkworm rearing; silk reeling; and re-reeling. According to George Williamson's account, the moths were placed on a mat to mate so that the females would lay their eggs on this same mat (Figure 3.2.1). When buds appeared on the mulberry shrubs, the silkworm eggs were exposed to enough sunlight to make them hatch. The worms were given food the morning after hatching in order to ascertain which were the healthiest. Those worms that were able to climb onto the leaves given to them were transferred onto mats and fed with mulberry leaves (Figure 3.2.2). During the rearing of the silkworms, the mats were stored on trays (Figure 3.2.4) which were kept in special buildings (Figure 3.2.3). When the worms were ready to spin their cocoons, they were moved onto a different mat that had on it a spiral of bamboo to which the worms attached themselves and then spun their cocoons (Figure 3.2.5).

The Indian method of killing the moth inside the cocoon was considered by Europeans to be detrimental to the quality of the raw silk. In Italy the normal practice was to kill the chrysalis inside the cocoon before it could conclude its metamorphosis, either in an oven or through the use of steam at a temperature of 70–80°C.[37] In India the moths were killed by exposing the cocoon to sunlight (Figure 3.2.6).[38] However, this method was unreliable

rural industries of Europe. Frank Perlin, 'Proto-Industrialization and Pre-Colonial South Asia', *Past and Present* 98 (1), 1983, pp. 84–94.

36   GL, 1775 fol.: Williamson, *Proposals*, p. 15. The organisation of production in premodern India was also dependent on a large number of intermediaries in other sectors. For cotton textile production in India see: Riello, *Cotton*, pp. 63–4.

37   Richard Hills, 'From Cocoon to Cloth: The Technology of Silk Production', in Cavaciocchi (ed.), *La Seta in Europa*, p. 63.

38   Figure 3.2.6 shows the mat on which the worms were kept before being exposed to the sun.

because the cocoons could only be exposed to sun after all of them had been spun. As the rate at which silkworms spun their cocoons varied, some had already started the metamorphosis into a moth at the time when the cocoons were exposed to the sun. If the chrysalis was not killed inside the cocoon, the moth tore the cocoon as it emerged, which lowered the quality of the silk and could render the cocoon unsuitable for further use.[39]

The last four scenes of Figure 3.2 depict the 'country' method of reeling and the processes of re-reeling the 'country-wound' silk. The silk was either reeled in peasant households or by cuttanies, the reelers who travelled from village to village.[40] A cuttany using reels and a split bamboo for reeling cocoons is depicted in Figure 3.2.7. Silk reeled using this method was known as 'country-wound' or 'Putney', and was deemed to be of low quality because silk filaments of different lengths and fineness were reeled together.[41] A further problem was unevenness within the skeins as some contained single, double, triple or even quadruple parts.[42] Finally, it was often observed that much of the resulting silk was dirty or unfit for use.[43]

Country-wound silk did not have a market in Europe so the EEIC had to have the silk rewound before sending it to Britain, and so the country-wound silk was delivered to merchant agents and re-reeled by winders called nacauds.[44] The process of rewinding is depicted in Figures 3.2.8–10. First, threads of different fineness had to be separated from each other using a reel and bobbin (Figure 3.2.8). Then, threads of different colours were separated by reeling the thread from the bobbin onto a large reel (Figure 3.2.9), and after this the reel was placed in the sun for the thread to dry. Only then was the silk twisted into skeins (Figure 3.2.10).[45]

---

39 Hills, 'From Cocoon to Cloth', p. 63.
40 Cuttanies had a reputation for not paying attention to quality: 'the cuttanies who manufacture the Putney are dispersed all over the country neither under control or inspection; that they have no interest in the quality or sale of the silk nor any consideration beyond their daily pay which they receive from the chassars who rears the worm'. WBSA, BoT Prcds 23 June 1778, 'Observations on Raw Silk and Remarks on these Observations', as cited in Davini, 'Una Conquista Incerta', p. 127; Davini, 'History of Bengali Raw Silk', p. 8.
41 Chaudhuri, *Trading World of Asia*, p. 346. However, it would be a mistake to suppose that filaments of different fineness and length were reeled into one skein only in Bengal. It seems that these problems were connected with household reeling in general, especially in regions where incentives for high-quality silk production were wanting. For instance, low-quality raw silk was also reeled by households in Provence, France. See: Archives Nationales, Paris: Serie F12, F12 677A.
42 India Office Records, British Library (hereafter IOR), IOR/E/4/616: 'Bengal Raw Silk to be Investigated by Richard Wilder, 25 March 1757', p. 557. Unevenness in skeins arises when threads of different quality or threads consisting of different number of filaments are twisted together.
43 IOR, Bombay (Misc. Public Documents, etc.), 1793.m.17: 'Letter from Giuseppe Mutti', p. 7.
44 Davini, 'History of Bengali Raw Silk', p. 8.
45 GL, 1775 fol.: Williamson, *Proposals*, p. 16.

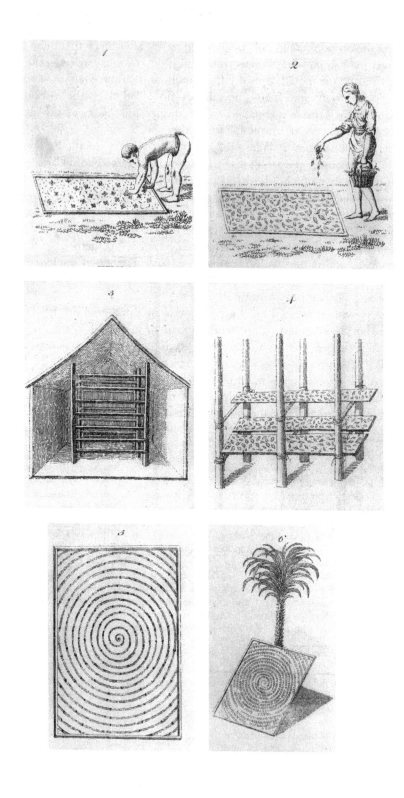

Figure 3.2 Drawings depicting the practices of sericulture (facing page) and silk reeling (above) in Bengal in 1775

Source: Goldsmiths' Library, 1775 fol.: G. Williamson, *Proposals Humbly Submitted to the Consideration of the Court of Directors, for Affairs of the United Company of Merchants of England, Trading to the East-Indies: For Improving and Increasing the Manufactures of Silk in Bengal* (London: n.p., 1775), pp. 17–18. Reproduced with the permission of Senate House Library, University of London.

The Initial Approach of the English East India Company to the Quality Problem

Though observing multiple issues in silkworm rearing, the Company identified reeling as the most urgent problem. Initially, the Company decided to have all silk rewound before sending it to Britain. However, rewinding only solved the problem of unevenness in skeins and it was detrimental to the quality of the silk filaments as they had to be soaked in water twice.[46] This practice also required more labour, gave rise to principal–agent problems and created a need for supervision of the re-reelers. These problems led the Company to experiment with new approaches.

Manufacturers' mounting dissatisfaction with the quality of exported silk led to new and more co-ordinated efforts to improve the standard of raw silk.[47] The Company sent silk specialists to Bengal from Europe to investigate the causes of the low quality of raw silk production, including, in 1757, Mr Richard Wilder, a expert in all stages of silk production.[48] The EEIC was especially eager to rectify the uneven quality of colour, fineness and length in skeins, and improve the system of 'marking' silk. All bales of raw silk had to be marked with the letters A to E according to the fineness of the thread, with A being the finest and E the most coarse.[49] This system was regularly ignored in Bengal: often bales marked D and E contained finer silk than those marked B and C. From London, the Company warned that 'these are Errors which must be looked into and rectified or the Company must drop the Importation

---

46   Ibid. It was especially detrimental to the gloss 'which is much and very visibly injured particularly in the lower letter of the country assortments'. WBSA, CCC, Vol. 2, Prcds 5 March 1772, as cited in Davini, 'Una Conquista Incerta', p. 137.

47   LSE Archives, W7204: East India Company, *Reports and Documents Connected with the Proceedings of the East-India Company in regard to the Culture and Manufacture of Cotton-wool, Raw Silk, and Indigo in India* (London: J. L. Cox, 1836); GL, 1795 fol. 16280, *Reports of the Committee of Warehouses of the East-India Company*, pp. 13, 16.

48   IOR/E/4/861: 'China, Canton, Raw Silk, Mr. Wilder to Make Enquiries', p. 980. IOR/E/4/616: 'Bengal Raw Silk to be Investigated by Richard Wilder, 25 March 1757', pp. 557–60. Richard Wilder was considered by the Court of Directors to be a 'Person extremely well qualified' in all stages of silk production. He was contracted by the Court on 25 March 1757 for a five-year period of service in Bengal. His task was to investigate the reasons for the production of low-quality silk in Bengal and to make amends. Wilder was paid £400 annually plus £10 for subsistence, and was also provided with accommodation. During his time in India he was also to make a journey to China, but the Company eventually realised that Wilder would be of no use in China because he would not be able to get involved in production there. His contract was extended for another two years during which he was allowed to get involved in private trade (with the exception of the trade in silk). Wilder remained in the Company's service until his death in 1765. IOR/E/4/616, 25 March 1757, pp. 557–60; IOR/E/4/617, 19 February 1762, p. 400; IOR/E/4/617, 15 February 1765, p. 1075; IOR/E/4/619, 17 March 1769, p. 339; IOR/E/4/620, 23 March 1770, p. 220.

49   IOR/E/4/616: 'Bengal Raw Silk to be Investigated by Richard Wilder, 25 March 1757', p. 557.

of the Article'.[50] Five grades made it more likely that the silk quality would be mismarked than if there were fewer categories, but it was typical to divide silk into five quality levels marked A to E for the European market.[51]

Apart from inspecting the production methods and the quality of the raw silk, Richard Wilder was also expected to supervise the rewinding of Putney at the Company's factory in Calcutta.[52] This was conceived as an experiment so that the Company could establish the cost of rewinding and identify the specific instructions that should be given to rewinders in order to improve the quality of the silk. However, it was also suggested that as much raw silk as possible should begin to be rewound at the Company's factory in Kasimbazar directly under Wilder's supervision.[53] Kasimbazar was the main area of silk production in Bengal and in the 1750s the Kasimbazar factory was the principal factory procuring raw silk from intermediary merchants.[54]

Richard Wilder was the Superintendent of the Company's Bengal silk investment from 1757 until his death in 1765. He was succeeded by John Chamier, who was a former 'free merchant' employed by the Board of the Kasimbazar factory because of his knowledge of raw silk production.[55] Joseph Pouchon was also employed by the Board, although he was to work under Chamier's direction.[56] Both Wilder and Pouchon attempted to implement several changes to reeling technologies,[57] but these changes remained just experiments and never became widely implemented practices. Pouchon, for instance, was able to produce a sample of raw silk reeled according to a

---

50 Ibid., p. 558.
51 According to the Company's documents it was common in Europe to divide silk according to its fineness into five categories designated by the letters A to E, where A was the finest with the lowest number of filaments in a thread. The Company attempted to implement such a system in Bengal. The five-letter system was sometimes expanded to six using the letter F when the silk of letter E was very coarse. The secondary literature on the silk industry does not mention this system of marking but the EEIC's documents imply that it was in widespread use and that buyers relied on it. The literature on the European silk industry mentions different systems of categorising the quality of silk so this was probably not the only one. Luca Molà, for instance, points to the fact that silk was divided into categories according to the region of origin and several other characteristics. Molà, *Silk Industry*, pp. 55–6.
52 IOR/E/4/616, 'Bengal Raw Silk to be Investigated by Richard Wilder, 25 March 1757', pp. 656–7.
53 Ibid.
54 The EEIC used the term 'factories' for trading posts; factories procured export goods but did not directly produce them.
55 IOR/G/23/13: 'Factory Records: Kasimbazar, 1757–59, 19 January 1759'. Before John Chamier became a silk superintendent he was a member of the Board of the Kasimbazar factory. The Court had a very favourable opinion of his experience in silk production and reported to the Board in Bengal that Chamier 'has a complete knowledge of the Manufacture of Raw Silk, having been bread up and many years engaged in the Silk Trade'. Ibid.; IOR/E/4/617, 15 February 1765, p. 1075.
56 Ibid.; IOR/E/4/619, 17 March 1769, p. 339; IOR/E/4/620, 23 March 1770, p. 220.
57 LSE Archives, W7204: East India Company, *Reports and Documents*, p. v.

method he invented, but the Company did not consider the experiment to be economically viable.[58]

The EEIC's Factory Records from the Kasimbazar silk factory from the late 1750s are an excellent source of information about the new practices that the Company attempted to adopt in the Bengal silk industry.[59] The role of the Kasimbazar factory (established in 1658) was to procure raw silk as well as finished silks for export markets.[60] No silk was produced in the factory itself as prior to the 1760s the Company relied exclusively on a putting-out system. Many techniques proposed by the Company's silk specialists could not be adopted because they were opposed by the winders: for example, knotting of the silk was not implemented.[61] Silk knotting was proposed to rectify the unequal widths of threads; it was also supposed to make the silk thread more round.[62] Although it was seemingly a simple adjustment to the established method of re-reeling, the implementation of knotting proved to be an insurmountable problem.

Initially, the Kasimbazar Factory demanded the winders knot the silk according to the method used in England. However, the winders refused to implement knotting and deserted their work. The factory records summarised the consequences as follows:

> the Method of knotting Silk proposed by Mr Wilder being introduced [...] into the Nacaud Connah caused a great Mutiny and desertion among the Winders, as they were not able to wind off so great a Quantity as they formerly could by the great Delay caused in endeavouring to the Knott proposed by Mr Wilder.[63]

To enable the introduction of knotting the EEIC had to agree to the introduction of a simpler knot as designed by the winders themselves.[64] However, the Company faced further problems: the winders refused to knot the finest grades of silk as it took considerably longer.[65] Moreover, the winders would only start knotting the silk when their allowance was increased.[66] In

---

[58]   This method was different from the Piedmontese reeling method adopted later. J. Geoghegan, *Some Account of Silk in India, Especially of the Various Attempts to Encourage and Extend Sericulture in that Country* (Calcutta: Department of Revenue and Agriculture, 1872), p. 2.

[59]   IOR/G/23/13.

[60]   Thomas Bowrey, *A Geographical Account of Countries round the Bay of Bengal, 1669–1679* (Cambridge: Hakluyt Society, 1905), p. 213.

[61]   This illustrates the lack of control that the EEIC had over the agrarian economy of Bengal. The EEIC had to rely on market incentives and could not control the existing silk market. Benoy Chowdhury, *Growth of Commercial Agriculture in Bengal 1757–1900* (Calcutta: R. K. Maitra, 1964), vol. 1, p. i; Davini. 'Una Conquista Incerta', p. 7.

[62]   IOR/G/23/13: pp. 93–4, 96, 108.

[63]   IOR/G/23/13: 7 October 1758, p. 108.

[64]   Ibid.

[65]   Ibid., 28 February 1759.

[66]   Ibid.

spite of concessions on the part of the Company, it remained difficult to convince winders to knot the silk carefully and complaints about the quality of knotting increased.

The Company encountered similar problems with compliance to the musters (samples) of silk. The Kasimbazar Factory based its decisions about the price it would pay for silk from a particular merchant agent and the quantity to be purchased on the musters of re-reeled silk it received. Musters were supposed to indicate the quality of the whole quantity of silk purchased but the silk procured by the Company often did not resemble the musters sent out.

The problems encountered in implementing knotting and matching the quality of silk thread to the musters are indicative of several issues. First, they show the Company's lack of power in enforcing the adoption of new practices. The winders were independent economic actors who often chose the merchants they worked for, and in many cases they chose to work for merchants who were not in the service of the EEIC. The factory records contain many reports which show that orders from London could not be fulfilled due to a lack of winders working for the Company.[67] Second, they demonstrate that the Company was subject to market laws. The Company was aware that it could not coerce the winders and that the only way to encourage them to adopt new practices and induce them to follow its directives was to increase their wages. Hence, the board of the Kasimbazar factory increased the allowance given to the winders on the grounds of it 'being assured that all other measures taken for the Improvement of the Quality, or increase of the Quantity of Silk required for the Company, will be ineffectual without it'.[68] However, this increase did not improve the standard of the raw silk produced. First, the changes in reeling practices were too marginal to lead to a significant improvement in quality, and second, even such minor changes were not enforced effectively due to the Company's reliance on a putting-out system.

The System of Procurement of Bengal Raw Silk for the British Market

As was true for other commodities traded by the English East India Company, the EEIC was dependent on intermediary merchants to procure raw silk. Intermediary merchants linked export merchants, such as the EEIC, with producers. The reliance on intermediaries, however, meant that the European companies were often unable to procure the quantity and quality of goods

---

67   IOR/G/23/13, 12 August 1758, p. 83; 30 August 1758, p. 94.
68   Ibid., 15 January 1759.

needed, and could not punish the fraudulent behaviour of some merchants. These problems were embedded in the procurement system.

In the case of raw silk, the system of procurement was also highly fragmented, with many intermediaries involved. The necessity of rewinding 'country-wound' silk introduced an additional stage of production and further complicated the procurement process. The Company lacked the power to enforce the supply both of the quantity and quality of silk it demanded.

The procurement process most widely used by the European companies was the dadni system.[69] A merchant was contracted to supply the Company with an agreed quantity of a specific commodity for which he received an advance payment, or 'dadni'.[70] Apart from its inability to fully control the quantity and quality of procured goods, the EEIC often faced the threat of losing its investment as merchants 'refused to give security for the dadni advanced to them'.[71] In 1753 the EEIC decided to switch to the gomasta system.[72] Gomastas were paid agents who procured goods on behalf of the Company.[73] The EEIC was not the first European company to make this switch as the Dutch East India Company had experimented with the gomasta system from 1747 to 1749. However, the gomasta system also created problems. In particular, the Dutch East India Company experienced 'considerable difficulty in finding a sufficient number of capable gomastas and in maintaining uniformity of standards'.[74] Similarly, the EEIC also encountered several issues using the gomasta system as can be illustrated for raw silk procurement.

The gomasta system was considerably fragmented and the silk passed through the hands of several intermediaries before reaching the EEIC

---

[69]   Sushil Chaudhury, 'Merchants, Companies and Rulers: Bengal in the Eighteenth Century', *Journal of the Economic and Social History of the Orient* 31 (1), 1998, p. 76. Dadni merchants retained a great deal of power because they could act together and stand against the EEIC. R. Mukherjee, 'The Story of Kasimbazar: Silk Merchants and Commerce in Eighteenth-Century India', *Review Fernand Braudel Center* 17 (4), 1994, pp. 500, 520; Davini, 'Una Conquista Incerta', pp. 23–4.

[70]   Chaudhury, 'Merchants, Companies and Rulers', pp. 76–7.

[71]   Ibid. p. 77.

[72]   This meant a very sudden decline in power for the dadni merchants. Mukherjee, 'Story of Kasimbazar', p. 531.

[73]   In his Ph.D. thesis, Roberto Davini argues that the gomasta system gave the Company more power over producers. The system of procurement became more bureaucratised, and contracts were written that specified the quantity and quality of goods to be delivered and set the deadline for their delivery. However, in practice the system did not work as smoothly as intended and the issues described below illustrate that the gomasta system was not a solution to problems of silk quality. Moreover, it is questionable whether the system increased the power of the EEIC over procurement. The gomasta system was unable to eliminate intermediary merchants from the system of procurement or make them accountable, thus the EEIC continued to face principal–agent problems. See: West Bengal State Archive (WBSA), Committee of Circuit at Cossimbuzar, Letter from Pattle to Committee of Circuit, 25 July 1772, as cited in Davini, 'Una Conquista Incerta', p. 28.

[74]   Chaudhury, 'Merchants, Companies and Rulers', p. 86.

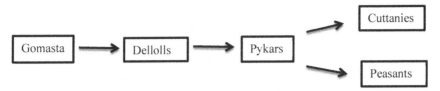

Figure 3.3   Actors involved in the procurement of 'country-wound' silk in Bengal, 1750s

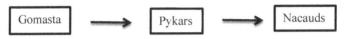

Figure 3.4   Actors involved in the re-reeling of silk in Bengal, 1750s

(Figure 3.3). Before the cultivating season started, the EEIC had to advance money to its gomasta merchants, who then advanced it to the principal producers for the promise of silk. The system was further fragmented because these merchants employed other intermediaries. The principal brokers, Dellolls, employed agents of their own called Pykars to purchase the Putney. Pykars were supplied with money by the Dellolls and they were to advance this money to the Chassars (the peasants rearing silkworms) so that they could purchase silkworm eggs, prepare huts in which to rear silkworms, till the land for the planting of mulberries, and pay Cuttanies for silk reeling.[75]

Once procured, the Putney had to be re-reeled. This was done by nacauds under the supervision of the head winders, the Sirdars. The employment of Sirdars was crucial because winders were prone to shirking. Nacauds apparently needed supervision because otherwise they would not wind properly, and would steal the Putney, tear it or take the advance and work for someone else.[76] The Kasimbazar factory records show that the EEIC also relied on gomastas for the rewinding of silk (Figure 3.4). In each aurung (silk region) around the beginning of each harvest season, the Company advanced money to a gomasta, who employed winders for rewinding Putney into the various quality categories. The Commercolly factory required the gomastas to send musters of the rewound silk before it made a decision about the quantity of silk it was going to purchase from a particular aurung.

The gomastas who proved reliable were advanced higher amounts of money before they sent musters, but finding such merchants often proved a difficult task. In several cases, gomastas did not have enough rewinders in their service.[77] The Kasimbazar factory encountered fraudulent behaviour

---

[75] GL, 1775 fol.: Williamson, *Proposals*, pp. 15–17.
[76] Ibid., p. 17.
[77] IOR/G/23/13, 5 December 1757, p. 2; 30 December 1757, p. 10; 24 September 1758, p. 105.

by gomastas who sent musters of higher quality than the silk procured, or who overcharged the Company.[78] Worse still, in some cases the factory could not even dismiss them as it would negatively affect the procurement of other goods. This occurred in the case of Hissenda, a gomasta involved in both raw silk and piece goods procurement. When the servants in the Kasimbazar factory compared the prices Hissenda charged the Company for raw silk procurement with those charged by one of the Assamys – gomastas not in the service of the EEIC – they found that:

> [Hissenda] has overcharged the Goods he has delivered into the Company's Cottah here, and by that means endeavoured to defraud his Employers of sicca rupees 8427 7 Annas 3 Pice [£913] but notwithstanding we have plainly discovered the above yet we are under a Necessity of continuing him at present in the provision of the Investment, he is already providing for should we turn him out of his Employ, and take the Assammys under our own Care, the Silk Piece Goods Investment would fall greatly short, as we are already informed the Weavers are beginning to sell their goods provided for the Company to other Merchants.[79]

This case shows just how difficult the situation was for the Company when the procurement of raw silk was involved. It is not surprising that the adoption of new reeling practices proved impossible. Neither the system of procurement of raw silk, nor the putting-out system under which raw silk was produced, were favourable to introducing changes to production techniques.

Piedmontese Methods of Silk Reeling

By the 1750s the EEIC was thus aware that an improvement in quality could not possibly be achieved under a putting-out system. At the same time, without an improvement in quality, Bengal raw silk would not increase its share of the raw silk market in Britain. Spurred on by the mounting dissatisfaction of British silk weavers with the quality of Bengal raw silk and encouraged by the assumption that the 'Piedmontese technology [had] a universal capacity to upgrade local production', the EEIC decided to rely on knowledge and technologies from Europe to alter the method of reeling Bengal raw silk.[80]

The EEIC was not alone in being confident that adopting Piedmontese technologies would bring success. The excellent quality of the Piedmontese reeled and thrown silk inspired the transfer of Piedmontese technologies to various European countries. For instance, attempts to implement the

[78] For instance, IOR/G/23/13, 21 October 1758, p. 114.
[79] IOR/G/23/13, 14 July 1758, p. 70.
[80] Davini, 'Piedmontese Reeling Technologies', pp. 90–1.

Piedmontese system of silk reeling were carried out in Midi France, in Portugal and in Hungary, though without achieving long-term success.[81] Throwing technologies were transferred to Chacim in Portugal, Derby in England, and Stockholm in Sweden.[82] All these transfers suffered setbacks and none of these regions succeeded in producing reeled or thrown silk of Piedmontese quality. Among the key problems was insufficient knowledge, as silk production technologies were considered 'secret' in the early modern period and were transferred mostly due to migration.[83] Differences in climatic conditions also potentially threatened the transfers.[84] The quality of inputs, whether cocoons or silk threads, caused problems as well. Lower-quality cocoons meant that raw silk of Piedmontese standard could not be achieved even if appropriate technology was used. Silk threads of a lesser quality than the Piedmontese caused problems in the silk mills, since they often broke and stopped work in the mill. Lack of political stability also sometimes impeded technology transfers.[85] Lack of consideration for institutions in which the Piedmontese system was embedded was, however, the major reason why the transfer of the technologies proved to be troublesome.

Attention was paid solely to the technological aspects of the Piedmontese method, and in none of the cases was the institutional setting taken into consideration. Yet, implementing the admittedly superior Piedmontese reeling technology on its own was not sufficient to make such projects successful. Several studies show that the organisation of production was vital and that Piedmontese success depended on the system of sericulture, organisation of production and labour as well as quality enforcement, all of which played as important a role as the technological innovations.[86]

The precise date of invention of the Piedmontese reeling machine (Figure 3.5) is not known.[87] However, its use in the second half of the seventeenth century is well documented as the reeling machine was made compulsory

---

81 Davini, 'History of Bengali Raw Silk', p. 5.
82 José M. Lopes Cordeiro, 'A Technology Transfer in Portugal's Late Eighteenth Century: The Royal Silk Twisting Mill of Chacim', *Textile History* 23 (2), 1992, p. 182.
83 The EEIC relied solely on their Italian silk specialist for knowledge of the Piedmontese technologies.
84 This was especially evident in the case of Bengal, where the monsoon climate proved to be incompatible with the use of wooden machinery.
85 This was mostly the case in Hungary. Walter Endrei, 'The Italian Contribution to the Development of Sericulture in Hungary', in Cavaciocchi (ed.), *La Seta in Europa*, pp. 301–2.
86 Davini, 'History of Bengali Raw Silk', p. 15; Claudio Zanier, 'Pre-Modern European Silk Technology and East Asia: Who Imported What?', in Debin Ma (ed.), *Textiles in the Pacific*, p. 131–9; Mauro Ambrosoli, 'The Market for Textile Industry in Eighteenth Century Piedmont: Quality Control and Economic Policy', *Rivista di Storia Economica* 16 (3), 2000, pp. 344–55.
87 The silk reeling machine depicted in Figure 3.5 represents an 1830s modification of the original. It is not a steam-driven machine.

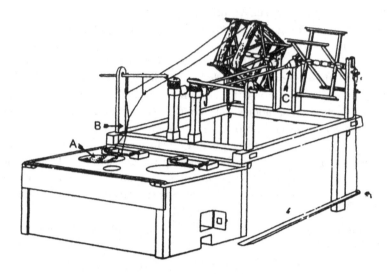

Figure 3.5   Piedmontese reeling machine (see Appendix A for further information)

Source: Piedmontese standard silk reeling machine, in Giacinto Carena, *Osservazioni ed Esperienze Intorno alla Parte Meccanica della Trattura della Seta nel Piemonte* (Torino, 1837) as reproduced from Claudio Zanier, 'Pre-Modern European Silk Technology and East Asia: Who Imported What?', in Debin Ma (ed.), *Textiles in the Pacific, 1500–1900. The Pacific World: Lands, Peoples and History of the Pacific, 1500–1900* (Aldershot: Variorum, 2005), p. 129.

throughout the Kingdom of Savoy by a Royal Decree in 1667.[88] More decrees ensued in the eighteenth century, detailing how reeling machines should be used and their modifications.[89] The main technical innovation of the reeling machine was a system for the crossing of silk threads. Zanier names several benefits: crossing silk threads meant that it was possible to 'squeeze water from the threads, remove impurities, render the thread more round, and compact the filaments in the thread'.[90]

Overall, silk crossing produced a silk of a higher standard. The Piedmontese reeling machine made a further contribution to quality improvement by reducing the number of filaments used for producing silk thread from eight or more down to three to five filaments, yielding a thinner and more delicate thread.[91] Moreover, the reeling machine introduced an oscillating ramping board for distributing the thread on the reel. This mobile board was

---

[88] Zanier, 'Pre-Modern European Silk Technology and East Asia', p. 128.
[89] Ibid.
[90] Ibid., pp. 130, 142, 146–9.
[91] Ibid., p. 129.

powered by a revolving reel with the use of a driving belt. The benefits of the introduction of the ramping board were twofold: it ensured that the threads already reeled did not stick together in the hank, which would happen if the threads just fell onto each other. Second, it was a substitute for the labour of an assistant who would otherwise have had to do the work by hand.[92]

Yet, as mentioned by Claudio Zanier, the 'Piedmontese revolution' in reeling technology was much more than the invention of the reeling machine. The use of machinery would not have been profitable if the organisation of production had not also been adapted. For instance, the introduction of the oscillating ramping board required increased technical knowledge for the maintenance of the mechanism. The production of thinner thread required higher-skilled reeling masters, which in turn necessitated a prolonged period of apprenticeship, usually up to seven years. On the other hand, in spite of the innovations introduced by the reeling machine, one reeler could still not operate the machine on their own. A master reeler was assisted by an apprentice turning the reel and by an assistant watching over the fire under the basin, where the cocoons were boiled before reeling.[93] Also the system of remuneration changed. As the Piedmontese system was focused on quality rather than quantity, reelers started to be paid time wages instead of a piece rate wages.[94]

Several other factors characterised the Piedmontese reeling system. Reelers were mostly women as it was said that their hands were more delicate and thus more skilful for reeling. It was also easier to employ female reelers as reeling was done only seasonally. Several studies show it was common for women in premodern Europe to take part in seasonal labour: it enabled them to carry out their domestic tasks and represented a source of additional income. Most importantly, the organisation of labour in silk reeling changed, and from the late seventeenth century silk began to be reeled in factory-like establishments called silk filatures. Representing an important move from the proto-industrial putting-out system, filatures were characterised by the supervision of reelers, by inflexible discipline and managerial hierarchy. The strict discipline was meant to ensure a high quality of reeling as well as the efficiency of reelers.[95] All the changes in the organisation of labour were implemented in the name of achieving a high standard of reeled silk. Moreover, locating the filatures in rural areas and employing women enabled the Piedmontese silk merchants to produce high-quality silk thread and still keep labour costs down.

The 'Piedmontese reeling revolution' did not only affect reeling practices, it also shaped sericulture. First, it affected the organisation of production. As with

---

92   Ibid., p. 132.
93   The work of watching over the fire was mostly done by young girls. Ibid., p. 131.
94   Davini, 'History of Bengali Raw Silk', p. 15.
95   Ibid., pp. 6–7, 15.

the other stages of production, sericulture had been controlled by merchants since the late seventeenth century. Merchants financed the industry, providing the peasants with advances for the following year's cocoon production, the sum given matching 'the commune, the price the cocoons fetched in all rural markets'.[96] This price was dictated by the merchants and was dependent on the expected demand for silk thread in the European markets.[97] Second, it was argued by Claudio Zanier that the changes to reeling techniques 'compelled producers to raise cocoon quality'.[98] Only the best cocoons were reeled in silk filatures, a step that ensured the production of the highest quality of raw silk for export or for throwing into organzine.[99] Cocoons graded as being of second-rate quality were not reeled in silk filatures but by small-scale manufacturers, while cocoons of worse than second-rate quality were reeled by peasants. These coarser raw silks did not reach the export market, nor were they thrown into organzine, but were twisted into trama. Only then were the silks exported or used in the domestic silk industry.[100]

Lastly, the process of silk thread production was regulated by the state and quality was strictly enforced. As emphasised by Mauro Ambrosoli, 'the striking difference from the rest of the Italian cities where similar trades were carried on, was that the state and not the local guilds had to supervise the whole process of production, issuing instructions, laws, and regulations, granting trading privileges'.[101] For instance, the best practice in reeling was 'enforced by minute regulations ordered by the Consulate of Commerce, a direct issue of the King himself'.[102] These institutional arrangements were an outcome of the specific form of mercantilism practised in Piedmont. The government favoured industrial development as manufacturing secured customs revenue. Silk was a principal export item and was thus given special attention. In contrast with Bologna, however, the objective of Piedmontese regulation was to increase the competitiveness of the silk industry. Such regulation did not become a source of rigidity but 'defended an innovative manufacturing process that aimed at the production of the best quality thrown silks'.[103] The ability to produce high-quality silk – which needs to be seen as a form of product differentiation – was key to the success of Piedmontese silk on the London market, especially as the supply of Asian silks increased in the late eighteenth century.[104]

---

[96] Ibid., p. 7.
[97] Ibid.
[98] Zanier, 'Pre-Modern European Silk Technology and East Asia', p. 139.
[99] After 1751 the export of raw silk was banned and only thrown silk could be exported. Davini, 'History of Bengali Raw Silk', p. 7.
[100] Ibid.
[101] Ambrosoli, 'Market for Textile Industry', p. 346.
[102] Ibid., p. 344.
[103] Ibid., p. 355.
[104] Ibid., p. 356.

The fact that the Piedmontese technologies relied on advanced machinery, hierarchical management of labour, and strict enforcement of quality made the technology transfer to Bengal such an intricate process. The geographical distance between the Court of Directors in London and its agents in Bengal precluded effective communication and created a further obstacle. Yet, the EEIC was aware that centralisation would allow it to overcome problems embedded in the putting-out system.

Conclusion

The English East India Company faced several obstacles in the trade of Bengal raw silk. As the silk exported from Bengal by the EEIC had to compete with superior raw silk from Italy and China as well as with silk from Turkey and Spain, quality became an issue of central importance for the Company. The raw silk produced in Bengal was of a comparatively low quality due to the technologically inferior production methods adopted, which meant that the standard was too low to gain a significant market share in Britain. Moreover, in India high-quality silk production was not promoted by the government as in Italy and China. In order to expand its trade the English East India Company decided to take steps to improve the quality of Bengal raw silk. The initial approach of the Company was to contract reelers to re-reel the so-called 'country-wound' silk. As this step did not lead to a sufficient increase in quality, the Company's silk specialists attempted to implement wider changes to silk-reeling practices. However, enforcement of changes under a putting-out system was impossible. The EEIC thus started to experiment with silk reeling straight from cocoons under its own direct supervision in establishments owned by the Company.

Chapter 4

THE BENGAL SILK INDUSTRY AND THE ENGLISH EAST INDIA COMPANY

The Company's commercial interest in Bengal raw silk dated back to the breakdown of the negotiations between Sir Thomas Roe and the Sophy of Persia in 1617, which aimed to secure for the EEIC the monopoly in trading Persian silk.[1] Trade in Bengal silk was promoted from 1675.[2] As the legislation of 1699, 1702 and 1720 curtailed the Company's opportunities for legally importing finished silk fabrics into Britain, it turned its attention to Bengal raw silk.[3] However, the reputation of Bengal raw silk among European silk manufacturers and weavers was one of low quality. The main complaint was that it was coarse and unequal in skeins.[4] Its quality did not allow for immediate use in weaving, and the fact that Bengal raw silk required reworking prior to utilisation diminished demand.[5] Problems with the quality of raw silk were so serious that at times they threatened to halt trade altogether.[6] Aware of the issues, the Company decided to adopt the Piedmontese system of silk reeling in Bengal. The Piedmontese technologies relied on centralisation of silk

---

[1] J. Geoghegan, *Some Account of Silk in India, Especially of the Various Attempts to Encourage and Extend Sericulture in that Country* (Calcutta: Department of Revenue and Agriculture, 1872), p. 1.

[2] Streynsham Master, *The Diaries of Streynsham Master 1675–1680*, ed. Richard Temple (London: J. Murray, 1911), p. 204.

[3] K. N. Chaudhuri, *The Trading World of Asia and the English East India Company, 1660–1760* (Cambridge: Cambridge University Press, 1978), p. 344. Prior to 1757 the Company was interested in both wrought and raw silk, and only after that date did it start to focus mainly on raw silk. Indrajit Ray, 'The Silk Industry in Bengal during Colonial Rule: The "De-Industrialisation" Thesis Revisited', *Indian Economic Social History Review* 42 (3), 2005, p. 340.

[4] Goldsmiths' Library (hereafter GL), 1796 fol. 16654, *Considerations on the Attempt of the East-India Company to Become Manufacturers in Great Britain* (London: n.p., 1796), p. 21; GL, 1795 fol. 16280, *Reports of the Committee of Warehouses of the East-India Company relative to Extending the Trade on Bengal Raw-Silk* (London: n.p., 1795), p. 13; Chaudhuri, *Trading World of Asia*, p. 346.

[5] The silk could not be used for throwing or weaving without first being re-reeled.

[6] LSE Archives, W7204, East India Company, *Reports and Documents Connected with the Proceedings of the East-India Company in regard to the Culture and Manufacture of Cotton-wool, Raw Silk, and Indigo in India* (London: J. L. Cox, 1836), p. iv.

reeling and made the Company's direct involvement in production essential. This explains why the EEIC set up what I call 'the Bengal Silk Enterprise'. This label aims to emphasize the fact that it was the only instance in which the Company expanded its activities into manufacturing.

This chapter first examines the transfer of Piedmontese technologies to Bengal and second, it focuses on the changes that the adoption of the new technologies had on sericulture. It then considers the effects that adoption of the Piedmontese silk technologies had on the Company's trade in Bengal raw silk. Finally, the chapter examines the system of quality control.

Transfer of the Piedmontese Silk-Reeling Technology to Bengal

Aware of the inadequate quality of Bengal raw silk the Court of Directors – the highest managerial body of the Company – decided in 1769 to transfer the Piedmontese method of reeling to Bengal.[7] This was not the first time the Company had attempted to make changes to the reeling method: experiments were first carried out in the 1750s but did not succeed. In what was then a putting-out system, the reelers refused to implement new practices, fearing that these would reduce the speed of reeling and therefore the quantities of reeled yarn produced. The key advantage of the Piedmontese system was the centralisation of silk reeling in filatures – a type of factory establishment. In Piedmont, relocating reeling to filatures was supposed to facilitate the enforcement of quality control and efficient use of the Piedmontese reeling machine, as the equipment represented a significant capital investment. In Bengal, relocating reeling to filatures had further advantages. Centralisation enabled the training of multiple reelers in the new method at the same time, and eased the process of learning as it was based on a transfer of tacit knowledge and manual skills for which demonstration was crucial. Moreover, in contrast with the previous putting-out system, reelers in filatures did not bear the full cost of training and so became willing to implement the new method of reeling.

The EEIC relied on European silk specialists to transfer the Piedmontese method to Bengal. Initially, three silk specialists – James Wiss, Pickering Robinson and William Aubert – were sent to India. Their task was to set up silk filatures and thereafter become the superintendents of those establishments.[8] Pickering Robinson already had experience with transferring sericulture and silk reeling to Georgia.[9] The key figure was James Wiss

7   LSE Archives, W7204, East India Company, *Reports and Documents*; GL, 1795 fol. 16280, *Reports of the Committee of Warehouses of the East-India Company*, p. xi.
8   India Office Records, British Library (hereafter IOR), IOR/E/4/619, 31 January 1770, pp. 655–6.
9   Ben Marsh, *Georgia's Frontier Women: Female Fortunes in a Southern Colony* (Athens and London: University of Georgia Press, 2007), p. 60.

from Novi in Italy, whose real name was Giacomo. His knowledge of silk production and English made him a very valuable asset, and Wiss became instrumental in silk manufacturing in Bengal. He worked for the Company in Bengal until 1777 when due to his abilities he was appointed Inspector of the Bengal Raw Silk in London and 'continued in the Company's home service for many years'.[10] William Aubert came from France but his influence on the transfer was limited as he died shortly after reaching Bengal.[11]

The silk specialists relied on their personal networks to recruit reelers and mechanics to accompany them to Bengal. James Wiss, a resident of Piedmont, was accompanied by four Italian reelers (J. Rugiero, Dominicus, C. P. Bricola and Augustus Della Casa); Pickering Robinson, an Englishman, was accompanied by three Italians (Francis Clerici, Pielo [*sic*] Spera and Paulo [*sic*] Erva); and William Aubert was accompanied by three reelers from Languedoc (Anthony Broche, Anthony Burgnier and John Peter Angoia) and the mechanic James Demarin.[12]

The initial setting-up period took approximately six years, and during this time Wiss and Robinson established filatures in the major silk regions of Bengal. Figure 4.1 shows the location of the filatures at Bauleah, Commercolly and Kasimbazar, which were the first to start producing raw silk for the British market. The cost of setting up a filature was significant: in Bauleah, Commercolly and Kasimbazar, the cost was estimated to be 284,287 Sicca Rupees (£30,798).[13] However, costs differed among filatures. The system of filature building worked on the principle of cost estimation: the superintendents calculated the necessary costs, received approval from the EEIC for the estimated sum and committed themselves to building the filature for that amount. It seems that the actual costs matched the estimates, as the only case in which the Company enquired about high expenditure was for the construction of the Kasimbazar filature by James Wiss in the early 1770s.[14]

The investigation into the building of the Kasimbazar filature provides important data, as two specialists were contracted in Bengal in the late 1770s to estimate the costs of constructing a filature of 208 furnaces. They suggested the cost of setting up a filature to be between 67,801 and 84,775 Sicca Rupees (£7,345 to £9,184). The difference in the estimates is due to the later silk specialist being new to Bengal and dependent on information from natives and Company servants in Bengal.[15] A similar explanation was used

10   LSE Archives, W7204, *Reports and Documents*, p. xvii; IOR/E/4/625, 9 April 1777, p. 171.
11   LSE Archives, W7204, *Reports and Documents*, p. xi.
12   Ibid.
13   IOR/E/4/625, 9 April 1779, pp. 131–2.
14   In this case the costs exceeded the initial estimate due to the increased capacity of production. The filature was initially to have only a hundred furnaces, but during construction James Wiss changed the plan and built a filature with a capacity of 208 furnaces.
15   IOR/E/1/61, fols 355–357v: 3 September 1777, p. 356.

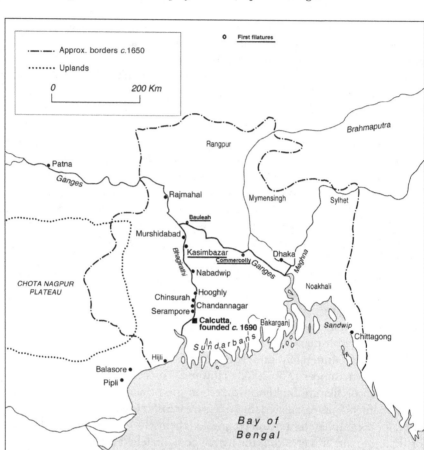

Figure 4.1   Map of Bengal showing the initial silk filatures

Source: Map reproduced and adapted from Tirthankar Roy, 'Where Is Bengal: Situating an Indian Region in the Early Modern World Economy', *Past and Present* 213 (1), 2011, p. 117.

by James Wiss to explain why the estimated costs were surpassed: there was a 'want of knowledge in the language of a country he was newly arrived in, and his being forced to rely entirely on the Banians, Sircars, Servants during the whole time of the execution of so extensive works'.[16] Overall, this reveals two issues: first, the cost of setting up filatures depended on the superintendent's degree of knowledge of the local environment and familiarity with the local language; second, the cost of building larger-scale filatures was

[16]   Ibid., p. 357.

not significantly higher than that of building smaller ones. James Wiss, for instance, was granted the finances required for constructing the Kasimbazar filature once the Court in London recognised that the 208-furnace filature was completed for 99,452 Sicca Rupees (£10,774), whereas the combined costs of building the Bauleah and Commercolly filatures, with 104 furnaces each, amounted to 184,835 Sicca Rupees (£20,024).[17]

The materials used for building filatures and the machinery involved explain why constructing filatures was costly. Filatures needed to be adapted to the Bengal climate: they had to be built of brick and of wood such as bamboo, teak and malaca, as it was necessary to use materials suitable for the monsoon climate.[18] Moreover, filatures had to be closed rather than semi-open because of the rainy weather.[19] The weather was also detrimental to the use of wood in the reeling machinery: wooden cog wheels had to be replaced by brass ones and the axis of the reels had to be made from steel.[20] Initially, the Piedmontese reeling machines were produced in Novi in Piedmont, and were transported to Bengal.[21] From the second half of the 1770s, models of the equipment were produced in Britain, and sent to Bengal where copies were made.[22] From 1769 to 1796 the Company sent 3,825 sets of cog wheels and 3,833 double-crossing machines to Bengal.[23]

No surviving image of the reeling machine used in Bengal exists. According to an 1838 EEIC publication, however, the machinery used was identical to that described in Dionysius Lardner's book of 1832 *A Treatise on the Origin, Progressive Improvement, and Present State of the Silk Manufacture* as shown in Figure 4.2. The problem with this image is that it does not contain a double-crossing implement, which was the main innovation of the Piedmontese machine. Yet, double-crossing machines had been adopted as part of the Piedmontese machine in Bengal as early as the 1770s, thanks to the fact that James Wiss was familiar with the machines used in Novi, Piedmont.[24]

The image and Lardner's description shows that the reeling machine

---

17 IOR/E/4/625, 9 April 1779, pp. 131–2.
18 Roberto Davini, 'Una Conquista Incerta: La Compagnia Inglese delle Indie e la Seta del Bengala, 1769–1833' (unpublished Ph.D. thesis, European University Institute, 2004), pp. 230–2, 247.
19 However, this created the problem of how to dispose of the fumes created by the furnaces. Ibid., pp. 230–2.
20 IOR/E/4/625, 14 July 1779, pp. 484–6. For further information on adaptations of the Piedmontese technologies in Bengal see: Karolina Hutková, 'Transfer of European Technologies and their Adaptations: The Case of the Bengal Silk Industry in the late-eighteenth century', *Business History* 59 (7), 2017, pp. 1111–35.
21 IOR/E/4/620, 27 January 1771, p. 396.
22 IOR/E/4/625, 14 July 1779, pp. 485–6; IOR/E/4/626, 12 May 1780, p. 107; IOR/E/4/640, 25 June 1793, p. 523.
23 IOR/E/4/626, 12 May 1780, p. 99; IOR/E/4/625, 14 July 1779, p. 484; IOR/E/4/629, 8 July 1785, p. 91.
24 LSE Archives, W7204, *Reports and Documents*, p. 16. Lardner's work, as well as other

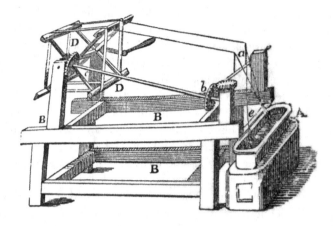

Figure 4.2   Piedmontese reeling machine as depicted in Lardner's *Treatise* (1832)

Source: Dionysius Lardner, *A Treatise on the Origin, Progressive Improvement, and Present State of the Silk Manufacture* (Philadelphia: Carey & Lea, 1832), p. 155.

consisted of three parts: component A depicts the boiler (or basin), B the frame, and D the reel (a full description of the machine can be found in Appendix A). The fire in the furnace brought water in the basin to the boil and the cocoons were placed into the basin in order for the gummy substance covering the filaments to dissolve. A number of filaments were then passed through the reel (D). The reel consisted of wheels with a specific number of teeth, as well as cog-wheels and staves, and had a double-crossing machine, which was introduced by James Wiss to make sure that the thread did not have any lumps.[25] Precision during the construction of the reel was essential, because the wheels had to have a specific number of teeth in order to produce a skein of high-quality silk thread to a particular dimension. The staves had to be set at a defined distance from each other in order to reel a skein of the dimension generally demanded by the European market: 40 inches long and 80 inches in circumference.[26]

Reeling was done by Bengalese reelers and, although it cannot be said definitively, it appears that reelers were paid piece wages.[27] Each furnace was

contemporary sources on silk, shows a lack of knowledge in Britain about double crossing in silk reeling.

[25] IOR/E/4/625, 9 April 1777, p. 209; IOR/E/4/627, 12 July 1782, p. 349; IOR/E/1/65, fols 440–441v, 20 December 1779, p. 440.

[26] IOR/E/4/626, 12 May 1780, p. 105; IOR/E/1/66, fols 422–424v, 'Letters 212–213', 10 May 1780, p. 424.

[27] This was a major difference compared with the system at filatures in Piedmont, where reelers were paid time wages. This was supposed to incentivise the reelers to favour quality over quantity of production. Roberto Davini, 'The History of Bengali Raw Silk as Interplay

Figure 4.3   Hierarchical structure of control over raw silk manufacturing

furnished with three reels and thus accommodated three reelers.[28] That means that a filature with 104 furnaces employed 312 reelers. Reelers were supervised by overseers, whose task was to ensure that the quantity and quality of the reeled silk met the Company's requirements. It was the wish of the Court in London to have one overseer for every 40 furnaces (120 reelers) as was the rule in Italy.[29] However, it can be inferred that the number of reelers per overseer differed among the filatures. Each filature was managed by a director or a superintendent, who was to give instructions and check that the quality of the silk produced in the filature conformed to the Company's requirements.[30] Commercial Residents held a special position in the system. These were servants of the EEIC in India in charge of commodity procurement in a specific area, in this case the procurement of raw silk. In the hierarchical structure, Commercial Residents were above the directors of filatures.[31] The foreign silk specialists who assumed the role of silk superintendents likewise were above directors of filatures in the hierarchical structure. The principal managerial body in Bengal was the Board of Trade, which had ultimate control over trade and manufacturing. This hierarchical structure is depicted in Figure 4.3.

The introduction of the Piedmontese system was accompanied by further innovations, such as the adoption of ovens for killing the moths inside the cocoons. Killing moths by heat was an essential improvement because it was

between the Company Bahadur, the Bengali Local Economy and Society, and the Universal Italian Model, c.1750–c.1830', *Commodities of Empire Working Paper* 6 (2008), p. 15.

28   IOR/E/1/61, fols 486–487v, 18 November 1777, p. 486.

29   IOR/E/4/625, 9 April 1777, p. 219.

30   Ibid., pp. 176–212.

31   During the contract system in silk procurement implemented by Warren Hastings from the 1770s to the 1790s, Commercial Residents often rented silk filatures from the Company and produced raw silk for the EEIC. I will discuss their role in more detail in chapter 6 when focusing on the role of private entrepreneurs in silk manufacturing.

far more effective than the previous method of exposing cocoons to the sun.[32] The Company started to procure cocoons from Bengalese peasants; upon arrival at the filature, the cocoons were placed into the oven for the moth to be killed, and the cocoons were then cleaned.[33] It was emphasised that only 'good cocoons', meaning cocoons that had not undergone the process of fermentation – a process of decomposition – were to be used for reeling in the Bengalese filatures.[34]

The establishment of filatures inevitably altered the procurement and organisation of labour in silk production. The number of intermediaries involved in silk production declined but the EEIC still needed to rely on intermediary merchants. Instead of the Company contracting gomastas to procure reeled silk and then contracting them to organise the re-reeling of the country-wound silk, the Company now procured cocoons. At the beginning of each season, Pykars – contracted agents described by the Company as 'men [...] who go around the country collecting [cocoons]' – were provided with advances to pay Chassars.[35] Chassars were defined as men who rented plantations of mulberry trees, produced mulberry leaves, reared silkworms and produced cocoons.[36] At the end of the rearing season Pykars collected cocoons for the Company.

Changes in Bengalese Sericulture

In contrast with silk reeling, only minimal changes were implemented in sericulture. This was in spite of the fact that, in the case of silk reeling, access to good-quality cocoons was key to determining the eventual quality and cost of the thread produced. From this perspective, the EEIC suffered a considerable disadvantage as innovations in sericulture never got beyond the experimental stage. This should be considered the key difference between the adoption of European silk technologies in Bengal and then fifty years later in Japan, where the technological upgrading of sericulture underlined Japanese success in becoming a major exporter of raw silk.[37] Similarly, the Piedmontese

---

[32] Ibid., pp. 177–200.

[33] Ibid., pp. 199–200, 220.

[34] Ibid., pp. 173–84.

[35] Before the implementation of the Piedmontese system, the EEIC relied on several merchant agents to procure raw silk for the European market. After the new system was adopted, the Company only depended on contractors for the procurement of cocoons. At the beginning of each season, Pykars were given advances intended for the peasants, the Chassars. These advances were supposed to enable the peasants to buy silkworm eggs. IOR/E/4/630, 21 July 1786, p. 548. The Chassars were often unwilling to sell cocoons to the Company because they could earn more if they reeled the cocoons and sold the silk thread on the local market. Davini, 'Una Conquista Incerta', p. 47.

[36] IOR/E/4/630, 21 July 1786, p. 547.

[37] Debin Ma, 'Why Japan, Not China, Was the First to Develop in East Asia: Lessons from Sericulture, 1850–1937', *Economic Development and Cultural Change* 52 (2), 2004, p. 370.

success relied on an improvement in the quality of cocoons.[38] However, it needs to be pointed out that the EEIC was aware of the connection between the quality of cocoons and the quality of the final thread. To understand its position it is necessary to acknowledge that it was impossible for the Company to facilitate an overall change in sericulture under the putting-out system. At the same time, assuming direct control would be too expensive as sericulture in Bengal was scattered over a large area.

According to the Company's silk specialists, several defective practices employed in Indian sericulture negatively affected the quality of the cocoons. Among these were training the mulberry as a shrub; opposition to feeding the worms with mulberry tree leaves; economising on mulberry leaf consumption; keeping the worms crowded together on mats; the method of killing the moth inside a cocoon; and the improper handling of silkworms and eggs which facilitated their 'degeneration'.[39] Training the mulberry as a shrub instead of a tree – which was the general practice in India – was based on the assumption that mulberry trees could not otherwise survive the climatic conditions of Bengal. This assumption was proven to be false by experiments carried out in the eighteenth century.[40] It was strongly criticised in particular by the Company's silk specialist Giuseppe Mutti.[41] He cited cultivating the mulberry as a shrub to be among the most serious obstacles to getting better-quality cocoons. A mulberry shrub does not yield as many leaves as a tree, and those leaves are less suitable for silkworms. Moreover, the training of a mulberry as a shrub is more labour intensive and necessitates higher land input. Although the shrub system allowed the Company to purchase silk five or six times a year in comparison with just three or four times under the tree system, the silk obtained was lower in both quality and quantity.[42]

The opposition to feeding worms mulberry tree leaves was due to it being

---

[38]   Claudio Zanier, 'Pre-Modern European Silk Technology and East Asia: Who Imported What?', in Debin Ma (ed.), *Textiles in the Pacific, 1500–1900. The Pacific World: Lands, Peoples and History of the Pacific, 1500–1900* (Aldershot: Variorum, 2005), p. 139.

[39]   IOR, Bombay (Misc. Public Documents, etc.), 1793.m.17: 'Letter from Giuseppe Mutti to John Bell Esquire on 20th October 1838', pp. 5–7. The issues surrounding the improper handling of silkworms and eggs were highlighted by a Mr. Atkinson who was Resident at the Jungypore filature. His analysis of sericulture from 1779 is cited in full in Geoghegan, *Some Account of Silk in India*, p. 7.

[40]   These experiments were carried out by Giuseppe Mutti who proved that mulberry trees could be cultivated in Deccan.

[41]   The practice of cultivating mulberries as shrubs was also criticised by James Frushard, the superintendent of silk investment in the 1780s. IOR, Bombay (Misc. Public Documents, etc.), 1793.m.17: 'Letter from Giuseppe Mutti', p. 5; WBSA, BoT (Comm) Prcds 13 January 1789. Observations of the Superintendent of Silk Investment, as cited in Roberto Davini, 'Una Conquista Incerta', p. 67.

[42]   IOR, Bombay (Misc. Public Documents, etc.), 1793.m.17: 'Letter from Giuseppe Mutti', pp. 5–7.

thought that this produced a coarser silk.[43] Economising on leaf consumption or keeping worms in crowded conditions on the mats would not allow them to be properly fed, thus having a detrimental effect on their health. The outcome was that the worms needed a longer time to spin and the cocoons that they produced were of a lower quality.[44] Giuseppe Mutti also argued that worms that are crowded together produce less silk. He assumed that if they were kept under better conditions, only some 10,000 worms would be needed to produce as much silk as 15,000 worms left crowded together. Yet, in spite of these observations, the Company did not attempt to alter the practices of sericulture.

The EEIC was well aware that the quality of cocoons had an important effect on the quality of reeled thread: 'Mr. Wiss had succeeded to admiration in drawing a tolerable silk from the most ungrateful cocoons, that the sickliest worms under the most unfavourable season' gave.[45] However, the Company was convinced that the most decisive factor for the quality of cocoons was the quality of the silkworm breed. Therefore, the Court was concerned with attempts to introduce foreign breeds of silkworms rather than with facilitating an overall change in sericulture.

Yet for several reasons the Company's efforts towards introducing new silkworm breeds to Bengal never progressed beyond the experimental stage. The EEIC was most interested in introducing the breed of silkworm reared in Italy. However, attempts were hindered by geographical distance and problems with keeping at least some of the worms alive during the passage to India.[46] Considering the long duration of the journey, maintaining a supply of leaves for feeding the silkworms became the principal obstacle.[47] In 1836 the EEIC summed up these efforts by stating that: 'It must be obvious, that the introduction of the Italian worms into India could not have been effected without great difficulty, on account of the length of the voyage, and the danger of the worms perishing from being deprived of food during the passage.'[48] Attempts to introduce silkworms from China were similarly unsuccessful. For the same reasons as with the Italian silkworms, the EEIC was also unable to secure a sufficient quantity of silkworms to make a decisive impact on cocoon production in Bengal.[49]

---

[43] Geoghegan, *Some Account of Silk in India*, p. 3.

[44] IOR, Bombay (Misc. Public Documents, etc.), 1793.m.17: 'Letter from Giuseppe Mutti', pp. 6–7.

[45] LSE Archives, W7204, *Reports and Documents*, pp. xiii, xiv.

[46] The Company sent silkworm eggs from Europe, but they hatched during the voyage.

[47] In this respect the EEIC cites the problems encountered in the attempt to bring sericulture to St Helena. Most of the silkworms died during the journey due to lack of nourishment. LSE Archives, W7204, *Reports and Documents*, p. xv.

[48] Ibid., p. xiv.

[49] Geoghegan, *Some Account of Silk in India*, pp. 5–7.

A further issue was the so-called 'degeneration' of the imported silkworms.[50] Degeneration was a term used for describing the process in which the succeeding generations of imported silkworms lost their ability to produce silk of a quality that was superior to that of the Bengal breed. This was the case for the silkworms imported from China in 1771: it was argued that the worms degenerated due to 'carelessness and improper management'.[51] The degeneration of silkworms was thus a serious obstacle for improving the quality of cocoons.[52] The Court also registered such concerns in the 1790s when it decided against the introduction of the apparently superior breed of silkworms from the Coromandel Coast.[53] Similarly, contemporary publications by the EEIC considering Bengal raw silk production often mention degeneration as a problem.[54]

Considering the fact that degeneration was a recurring topic, it might seem surprising that the EEIC never attempted to tackle the issue. However, addressing the causes of silkworm degeneration would mean dealing with the defective practices employed in sericulture, and such practices could not be changed under a putting-out system. The cause of silkworm degeneration was said to be improper rearing: in particular, the practices of feeding the silkworms not enough mulberry leaves, feeding them leaves of inappropriate quality and keeping the silkworms in an unhealthy environment.[55] Thus, the same practices that were said to be the cause of the production of low-quality cocoons were also behind the 'degeneration' of silkworms. The key problem was that the reason for employing such methods was not a lack of knowledge of the best practices, but the opportunistic behaviour of peasants. It was argued that the peasant:

> may pay attention to a portion of his cocoons, for the purpose of delivering the same as a sample for fixing the factory prices for a silk harvest, yet no sooner are their prices established and published, then it becomes his immediate interest to distribute the mulberry plant he can command to as many silkworms as the same can possibly keep alive.[56]

The problem was very similar to that faced by the Company when procuring

---

50   The expression 'degeneration' is widely used in the EEIC's correspondence and documents; it was also used by the foreign silk specialists.
51   According to Atkinson as quoted in Geoghegan, *Some Account of Silk in India*, p. 7. The main causes were said to be 'improper food' and 'improper management' of silkworms. WBSA BoT (Comm) Prcds 21 April 1789, Letter from Jungypore, 21 April 1789 as cited in Davini, 'Una Conquista Incerta', p. 96.
52   WBSA, BoT (Comm) Prcds 3 May 1796, Letter from Jungypore dated 25 April 1796, as cited in Davini, 'Una Conquista Incerta', p. 95.
53   The project was never realised. IOR/E/4/640, 25 June 1793, p. 518.
54   Interestingly, the term 'degeneration' is still used in the literature on sericulture today.
55   As argued by Atkinson, cited in Geoghegan, *Some Account of Silk in India*, p. 7.
56   Atkinson, as cited in ibid.

re-reeled silk from gomastas in the 1750s. The system of fixing prices for cocoons according to samples provided at the beginning of the rearing season motivated peasants to focus on the quality of cocoons only when rearing silkworms for the sample cocoons. After the price was fixed, the peasants aimed instead at producing the highest quantity of cocoons possible. Thus, the quality of cocoons delivered to the Company at the end of the rearing season was significantly lower than that of the sample cocoons. If the peasants did focus on production of high-quality cocoons, these were mostly intended for local trade. This was detrimental to the Company's business, especially since rearing the whole crop of silkworms was financed from the Company's advances.[57] Peasants reportedly reeled some of the cocoons that they produced to sell raw silk on the local market.[58] However, this needs to be assessed in the context of premodern production under a putting-out system, in which embezzlement of part of the advanced material was largely tolerated and anticipated.[59]

The fact that peasants could sell part of their produce on the local market was not the only impediment to getting high-quality cocoons. The more serious obstacle was the system of cocoon procurement. When obtaining cocoons from peasants, the EEIC relied on intermediaries called Pykars who brought cocoons from the countryside to the Company's filatures.[60] Relying on Pykars solved the problem of how to procure cocoons from peasants scattered across the large expanse of Bengal.[61] Such dependence, on the other hand, created new problems: in the 1780s the Company found that the Pykars

> sometimes use the most unjust oppression in forcing from the Chassars the Cocoons at their own prices. The Pykars after putting a profit and we have no doubt a handsome one upon them sell them to those engaged in the Silk Filatures by whom they are manufactured into Silk.[62]

The reliance on Pykars was also problematic because the Company was being overcharged for cocoons.[63] Moreover, and more importantly, Pykars

---

57   Ibid.

58   Ibid.

59   Douglas W. Allen, *The Institutional Revolution: Measurement and the Economic Emergence of the Modern World* (London: University of Chicago Press, 2012), pp. 196–9.

60   IOR/E/4/630, 21 July 1786, p. 548.

61   GL, 1775 fol.: George Williamson, *Proposals Humbly Submitted to the Consideration of the Court of Directors, for Affairs of the United Company of Merchants of England, Trading to the East-Indies, For Improving and Increasing the Manufactures of Silk in Bengal* (London: n.p., 1775), p. 15.

62   IOR/E/4/630, 21 July 1786, p. 548. Roberto Davini mentions that Chassars preferred to reel cocoons into country-wound silk and then sell it on the local market because they could get a better price for their silk this way. Davini, 'Una Conquista Incerta', p. 47. I argue that the low prices offered by Pykars and their behaviour towards Chassars needs to be considered as the main reason why Chassars preferred to sell their production on the local market.

63   The Company suspected that there was a 'secret understanding between the Pykars, the

made the use of price mechanisms to stimulate production of high-quality cocoons impossible. If the price of cocoons was set by the Pykars, the EEIC could hardly reward the production of high-quality cocoons through higher purchasing prices.[64]

Under both the putting-out system and the system of cocoon procurement, the EEIC was unable to implement changes to silkworm rearing practices. The problem was also recognised by the Company's employees. Mr Atkinson and George Williamson, for instance, acknowledged the fact that the Company needed to get directly involved in sericulture if the quality of cocoons was to improve.[65] Mr Atkinson commented on both the quality of the silkworm breed in India and the issue of 'degeneration', and linked them to the system of cocoon procurement as well as arguing for the introduction of foreign breeds. However, Atkinson also warned against degeneration in foreign silkworms if they were to be distributed among the peasants 'as indeed is evident in the case of the China cocoons'.[66] The method he championed was the 'establishment of breeding houses, or nurseries, under the inspection of silk agents for the purpose of rearing cocoons for supplying the filature'.[67]

George Williamson, a former employee of the EEIC in Bengal, proposed that the grounds around filatures be appropriated for the cultivation of mulberry trees, with huts for rearing silkworms to be set up in the grounds as well.[68] That would have allowed the EEIC to control sericulture and to oversee every stage of silk thread production. Williamson further proposed that the Company employ whole families in the production of silk thread: men in mulberry cultivation, women in the rearing of silkworms and children in silk reeling.[69] Although such an approach would undeniably have given the EEIC greater control over cocoon production, Williamson's plan was difficult to implement. This is because, notwithstanding the political control of Bengal, the EEIC was never able to monopolise Bengal's rural production and trade. There are numerous examples in the literature showing the

---

Banians [merchants] and the Contractors [of private filatures]' which was driving up the prices of cocoons. WBSA, CCC Prcds 25 July 1771, Letter from Cossimbuzar, 8 July 1771, as cited in Davini, 'Una Conquista Incerta', p. 131.

[64] In all likelihood, Pykars must have created an incentive for the peasants to focus on production for the local market. The discontent of peasants with the oppressive practices of Pykars was registered even before the filature system of raw silk production was put in place, and it was considered by the Company to be a serious threat to its investment policy. IOR/E/4/620, 23 March 1770, pp. 61–3.

[65] See Atkinson as cited in Geoghegan, *Some Account of Silk in India*, p. 7; GL, 1775 fol.: Williamson, *Proposals*, p. 17.

[66] Atkinson as cited in Geoghegan, *Some Account of Silk in India*, p. 7.

[67] Ibid.

[68] GL, 1775 fol.: Williamson, *Proposals*, pp. 17–18.

[69] Ibid., p. 18.

Company's inability to change trade patterns or to alter production in India in order to suit its own export needs.[70]

Altering the system of sericulture would be exceedingly difficult.[71] Rearing silkworms remained a household activity at least until the late nineteenth century in all silk-producing regions of the world. Coercing whole families to become involved in sericulture under the EEIC's management and control would require more political power than the Company commanded. Moreover, direct supervision of silkworm-rearing activities would be very expensive. Giovanni Federico has argued that the principal reasons for sericulture remaining a household activity were its labour intensity and the high costs of supervision that the centralisation of sericultural production would elicit.[72]

The fact that the Court never attempted to control sericulture should be seen as part of the general policy of the Company in procurement of goods for export: the Court emphasised that under all circumstances preference should be given to contracting for finished products rather than the Company becoming involved in production.[73] Silk reeling was an exception to this rule. The Court believed that amending reeling practices was a sufficient measure in order to attain Italian-quality raw silk. Moreover, the Court was convinced

[70]   Giorgio Riello, *Cotton: The Fabric that Made the Modern World* (Cambridge: Cambridge University Press, 2013), pp. 62–4; Bishnupriya Gupta, 'Competition and Control in the Market for Textiles: Indian Weavers and the English East India Company in the Eighteenth Century', in Giorgio Riello and Tirthankar Roy (eds), *How India Clothed the World: The World of South Asian Textiles, 1500–1850* (Leiden: Brill, 2009), pp. 292–7.

[71]   LSE Archives, W7204, *Reports and Documents*, p. xxxiv. 'That mulberry plantations can be established on account of the Company, so as in time to render the public investment in a considerable degree independent of the other sources of supply of cocoons, is not, we conceive, to be expected, considering that, for the accomplishment of such an ends, lands to so great an extent must be cultivated, and servants so numerous must be employed, as well as buildings be erected for rearing of cocoons comprehending altogether such a field of care and superintendence, as no Resident [director of a filature] could be competent to, in addition to the minute and constant attention requisite to the peculiar and important duty of manufacturing silk. Such a plan, even if it were found to be practicable, should, in all probability, from the greatness of the expense attending it, prove decidedly objectionable.' Ibid., p. 63.

[72]   In many regions sericulture remained a household activity even in the twentieth century, and entrepreneurs gained control over the production process by creating dependence. For instance, in Japan raw silk manufacturers gained control 'by providing scientifically bred silkworm eggs and detailed technical guidance', as well as by signing long-term direct purchase contracts with the farmers. Ma, 'Why Japan, not China', p. 381. Giovanni Federico, *An Economic History of the Silk Industry, 1830–1930* (Cambridge: Cambridge University Press, 1997), p. 16. In Japan the problems with cocoon quality were overcome under the household system of production thanks to institutional innovations. A new type of contract called the 'sub-contractual long direct purchase system' emerged, and institutionalised a long-term procedure of purchase contracts between farmers and filatures. Ma, 'Why Japan, Not China', p. 379.

[73]   IOR/E/4/630, 12 April 1786, p. 272.

that considerable improvement to the quality of reeled silk would be achieved if cocoons were handled in an appropriate manner.[74] The Court sent detailed guidelines to Bengal describing the preferred methods of storing cocoons. Attention was supposed to have been paid to the separation of 'good' and 'spoiled' cocoons – that is, mouldy cocoons or cocoons in which the moth was decomposing. The essential issue was to prevent cocoons becoming mouldy or undergoing fermentation or decomposition before they could be reeled.[75] Mixing 'good' and 'spoiled' ones increased the number of decomposing cocoons. Moreover, if these 'spoiled' cocoons were used in reeling they negatively affected the elasticity, strength and colour of the resulting silk thread, ultimately decreasing the price of such raw silk.[76]

Effects of the New Technologies on the Company's Silk Trade

After discussing the adoption of the Piedmontese technologies and the lack of change in sericulture, it is necessary to assess the effectiveness of the new system in Bengal. The quantities of exports and the share of Bengal raw silk on total imports, as well as the quality of the filature-made silk, needs to be considered to gain an accurate picture. The quality of raw silk was the single most important factor determining the demand for and price of Bengal silk on the British market. The adoption of the Piedmontese system of silk reeling led to significant quality improvements with positive effects on demand and prices. However, quality issues remained, driving down both prices and demand. Both contemporary and current research focused mostly on the quality of Bengal raw silk to argue that the Company's venture was a failure. Yet, the quantitative data shows that Bengal raw silk as a share of total raw silk imports to Britain from 1773 to 1829 exceeded 40 per cent, which made Bengal the largest exporter of raw silk to Britain. This surely does not suggest a failure.

Overall, the adoption of the Piedmontese technologies had a positive impact on the EEIC's capacities to export silk to Europe (Table 4.1). From the 1770s Bengal became quantitatively the most important exporter of raw silk to Britain. As the importation of raw silk from Bengal increased, the amount of raw silk imported from Aleppo, Valentia, Naples, Calabria and other places in the Mediterranean decreased.[77] Filature silk started to be produced in Bengal in 1773 and on a larger scale in 1775. Table 4.1 shows

---

[74] The guidelines produced by James Wiss, summing up the best practices that were to be implemented in filature silk production, contain a long passage with a detailed description of how the cocoons should be handled. IOR/E/4/625, 9 April 1777, pp. 173–85.

[75] Ibid., pp. 172–4.

[76] Ibid., pp. 182–4.

[77] LSE Archives, W7204, *Reports and Documents*, p. xxiv.

Table 4.1   Bengal raw silk as a share of the total imports of raw silk to Britain, 1750–1835

Year	Total average annual imports of raw silk (lbs.)	Quantity of Bengal raw silk as % of total
1750–60	388,091	8.7
1773–79	930,202	43.2
1780–89	889,371	45.0
1790–99	775,188	53.5
1800–09	786,183	51.1
1810–19	1,270,320	63.7
1820–29	2,638,144	45.6
1830–35	3,590,963	26.2

Source: Compiled from B. R. Mitchell, *British Historical Statistics* (Cambridge: Cambridge University Press, 1988), p. 343; K. N. Chaudhuri, *The Trading World of Asia and the English East India Company, 1660–1760* (Cambridge: Cambridge University Press, 1978), p. 534, Goldsmiths' Library, 1795 fol. 16280, *Reports of the Committee of Warehouses of the East-India Company relative to Extending the Trade on Bengal Raw-Silk* (London: n.p., 1795), pp. 6, 10, 14; House of Commons, *An Account of the Quantity and Value of Raw and Thrown Silk Imported into, and Exported from, Great Britain, For Twenty Years, ending the 5th January 1806* (London: n.p., 1806); House of Commons, *An Account of all Raw and Waste Silk Imported and Entered for Home Consumption in Each Year, from 1814 to the 5th day of January 1842* (London: n.p., 1842); LSE Archives, W7204, East India Company, *Reports and Documents Connected with the Proceedings of the East-India Company in regard to the Culture and Manufacture of Cotton-wool, Raw Silk, and Indigo in India* (London: J. L. Cox, 1836), pp. 3–4.

that the largest growth in raw silk imports occurred in the period from 1810 to 1830–35, which also saw an increase in total imports of raw silk to Britain. Yet, it should not be inferred that the figures were stable year on year; Table 4.1 does not capture the fact that annual imports fluctuated a great deal. This was caused by external factors such as droughts and natural disasters, as well as internal factors such as the lack of investment. However, fluctuations did not affect the buyers of raw silk as the Company kept reserves of raw silk at its London warehouses.

Adoption of the filature system played an important role in the growth of exports, as the evidence shows. Considering the quantity of production, the Bauleah filature with 104 furnaces produced 533 maunds 10 Seers 9 chhattaks (39,998 lbs.) of silk in the first four years of its existence. The Commercolly filature with 208 furnaces produced 1,096 maunds 32 seers 3 chhattaks (82,260 lbs.). Overall the establishment of the Bauleah, Commercolly and Kasimbazar filatures enabled the Company to double the value of silk procured from the Kasimbazar region in the years between 1772 and 1776.

It is clear that the filatures played an essential role in expanding imports to Britain. Unfortunately, the number of filatures and their production capacity is not known for the majority of the 1770s to the 1830s. Tables 4.2 and 4.3 offer a glimpse of the total capacity of filature production in 1833. The tables show that silk was produced in the major silk regions of Bauleah, Commercolly, Kasimbazar, Hurripaul, Malda, Radanagore, Rungpore, Santipore, Soonamooky and Surdah. In each of these regions there was one head factory which managed several filatures but, unfortunately, the exact number of filatures managed by each head factory is not known. The issue is even more complicated due to the fact that not all filatures were owned by the Company – some were hired. Thus, the most important information is the total number of basins since this number shows the capacity of filature silk production. If we add the number of hired basins to the number owned by the EEIC, it amounts to almost 16,000 basins.

Yet, despite the improved production capacity thanks to the establishment of filatures, the Company still needed to continue to import both filature and country-wound silk to fulfil the target quantity of exports to Britain. Between the 1770s and 1800s the Company did not differentiate between the two in its statistics, thus the quantity of filature production cannot be definitely ascertained for this period. We know for sure that the Company endorsed the importation of both types of raw silk from Bengal but gave preference to filature silk. This can be inferred from the instructions given to the Board of Trade in Bengal: in 1785, for instance, the Court in London demanded the proportion of silk to be 180,000 sm. lbs. of country-wound silk and 360,000 sm. lbs. of filature silk.[78] The orders for filature silk were further increased in 1796, when the quantity requested grew to 420,000 sm. lbs., while orders of country-wound silk remained stable (Figure 4.4).[79] The importation of filature silk continued to depend on expanding the capacities of filatures. Imports of country-wound silk were driven by the aim of the Company to meet the target of 540,000 sm. lbs. (later 600,000 sm. lbs.) per annum, rather than by the demand for this type of silk. The Court in London did not view the imports of country-wound silk favourably and demanded that production of filature silk be increased. In 1796 it was reported from London that country-wound silk had been a loss-making item of trade in several past sales.[80] It was therefore stated that 'the proportion (180,000 sm. lbs.) of Country Wound Silk ... is so ample as not to leave room for any addition. It is the Filature Sort only that can be looked to for any increase'.[81] Since the Company's records do not contain suggestions that increases in exports of Bengal raw silk after

78   IOR/E/4/628, 11 April 1785, p. 552.
79   IOR/E/4/645A, 27 July 1796, pp. 334–8.
80   IOR/E/4/645A, 27 July 1796, p. 338.
81   IOR/E/4/643, 3 July 1795, p. 595.

Table 4.2   Filatures hired by the English East India Company, 1832

Aurung	Number of basins	Silk procured by contract
Bauleah	0	No
Commercolly	0	No
Kasimbazar	792	Yes
Hurripaul	0	Yes
Malda	1,002	Unknown
Radanagore	200	Unknown
Rungpore	240	Unknown
Santipore	0	Yes
Soonamooky	1,350	Unknown
Surdah	100	Unknown
Total number of basins	3,684	

LSE Archives, W7204, East India Company, *Reports and Documents Connected with the Proceedings of the East-India Company in regard to the Culture and Manufacture of Cotton-wool, Raw Silk, and Indigo in India* (London: J. L. Cox, 1836), pp. 219–21.

Table 4.3   Filatures owned by the English East India Company, 1833

Head factory	Number of filatures comprising head factory	Number of filatures controlled by head factory	Total number of basins
Bauleah	10	24	2,018
Commercolly	6	7	1,716
Kasimbazar	1	0	152
Hurripaul	0	6	766
Jungypore	6	4	923
Malda	3	3	480
Radanagore	5	N	2,594
Rungpore	N	N	1,300
Santipore	N	N	800
Soonamooky	N	N	302
Surdah	N	N	888
Experimental	1		100
Total number of basins			12,039

LSE Archives, W7204, East India Company, *Reports and Documents Connected with the Proceedings of the East-India Company in regard to the Culture and Manufacture of Cotton-wool, Raw Silk, and Indigo in India* (London: J. L. Cox, 1836), pp. 215–18. N – signifies that the number is not known.

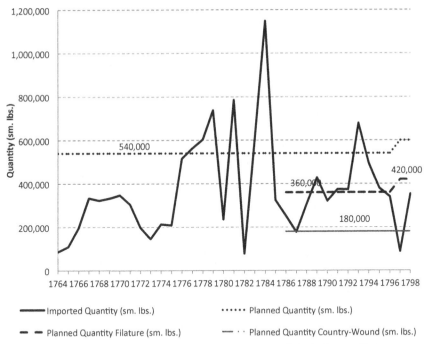

Figure 4.4   Quantities of Bengal raw silk imported into Britain (in sm. lbs.), 1764–1798

Source: Goldsmiths' Library, 1795 fol. 16280, *Reports of the Committee of Warehouses of the East-India Company relative to Extending the Trade on Bengal Raw-Silk* (London: n.p., 1795), pp. 6–10; LSE Archives, W7204, East India Company, *Reports and Documents Connected with the Proceedings of the East-India Company in regard to the Culture and Manufacture of Cotton-wool, Raw Silk, and Indigo in India* (London: J. L. Cox, 1836), p. 3; IOR/E/4/628, 11 April 1785, p. 552; IOR/E/4/645A, 27 July 1796, pp. 334–8. The sharp decline in imports in 1782 and the sudden increase in 1783 was due to a delayed harvest and problems with transportation.

1800 were driven by the expansion of imports of country-wound silk, it is safe to infer that the capacity of filature silk production grew significantly in this period.

The Company's silk investment policy was also of key importance. Investment in silk changed in conjunction with demands for military and administrative provision. Although precise information about the Company's yearly investments in raw silk is incomplete, the documents show that it fluctuated between £275,894 and £715,281 in the 1780s. However, when waging war, the annual investment fell to as low as £102,183.[82] The EEIC

---

[82]   GL, 1795 fol. 16280, *Reports of the Committee of Warehouses of the East-India Company*, pp. 18–19. Such evidence runs contra to Lucy S. Sutherland's findings that in the late 1760s and early

on several occasions, and particularly in the period of the 1770s to the 1790s, tried to offset the lack of funds available for investment in silk by allowing private individuals to build silk filatures in Bengal or to let them rent the Company's filatures.[83] The Company then procured the raw silk produced by these filatures.

Equally important to imports is analysis of the volume of Bengal raw silk sold on the British market. Once again the data is incomplete (Figure 4.5),[84] but it does show that fluctuations were not uncommon and, most importantly, that imports of Bengal raw silk surpassed its sales. During 1773–95 the EEIC accumulated 651,783 sm. lbs. of unsold Bengal raw silk in its warehouses, rising to an astonishing 2,658,693 sm. lbs. during 1801–05. This became a serious issue that the EEIC needed to address. Besides adopting measures to further improve the silk quality, the Court in London also tried to find new channels of consumption for Bengal raw silk, and in the late eighteenth century it promoted throwing Bengal raw silk in British mills.

Besides imports and sales it is also important to examine the prices of Bengal raw silk on the British market. The EEIC expected that Bengal raw silk reeled according to the Piedmontese method would attain a price increase of about 25 per cent.[85] The data shows that filature silk attained prices 26 per cent higher than country-wound silk, which implies that the adoption of the Piedmontese methods had a positive effect.[86] The Company's data on Bengal silk prices for the period 1770–1800 is incomplete; the existing data shows considerable year-on-year fluctuations rather than any steady trend. For instance, whereas in 1765 one gr. lb. of Bengal raw silk was sold for 26s. 12d, in 1771–72 it fetched around 18s. 8d. In 1772–75, when the first filature-wound silk reached the British market, it was sold at around 24s. However, such price fluctuations reflected the development of the British silk industry – characterised by expansion in the 1760s, a slump in the 1770s and subsequent stagnation until 1810 – rather than being an indication of the quality of Bengal raw silk.[87] In the period 1792 to 1796, filature silk sold on

1770s the Company was increasing its Bengal investment in spite of financial difficulties. Lucy S. Sutherland, *The East India Company in Eighteenth-Century Politics* (Oxford: Clarendon Press, 1952), p. 225.

[83] IOR/E/4/618, 24 December 1765, p. 97; IOR/E/4/638, 30 May 1792, p. 470; IOR/E/4/621, 7 April 1773, p. 506; IOR/E/4/623, 5 April 1776, pp. 269–76. IOR/E/4/628, 16 March 1764, pp. 261–5 and 11 April 1785, p. 555.

[84] Sales were most probably also affected by the decline of the British silk industry, which I discuss below.

[85] IOR/E/1/61, fols 486–487v, 'Letter 240 James Wiss in London to the Court Outlining the Advantages of the Italian Method of Spinning Silk in Bengal, 18 November 1777', p. 486.

[86] IOR/E/4/640, 25 June 1793, pp. 513–14; IOR/E/4/643, 3 July 1795, p. 597; IOR/E/4/645A, 27 July 1796, p. 330.

[87] D. C. Coleman, *Courtaulds: An Economic and Social History*, vol. 1: *The Nineteenth Century Silk and Crape* (Oxford: Clarendon Press, 1969), pp. 14–20.

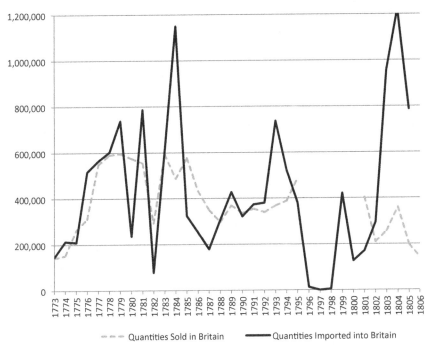

Figure 4.5 Bengal raw silk imported and sold in Britain by the EEIC, 1773–1806

Source: Compiled from: Goldsmiths' Library, 1795 fol. 16280, *Reports of the Committee of Warehouses of the East-India Company relative to Extending the Trade on Bengal Raw-Silk* (London: n.p., 1795), p. 6; L/PARL/2/55: Appendix to the Fourth Report of the Select Committee on the Affairs of the East India Company', pp. 218, 232; IOR/E/4/645, 27 July 1796, p. 552.

average for 24s. 7d. Although on some occasions filature silk sold for as little as 22s. 16d or even 16s. 7d, overall the fluctuations were not so severe and there is reason to expect that the price for which the Company sold its silk oscillated around 24s. per gr. lb. in the period from the 1770s to the 1800s.[88] In 1801–06 the average price was 19s. 4d per sm. lb. In the 1820s Bengal raw silk fetched between 14s. and 30s. on the London market depending on its quality.[89] In the 1830s one sm. lb. of Bengal raw silk sold for approximately 17s. 6d.[90]

In spite of the fact that the data is incomplete and caution needs to be taken when considering weights, several conclusions can be drawn.[91] First,

88 IOR/E/4/645A, 27 July 1796, p. 330; IOR/E/4/643, 3 July 1795, p. 597.
89 House of Lords, *Journal of the House of Lords*, vol. 54, 1821, p. 483.
90 House of Commons, *Report from Select Committee on the Silk Trade with Minutes of Evidence, Appendix and Index* (London: n.p., 1832), p. 698.
91 The essential problem for comparing sale prices in eighteenth century with those in the nineteenth century is the fact that in the period from the 1770s to the 1800s the Company

Bengal raw silk fetched lower prices on average than Chinese or Italian silk. Second, its price reflected quality, with finer sorts fetching higher prices. Third, the price of Bengal raw silk, as well of other silks, fluctuated from year to year rather than following an upward or downward shift in the period from the 1790s to the 1830s.[92]

Lastly, it is necessary to examine the quality of the silk as, in the silk trade, quality is the most important factor for determining sales and prices. Despite the innovations implemented, Bengal raw silk continued to be viewed as the lowest-quality silk on the market. The Company had to wrestle with the continuing perception by British manufacturers and contemporary economic writers that Bengal raw silk was a material 'fit only to be used in the lowest descriptions of manufactured goods, and its price in the English market, generally, was equal to about one-third of that of Italian silk'.[93] A contemporary silk expert claimed Bengal raw silk was 'of the commonest kind and fit only for inferior purposes, acceptable to the English manufacturer'.[94] The general consensus of the pamphleteers was that the lower quality of Bengal raw silk meant that it could fetch only a third or half of the price of Italian raw silk on the British market.[95] Yet, there was high demand for middling-quality raw silk on the British market as the British silk industry focused on production of smaller wares and haberdashery. Demand for middling-quality silk was increasing especially in the nineteenth century, when production of smaller wares and haberdashery further expanded as production of broad woven silk cloth declined. Thus, the key problem was not that the Bengal raw silk was of the coarser sort, but that it was not of a standard quality. The standardisation of quality was of pressing importance with the rise of mechanisation in throwing as the mills needed the input of a standard quality of silk thread in order to avoid breakages.[96]

---

sold silk in both sm. lbs. of 16 oz and gr. lbs. of 24 oz. Naturally gr. lbs. sold for higher prices yet there does not seem to be a stable relationship between the price of sm. lbs. and gr. lbs. The difference was approximately 6s. to 9s.

[92]   This conclusion can also be drawn from data presented in Appendix B. However, caution needs to be taken as this data represents averages of sale prices rather than reflecting the average price for which the Company sold its filature silk. This should explain why these prices often diverge from the Company's data. The Company seemed to be interested in the average selling price of its silk, as it was concerned with profitability rather than in giving information on prices per se. Besides it is not clear if the data always refers to sm. lbs. (16 oz) or gr. lbs. (24 oz) and what the qualitites of the different types of silks were.

[93]   John Crawfurd, *An Inquiry into some of the Principal Monopolies of the East India Company* (London: James Ridgway, 1830), p. 2.

[94]   Dionysius Lardner, *A Treatise on the Origin, Progressive Improvement, and Present State of the Silk Manufacture* (Philadelphia: Carey & Lea, 1832), p. 66.

[95]   Ibid.

[96]   IOR/E/4/627, 12 July 1782 p. 351; IOR/E/4/625, 9 April 1777, p. 175.

The System of Quality Enforcement in Bengal Raw Silk Manufacturing

The Company was keen to improve quality as it was aware that price and demand for Bengal raw silk were contingent on its reputation, the manufacturer's experience and the availability of information about its quality. In general, the quality of Bengal raw silk improved and it found a market especially among ribbon makers.[97] However, setting up an efficient system of quality enforcement proved to be challenging for the EEIC and, especially in the eighteenth century, a large part of the filature silk remained of non-standard quality. This meant that good-quality and inferior silk was often mixed in the same bale. This made buyers 'suspicious' about the quality of the raw silk and wary of being deceived. Such lack of quality enforcement became one of the most serious obstacles faced by the Company in the eighteenth century.[98] Problems with quality were caused by principal–agent problems that arose due to the distance between London and Bengal, and were aggravated by the system of contracting silk from private filatures from 1770 to the 1790s.

The introduction of the Piedmontese system meant a reduction of the principal–agent problems that existed between the Company and its gomastas on the one hand, and peasant producers on the other. Yet, the filature system brought about a new set of principal–agent problems: between the Court in London and the Board in Bengal; between the Court and the directors of the filatures; and between the directors of the filatures and the reelers (Figure 4.6).[99] The concept of the principal–agent problem is defined as the dilemma of how to motivate an agent to act in the best interest of the principal, and arises from asymmetries of information or conflict between the interests of principals and agents.[100] Geographical distance and slow communication were the key factors that gave rise to the possibility of agency problems as they negatively affected quality enforcement and created opportunities for fraud. Although the EEIC set up a multilevel procedure of quality inspection, the system was not fail-proof.

[97]   Royal Society of Arts (hereafter RSA) RSA/SC/EL/2/31, *Third Report of the Committee of Warehouses of the East-India Company relative to Extending the Trade on Bengal Raw-Silk* (London: n.p., 1795), pp. 6–7, 11–14; House of Commons, *Report from Select Committee on the Silk Trade*, pp. 41, 154, 174.

[98]   IOR/E/1/66, fols 422–424v, 'Letters 212–213 James Wiss in London to Peter Michell, 10 May 1780', p. 422.

[99]   Research has found that although vertical integration solves certain types of agency problems it also creates new types of agency problems related to the need for supervision. Rachel E. Kranton and Anand V. Swamy, 'Contracts, Hold-up, and Exports: Textiles and Opium in Colonial India', *American Economic Review* 98 (3), 2008, pp. 967–89.

[100]   See Sanford J. Grossman and Oliver D. Hart, 'An Analysis of the Principal–Agent Problem', *Econometrica* 51 (1), 1983, pp. 7–46; Ray Rees, 'The Theory of Principal and Agent, Part I', *Bulletin of Economic Research* 37 (1), 1985, pp. 3–26.

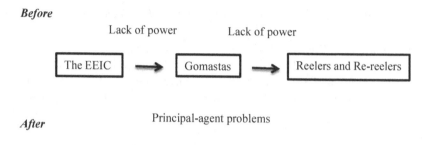

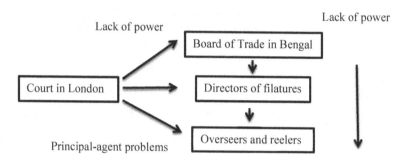

Figure 4.6   Agency problems before and after the implementation of the Piedmontese system

The quality of filature silk was to be supervised by the Superintendent General in Bengal and the Superintendents of Warehouses in Calcutta, and in Britain by the Inspector of Raw Silk in the EEIC's warehouses.[101] In filature production the system of quality control relied on labelling silk with the name of the factory, superintendent or director, overseer and warehouse keeper 'by which means we may in case of any deficiency discover to whose negligence the same is erring and accordingly require such Servants to make good any loss which shall be sustained by us on that account'.[102] However, the records do not contain any cases where a servant in Bengal was brought to account for the production of low-quality silk.[103] Moreover, the Company's documents note that the names of the persons responsible for the quality of the filature silk were often missing or changing very frequently due to turnover

---

[101] IOR/E/4/625, 9 April 1777, p. 171.

[102] IOR/E/4/621, 25 January 1772, p. 211; IOR/E/4/625, 9 April 1777, p. 226.

[103] The only case I found in which the EEIC dismissed employees due to misconduct related to silk production was a dismissal by the Board of Trade. Although this is a case of great magnitude, it is not connected to a neglect of quality enforcement in silk production but to fraudulent behaviour and embezzlement. See IOR/E/4/630, 12 April 1786, pp. 391–3.

of servants working in silk production.[104] Moreover, the system lacked any incentive in terms of financial rewards for reelers, overseers or filature supervisors to produce high-quality raw silk.

Asymmetries of information between the buyers (and the Court in London) and the producers were rife. Evidence shows that in 1780 it was found by the Company's London workers that 'fine and perfect silk reels over or is put upon coarse and inferior silk which makes it expensive and difficult to work and skeins are three times too large also'.[105] The Company was aware of the continuing problems with the standard of Bengal silk as instructions from London to Bengal repeatedly mentioned the necessity of quality enforcment. Correspondence from London also contained reports detailing the adverse effects of neglecting this issue:

> such a reception as is complained of may be productive of the worst consequences to the interest of the Company for if the appearance of the silk is so little to be expended upon from inspection, the buyers will grow so very suspicious that at the sales such silk as in reality might be worth 25 [shillings per gr. lb.] will not be bid more than 20 for, if this only for fear of being deceived.[106]

The silk specialists employed by the EEIC in London were well aware of the effect that fluctuating silk quality had on the buyers but could do no more than report the problem.

The Court was also well aware that the issue was caused by the faulty conduct of reelers and Bengal employees, and not by any technical difficulty. James Wiss – the EEIC's Inspector of Warehouses in London – drew attention to the fact that inconsistent silk quality was badly affecting the Company's profits:

> such a trick, which is certainly done intentionally by his people who can plead no excuse either from the quality of the cocoons, nor from the reels, not from the spinners, for the first reeling and the outside coat of the skeins is good silk, but the middle, which is very considerable in quantity for the skeins are three times as large, (that is too heavy – being 9 ounces in weight) consists only of rubbish and of very coarse bad silk perhaps not worth 8 s. a pound, and thus a deception by which the Sircars may have got a few hundred pounds, will make Company liable to suffer an immense loss upon the whole sale.[107]

Wiss's conclusions were well informed as they were based on several years

---

[104] IOR/E/4/625, 9 April 1777, pp. 225–6; IOR/E/4/626, 5 July 1780, p. 219.
[105] IOR/E/1/66, fols 422–424v, 'Letters 212–213 James Wiss in London to Peter Michell', p. 422.
[106] Ibid.
[107] Ibid., pp. 422–3.

of experience in setting up silk filatures, training reelers and adapting the Piedmontese technology in Bengal.

Such problems with quality that were discussed in the Company's documents with great frequency in the 1770s–90s almost ceased to appear in the later period. Not that the quality of Bengal raw silk was without problems in the later period but mixing became a lesser issue. The important thing to note is that in the period from the 1770s up to and including the 1790s the EEIC received a large part of its raw silk for export from private filatures.

The Company was pushed into contracting of silk from private filatures because of financial difficulties. Especially in the period from the 1770s up to and including the 1790s the Company invested in securing and expanding its territorial gains, and funds were channelled into military pursuits.[108] The Company needed to turn to other arrangements in order to be able to procure goods for Europe. In the case of silk production, it was decided that the easiest way to deal with a shortage of funds was to enable private individuals to build silk filatures in Bengal, or to let them rent the Company's filatures to produce raw silk there. Most of the silk produced by private filatures was bought by the Company although, as observed by Peter Marshall, private filatures also 'no doubt sold part of their silk to "country" traders, to the foreign companies, or to make up the "privilege" of officers on East Indiamen'.[109]

The procurement of silk from private filatures was based on contracts. The filatures entered into an agreement with the Board of Trade to deliver a determined quantity of silk at a set price, part of which was to be paid in advance.[110] The essential problem with contracting was that the authority to sign contracts was assumed by the Board of Trade. The Court in London had limited control over the Board and, as the evidence shows, the Board did not follow closely the directives received from London.[111]

The fact that contracts were fixed for several years added to the already suboptimal contracting system as it removed incentives for the filatures to compete for contracts by lowering their prices. Moreover, from 1774 to 1786 the system led to fraud and in 1789 the EEIC filed a suit in Chancery against eight former members of the Board of Trade in Bengal and several contractors.[112] The Court in London found that 'Contracts were a collusive business

---

[108] IOR/E/4/618, 24 December 1765, p. 97; IOR/E/4/638, 30 May 1792, p. 470; IOR/E/4/621, 7 April 1773, p. 506; IOR/E/4/623, 5 April 1776, pp. 269–76. IOR/E/4/628, 16 March 1784, pp. 261–5. IOR/E/4/628, 11 April 1785, p. 555.

[109] Peter Marshall, 'Private British Investment in Eighteenth-Century Bengal', in Patrick Tuck (ed.), *The East India Company, 1600–1858* (London: Routledge, 1998), vol. 4, p. 136.

[110] Ibid.; IOR/E/4/626, 12 May 1780, pp. 205–22.

[111] Ibid., pp. 215–22.

[112] Among the Board members were William Aldersey, Philip Milner, Mr Dacres, Charles Bentley, Alexander Higginson, Simeon Droz, William Rook and William Harwood. The contractors that were said to have derived most profit were Thomas Chapman, James Lucas Worship, James English Kegley, Joseph Barreto, James Burn, and John Fergusson. Several

between the Board of Trade and the Contractors, [...] the former reserved to themselves a certain share of the profits, or had contained sums paid them for granting this Contract at such high prices.'[113] The Board of Trade had signed contracts for raw silk reeled in private filatures for prices almost double the production cost.[114] The profit that the private contractors made in this way was then divided between the members of the Board and the contractors.[115] Furthermore, the quality of the silk from private filatures was considerably lower when compared with silk from the Company's filatures, and sold for considerably lower prices.[116]

The Court was well aware of the conflicting interests inherent in silk contracting, and of the consequences for the quality of the silk. Commenting on the conduct of the Board of Trade, the Court wrote to Bengal:

> this is among the mischiefs arising from our Board of Trade (and perhaps our Silk Inspectors at Calcutta) being interested in the Contracts, this interest has led them either not to examine, or if they did examine, shamefully to pass every bad Silk when the best was contracted for.[117]

The Court perceived the problem as one caused by a lack of penalties and was determined to rely on legal measures if necessary: 'until our Servants are made sensible of our determination to furnish as well as to warrant feeling the effect of legal proceedings we fear will not be deterred from the pursuing of improper conduct in the modes hereby practiced or by some new invention'.[118] At the same time the Court was determined to produce silk on its own account and not to rely extensively on private filatures. The fact that no large-scale scandal affected Bengal silk production in the nineteenth century should be evidence of its success.

Conclusion

The fact that the Piedmontese system relied on a centralised system of reeling proved to be key for the success of the venture. Relocating reelers into filatures enabled the specialist to instruct multiple reelers at the same time, adopt

---

of the members of the Board of Trade were also the directors of the Company's filatures in Bengal: for instance, Simeon Droz and William Aldersey. TNA C 12/175/27, 24 March 1789 to 11 November 1789.

113 IOR/E/4/630, 12 April 1786, p. 391.

114 Ibid., p. 390.

115 TNA C 12/175/27, 24 March 1789 to 11 November 1789; IOR/E/4/630, 12 April 1786, p. 392–3 and 21 July 1786, p. 537–42.

116 Ibid., 12 April 1786, p. 392.

117 Ibid.

118 Ibid., pp. 392–3.

practices such as killing moths in ovens, and supervise reeling. Any changes made only had a minimal effect on sericulture. The most important change was the reduction in the number of intermediaries involved in procurement. Attempts to adopt changes in sericulture did not extend beyond the experimental stage. The lack of improvement in cocoon quality represented an impediment to improvement in the quality of silk thread. Due to the lack of control over peasants – peasants could sell their cocoons on the local markets – the EEIC could impose no practical measures of quality improvement. Rearing silkworms under the Company's direct control would have been very expensive. Nevertheless, in the end the most serious problem was the inappropriate ways in which the EEIC's employees handled cocoons as these methods led to quality deterioration.

The transfer of Piedmontese silk-reeling technologies to Bengal enabled the EEIC to capture on average 50.4 per cent of the market for raw silk in the period 1773–1829 and made Bengal the largest exporter of raw silk to Britain. Yet the venture was not without challenges and the insufficient improvement in silk quality was the most significant problem. The fact that Bengal raw silk never matched the quality of Italian varieties was not of huge consequence, as historically the British silk industry specialised in the production of haberdashery and smaller items that relied on middling-quality raw silk rather than the finest varieties. Throughout the late eighteenth and early nineteenth centuries this specialisation gained momentum and demand expanded for coarser varieties of raw silk, such as that supplied from Bengal. The most serious problem was the production of sub-standard quality silk in the late eighteenth century, which had its origin in the institutional setting and was aggravated by contracting silk from private filatures.

Chapter 5

FILATURES AND PERFORMANCE IN THE BENGAL SILK INDUSTRY

The transfer of the Piedmontese technologies to Bengal represented a considerable investment. Overall, in the period 1760s–1810s the transfer and adaptation of the Piedmontese system to the Bengal climate cost the Company almost £1 million.[1] Thus, the questions to ask are: was the venture profitable for the Company? If yes, which factors underpin its profitability?

In economic history literature, technology transfers have been assessed from the point of view of factor-price ratios. The scholarship has shown that the similarity of factor prices between the country where a technology originates and the country to which that technology is exported is crucial to profitability in the new environment.[2] India has been labelled as a low-wage economy for which the adoption of a type of factory production in the eighteenth century would be premature.[3] This chapter considers the variation in the prices of labour and inputs between Piedmont and Bengal and shows that the difference, though not insignificant, did not undermine profitability. Control over further stage of raw silk commodity chain was instead the key factor that made the Piedmontese type of silk reeling profitable in Bengal. This enabled the EEIC to build a business model of raw silk production based on adapting the fineness and quantity of raw silk according to demand in Britain, on economies of scale in technology upgrading, and in the long run on learning-by-doing in production and management.

[1] IOR/E/4/625, 9 April 1779, pp. 131–2.
[2] Yujiro Hayami and Vernon W. Ruttan, 'Factor Prices and Technical Change in Agricultural Development: The United States and Japan, 1880–1960', *Journal of Political Economy* 78 (5), 1970, pp. 1115–41.
[3] Stephen Broadberry and Bishnupriya Gupta, 'Lancashire, India, and Shifting Competitive Advantage in Cotton Textiles, 1700–1850: The Neglected Role of Factor Prices', *Economic History Review* 62 (2), 2009, pp. 279–305.

Introduction

Economic history literature frequently cites factor prices as one of the main reasons why India did not adopt a factory system in the eighteenth century and early in the nineteenth century. In the scholarship, centralisation has been mostly related to the rise of factories and the substitution of labour with capital. Centralisation is thus associated with factor-price theories and the discussion of shifts in competitive advantage. Authors such as Stephen Broadberry and Bishnupriya Gupta, E. Rothbarth, Robert Allen, and Yujiro Hayami and Vernon W. Ruttan have focused on how high wages facilitated the development and adoption of capital-intensive technologies associated with high labour productivity.[4] Robert Allen has argued that the Industrial Revolution took place in Britain because it was a high-wage economy and high wages facilitated a search for technologies that could substitute labour with capital.[5] For the cotton industry, Broadberry and Gupta argued that in India comparatively low wages reinforced the focus on labour-intensive domestic cotton production.[6] Arguably, from this perspective, the EEIC's decision to implement a centralised system of production in raw silk manufacturing was therefore premature and thus the venture would be expected to be unsuccessful. Yet, the silk industry represents a case that does not support

---

[4]   Broadberry and Gupta, 'Lancashire, India', pp. 279–305. See also: E. Rothbarth 'Causes of the Superior Efficiency of USA Industry as Compared with British Industry', *Economic Journal* 56, 1946, pp. 383–90; Robert Allen, *The British Industrial Revolution in Global Perspective* (Cambridge: Cambridge University Press, 2009); Robert Allen, Jean-Pascal Bassino, Debin Ma, Christine Moll-Murata, and Jan Luiten van Zanden, 'Wages, Prices, and Living Standards in China, 1738–1925: In Comparison with Europe, Japan, and India', *Economic History Review* 64 (S1), 2011, pp. 8–38; Robert Allen, 'The High Wage Economy and the Industrial Revolution: A Restatement', *Economic History Review* 68 (1), 2015, pp. 1–22; Hayami and Ruttan, 'Factor Prices and Technical Change in Agricultural Development', pp. 1115–41.

[5]   Robert Allen considers macro-inventions decisive for industrial development and identifies James Hargreaves' spinning jenny (with Richard Arkwright's water frame) as a key invention of the Industrial Revolution. Allen argues that the invention of the spinning jenny was driven by factor supply conditions. Allen, *British Industrial Revolution*, pp. 182–216. However, the evidence collected by John Styles shows that spinning jenny was an 'inexpensive, low-tech, mechanical enhancement to household-based spinning' and, therefore, Allen's argument that it was a labour-saving, capital-intensive macro-invention cannot hold. John Styles, 'Fashion, Textiles and the Origins of the Industrial Revolution' (paper presented at the conference 'Anglo-Japanese Conference of Historians', Osaka, August 2015), pp. 3, 7–20, and especially 21. This undermines Allen's argument that factor prices are the sole factor driving technological development. In his book *The British Industrial Revolution in Global Perspective*, Robert Allen also attributes importance to coal, which gave Britain an important source of energy for the Industrial Revolution. Allen, *British Industrial Revolution*, pp. 80–106, 135–56; see also Allen, 'High Wage Economy', p. 2.

[6]   Broadberry and Gupta, 'Lancashire, India', pp. 281–2. For discussion of India as a high-wage economy, see for instance: Prasannan Parthasarathi, *The Transition to a Colonial Economy: Weavers, Merchants and Kings in South India, 1720–1800* (Cambridge: Cambridge University Press, 2002), especially pp. 3–5, 15–18.

the conclusions of theories either based on factor prices or drawn from the analysis of the cotton sector.

The organisation of a type of factory production was adopted in silk manufacturing sooner than in other industries in response to the introduction of complex reeling technologies.[7] The profitability of the centralised system of production in the eighteenth-century silk industry was underpinned by specific factors: the requirements for quality and the need to keep labour costs down. In Bengal, centralisation was a key for improvement in silk quality, for keeping labour costs low and increasing the productivity and precision of reelers. Moreover, centralisation proved to be profitable from the financial perspective. Statistics show that the EEIC was able to produce raw silk more cheaply than it could buy it finished on the market. Centralisation enabled the EEIC to capture a greater share of the commodity chain which proved essential for achieving economies of scale in production and when upgrading technology. The Company built its business model of raw silk manufacturing based on the control of reeling, access to cheap cocoons, and adapting the quantity and fineness of produced silk according to demand from the British market.

The handful of scholars who studied the Bengal silk industry did not perceive the Company's project as successful. Authors such as Gautam Bhadra, Sabyasachi Bhattacharya, Harbans Mukhia and Indrajit Ray drew attention to the fact that Bengalese peasants and reelers initially resisted the new methods.[8] Claudio Zanier considered the Company's attempts to innovate in the Bengalese silk industry to be inadequate and argued that efforts in this area had ceased by the 1790s. Roberto Davini pointed to the fact that the local market for raw silk was an important competitor of the EEIC and that the Company often could not get the best cocoons on the market.[9] Indrajit Ray argued that by the end of the nineteenth century technological

---

7   Claudio Zanier, 'Pre-Modern European Silk Technology and East Asia: Who Imported What?', in Debin Ma (ed.), *Textiles in the Pacific, 1500–1900. The Pacific World: Lands, Peoples and History of the Pacific, 1500–1900* (Aldershot: Variorum, 2005), pp. 131–9.

8   Gautam Bhadra, 'The Role of Pykars in the Silk Industry of Bengal (c.1765–1830) Part 2', *Studies in History* 4 (1/2), 1988, pp. 17–18, 34–5; Gautam Bhadra, 'Silk Filature and Silk Production: Technological Development in the Early Colonial Context, 1768–1833', in Deepak Kumar (ed.), *Science and Empire: Essays in Indian Context, 1700–1947* (Delhi: Anamika Prakashan, 1991), pp. 75–7, 82; Sabyasachi Bhattacharya, 'Cultural and Social Constraints on Technological Innovation and Economic Development: Some Case Studies', *Indian Economic and Social History Review* 3 (3), 1966, pp. 243–6; Harbans Mukhia, 'Social Resistance to Superior Technology: The Filature in Eighteenth-Century Bengal', *Indian Historical Review* 11 (1/2), 1984, pp. 56–64; Indrajit Ray, 'The Silk Industry in Bengal during Colonial Rule: The 'De-Industrialisation' Thesis Revisited', *Indian Economic and Social History Review*, 42 (3), 2005, p. 349.

9   Roberto Davini, 'Una Conquista Incerta. La Compagnia Inglese delle Indie e la Seta del Bengala, 1769–1833' (unpublished Ph.D. thesis, European University Institute, 2004), pp. 10–54.

upgrading petered out and Bengal was unable to compete with the major silk producers.[10] However, none of these authors consider the venture from the Company's point of view and thus fail to acknowledge the profits it made. Secondly, it is necessary to recognise the fact that the EEIC was not involved in the post-1833 development of the Bengal silk industry because the 1833 Act forced the Company to cease all its economic activities in India.

The Commodity Chain in Bengal Raw Silk Production and the Company's Business Model

Michael Morris, Minet Schindehutte and Jeffrey Allen pointed to the fact that 'ventures fail despite the presence of market opportunities, business ideas, adequate resources, and talented entrepreneurs'.[11] They argued that a faulty business model might be the explanation. Drawing on this finding I argue that in the case of the EEIC's silk manufacturing venture, a solid business model enabled the Company to succeed despite its organisational failures, strong market competition and the slow response of top management to the various challenges they faced.

Interest in business models has only grown since the late 1990s[12] but, despite this surge in research interest, no consensus yet exists regarding the definition of a business model.[13] Existing definitions can be categorised as economic, operational and strategic.[14] At the most basic level, a business model relates to the firm's economic model as 'a statement of how a firm will make money and sustain its profit stream over time'.[15] At the operational level, a business model refers to the firm's internal processes and its architecture that allows it to create value.[16] The strategic definition of a business model refers to 'the totality of how a company selects its customers, defines and differentiates its offerings, defines the tasks it will perform itself and those it will outsource,

---

[10] Ray, 'Silk Industry in Bengal', pp. 372–3.

[11] Michael Morris, Minet Schindehutte and Jeffrey Allen, 'The Entrepreneur's Business Model: Toward a Unified Perspective, *Journal of Business Research* 58, 2005, p. 726.

[12] Although this growing interest is connected to the rise of modern communication and computing technologies and the firms involved in these sectors, the topic of business models is in no way new. See for instance: David J. Teece, 'Business Models, Business Strategy and Innovation', *Long Range Planning* 43, 2010, p. 172.

[13] The term 'business model' is often confused with strategy, business concept, revenue model and economic model. Moreover, it is often understood in the literature to be architecture, design, pattern, plan, method, assumption or statement. Such a variation in perspectives makes the definition of a particular company's business model exceedingly difficult. Morris, Schindehutte and Allen, 'The Entrepreneur's Business Model', pp. 726–7.

[14] Ibid.

[15] David W. Stewart and Qin Zhao, 'Internet Marketing, Business Models, and Public Policy', *Journal of Public Policy & Marketing* 19 (2), 2000, p. 290.

[16] Morris, Schindehutte and Allen, 'The Entrepreneur's Business Model', p. 727.

configures its resources, goes to market, creates utility for customers and captures profits'.[17] The various definitions can be explained when we consider the range of theoretical backgrounds behind them. Business model theories build on the value chain concept, value systems and strategic positioning,[18] competitive advantage and resource-based theory,[19] the strategic network theory and co-operative strategies,[20] and choices about firm boundaries and transaction cost economics.[21]

Considering the several challenges the EEIC faced in its Bengal silk venture – especially faulty management leading to production of non-standard quality silk – the fact that the Company was able to make profits from trading Bengal raw silk raises questions. By examining the business model (Figure 5.1) we can make sense of this paradox. In defining the EEIC's business model in raw silk manufacturing I am relying on Morris, Schindehutte and Allen as their study offers a comprehensive theoretical framework that encompasses the economic, operational and strategic levels of business models. Figure 5.1 shows that knowledge of the British market for raw silk, transmission of information about demand on the British market, rules about the overall quantity and the fineness of silk to be produced and imported to Britain, setting of maximum prices to be paid for cocoons and maximum wages to be paid to reelers, and technological upgrading based on cutting production costs were the key principles on which the Company based its venture in Bengal raw silk manufacturing. These rules developed slowly throughout the 1790s–1830s thanks to learning-by-doing, as I will show. It is necessary to remember that eighteenth-century business and entrepreneurial practices were not characterised by advanced management and accounting systems, and so it would be misleading, for instance, to expect that the Company's decision to adopt

17 Adrian J. Slywotzky, *Value Migration: How to Think Several Moves Ahead of the Competition* (Boston, MA: Harvard Business Press, 1996), p. 4.
18 Michael E. Porter, *The Competitive Advantage of Nations* (New York: Free Press, 1990); Michael Porter, 'What Is Strategy?', *Harvard Business Review* 74 (6), 1996, pp. 61–78.
19 Jay Barney, Mike Wright, David J. Ketchen Jr, 'The Resource-Based View of the Firm: Ten Years After 1991', *Journal of Management* 27 (6), 2001, pp. 625–41.
20 J. Carlos Jarillo, *Strategic Network: Creating the Borderless Organization* (London: Routledge, 1995); Jeffrey H. Dyer and Harbir Singh, 'The Relational View: Cooperative Strategy and Sources of Interorganizational Competitive Advantage', *The Academy of Management Review* 23 (4), 1998, pp. 660–79.
21 Jay B. Barney, 'How a Firm's Capabilities Affect Boundary Decisions', *Sloan Management Review* 40 (3), 1999, pp. 19–32; Oliver E. Williamson, 'The Economics of Organization: The Transaction Cost Approach', *American Journal of Sociology* 87 (3), 1981, pp. 548–77; Ronald Coase 'The Nature of the Firm', *Economica* 4 (16), 1937, pp. 3–7; Oliver E. Williamson, 'The Vertical Integration of Production: Market Failure Considerations', *American Economic Review* 61 (2), 1971, pp. 112–13; Oliver E. Williamson, 'Transaction Cost Economics: The Governance of Contractual Relations, *Journal of Law and Economics* 22 (2), 1979, pp. 233–61; Oliver E. Williamson, 'The Organization of Work: A Comparative Institutional Assessment', *Journal of Economic Behaviour & Organization* 1 (1), 1980, pp. 25–9.

Figure 5.1　EEIC business model of raw silk

Foundation level	Proprietary level	Rules
Component 1: How did the EEIC create value? (factors related to offering)		
Sell products	Raw silk	Maximum prices at which filatures bought cocoons should not exceed internally agreed price
Standardised	Silk of qualities A (finest quality) to E (coarse variety)	
Narrow breadth	Focus on customers demanding raw silk of coarser varieties	Maximum wages of reelers should not exceed internally agreed wages
Shallow lines	Raw silk only (thrown yarn was only at an experimental stage)	In case of liquidity issues, partially outsource silk production to private manufacturers
Internal manufacturing	Reeling of silk from cocoons done in the Company's filatures	
Direct distribution	Raw silk sold at the Company's sales – two sales per year	
Component 2: Who did the EEIC create value for? (market factors)		
Type of organisation: business-to-business (B2B) and business-to-consumer (B2C) (sell silk to individual weavers and silk manufacturers as well as intermediary merchants)	Supplying British market with silk from dependent territory, relying on lower duties thanks to the government's favouring imports from colonies	Supplying defined quantities of raw silk annually in order not to decrease the silk price
International/national	Focus on British market which produces haberdashery and silk items of lower quality (in international comparison) and thus relies on medium-quality silk	Allocate annual production between categories of fineness A to E according to current market demand
Where customer is in the value chain: downstream supplier		Stressing the benefits the Company provides for British manufacturers to gain popular and government support
Broad market	Gathering information about the development of demand for raw silk on the British market	
Transactional		

Foundation level	Proprietary level	Rules
Component 3: What was the EEIC's source of competence? (internal capability factors)		
Production/operating systems	Hiring highly skilled European silk specialists to implement 'best practices' in production and technical innovations	Creating the positions of Superintendent of London warehouses and Superintendent General in Bengal
Information management	Gather information about the demand for raw silk at sales and from manufacturers, employ silk specialists to suggest improvements	Send silk specialist to Bengal to advise individual filatures – a maximum of three silk specialists in Bengal at any one time
Supply chain management	Procuring inputs: cocoons for silk reeling from peasants either directly or more often from intermediary merchants Directly managing the reeling phase Directly managing transport, sales and marketing Relying on market power and economies of scale	Buying cocoons at each of the five cocoon harvests of the year and adopting rules about the type of silk that is to be reeled at each harvest (rainy seasons focus on producing less fine silk) Setting advances to be given to peasants, attempt to set the quality required for cocoons Organising two sales per year in London
Component 4: How did the EEIC competitively position itself? (competitive strategy factors)		
Image of consistency/ dependability	Differentiation is achieved by stressing the reliability of silk supply in contrast to disruptions in supply of raw silk from non-British territories due to war or bans on exports	Make sure that there are two sales each year. If supply of silk from Bengal declines due to adverse weather conditions or other unforeseen events, rely on reserve supply in London warehouses
Low cost	Sell silk for market price rather than set price	

(ctd.)

(Figure 5.1 ctd.)

Foundation level	Proprietary level	Rules
Component 5: How did the EEIC make money? (economic factors)		
Fixed revenue source High operating leverage High volumes Low margins	Relying on cheap inputs (cocoons and wood) and cheap labour, favourable tariffs and demand for medium quality raw silk in Britain to make profits	Maintain production costs of 1 lb. of raw silk or decrease these costs through adoption of technological innovation and using market power and innovations in system of cocoon procurement to avoid a rise in their prices
Component 6: What was the time, scope and size ambitions of the EEIC?		
Subsistence model (income model at certain periods)	Emphasis on profits and avoiding losses, adoption of technologies that would decrease production costs	Avoiding losses, maximising profits rather than expanding business

the Piedmontese technologies was based on the detailed analysis of the future return on its investment that is common today.[22]

Initially, the EEIC based its decision to manufacture raw silk in Bengal on the knowledge that labour in India was cheap and it also counted on Bengal raw silk having preferential access to the British market. Primarily, the Company expected to be able to produce higher-quality silk at competitive prices if it integrated reeling into its business operations. Adopting a centralised system of production made direct control over silk reeling possible and allowed the Company to differentiate its product – Bengal raw silk – from other types of silk. Most importantly, the EEIC was aware that by integrating reeling into its business activities it would be able to manage a higher proportion of the global commodity chain in raw silk production and exports.

A commodity chain is defined as 'a network of labor and production processes whose end result is a finished commodity'.[23] A global commodity chain 'consists of sets of inter-organizational networks clustered around one commodity or product, linking households, enterprises, and states to

22   Sidney Pollard, *The Genesis of Modern Management: A Study of the Industrial Revolution in Great Britain* (London: Edward Arnold, 1965), pp. 190–3, 250–70.
23   Terence K. Hopkins and Immanuel Wallerstein, 'Commodity Chains in the World-Economy Prior to 1800', *Review Fernand Braudel Center* 10 (1), 1986, p. 159.

Figure 5.2 Commodity chain in raw silk production in Bengal, 1770s–1830s

Primary stage	Secondary stage	Tertiary stage
Controlled by peasants	**Controlled by EEIC**	**Controlled by EEIC**
Inputs: Silkworm eggs, mulberry leaves, water, peasant labour, land for mulberry cultivation and cocooneries.	**Inputs:** Land for filatures, filatures, labour of reelers, supervision, cocoons, wood.	**Inputs:** Freight, customs, charges for warehouses, etc.

Product

Cocoons ⟶ Reeled silk ⟶ Bengal raw silk on British market

one another within the world-economy'.[24] Many industries were already characterised by global commodity chains in the pre-industrial period.[25] The silk industry was identified as one such due to the diffusion of silk weaving to those regions with climatic conditions unfavourable to sericulture. Moreover, the global commodity chain in silk production was characterised by high levels of competition in both raw silk production and the silk textiles market. According to Porter, a firm can succeed in a global industry only if it 'manages linkages in a global commodity chain in an integrated and systemic fashion'.[26] Figure 5.2 shows the three stages of the raw silk commodity chain in Bengal. The EEIC already controlled the tertiary stage which consisted of transport, sales and marketing. By implementing the Piedmontese system, the EEIC took charge of the secondary stage and the process of reeling. This gave the Company control over reeling practices and the costs of reeling, and at the same time increased its power vis-à-vis the intermediary merchants and peasants involved in sericulture. Moreover, the reduction in the number

---

[24] Gary Gereffi, Miguel Korzeniewicz and Roberto P. Korzeniewicz, 'Introduction: Global Commodity Chains', in Gary Gereffi and Miguel Korzeniewicz (eds), *Commodity Chains and Global Capitalism* (Westport, CT: Praeger, 1994), p. 2.

[25] An example of this is early-modern shipbuilding: Eyüp Özveren, 'The Shipbuilding Commodity Chain, 1590–1790', in Gereffi and Korzeniewicz (eds), *Commodity Chains and Global Capitalism*, pp. 20–33. 'We think it is quite clear that for these two fundamental processes of the capitalist world-economy in the seventeenth and eighteenth centuries, the commodity chains were geographically extensive, complex, and in constant recomposition.' Terence K. Hopkins and Immanuel Wallerstein, 'Conclusions About Commodity Chains', in Gereffi and Korzeniewicz (eds), *Commodity Chains and Global Capitalism*, p. 48.

[26] Michael E. Porter, 'Changing Patterns of International Competition', in David J. Teece (ed.), *The Competitive Challenge: Strategies for Industrial Innovation and Renewal* (Cambridge, MA: Ballinger, 1987), p. 30.

of intermediaries involved in raw silk production gave the Company better control over cocoon prices by decreasing the margins gained by merchants.

Porter has argued that in industries characterised by global competition, a competitive advantage can be achieved by integrating activities on a worldwide basis.[27] He draws on a disaggregated view of the firm, which he has called a 'value chain'.[28] From this perspective a firm is a 'collection of discrete activities performed to do business in its industry', and these activities are called 'value activities'.[29] Firms can gain a competitive advantage either by focusing on product differentiation or by lowering their production costs.[30] From this point of view the EEIC focused its activities in the eighteenth century on achieving product differentiation. Such an approach was based on the structure of the contemporary market in raw silk, in which silk of a higher quality attained a higher price. A market for middling-quality silk also existed, however, as producers of haberdashery purchased large quantities of such silk. Silk manufacturers and weavers did not necessarily seek raw silk at the lowest price but silk of a suitable quality. In such a market, product differentiation was a source of competitive advantage because it enabled a firm to focus on a target market.

Figure 5.3 draws on Porter's definition of the firm as a value chain and adds the actual operations carried out by the Company in raw silk production. The primary 'value activities' were cocoon procurement, reeling, warehousing and transport, advertising and the organisation of sales. I have estimated the costs that the EEIC needed to incur for each activity for the production of 1 sm. lb. of raw silk.

Porter distinguishes between two sources of competitive advantage: cheap labour and 'higher order' competitive advantages (proprietary technology, product differentiation, brand reputation, customer relationships and constant industrial upgrading).[31] By implementing the Piedmontese system, the EEIC attempted to draw on two sources of 'higher order' competitive advantage mentioned by Porter: product differentiation and brand reputation. The EEIC adopted the most advanced European reeling technology with the aim of producing 'Bengal Italian silk'. Its intention was to differentiate the silk from other types and create a brand reputation for it.

The case of the EEIC's raw silk production in Bengal illustrates the importance of transnational companies in shaping technological paths by increasing

---

[27] Michael E. Porter, *Competition in Global Industries*, (Boston, MA: Harvard University Press, 1986), p. 19.

[28] Michael E. Porter, 'Changing Patterns of International Competition', *California Management Review* 28 (2), 1986, p. 13.

[29] Ibid.

[30] A competitive advantage as defined by Porter is a 'function of either providing comparable buyer value more efficiently than competitors (low cost), or performing activities at comparable cost but in unique ways that create more buyer value than competitors and, hence, command a premium price'. Ibid.

[31] Porter, *Competitive Advantage of Nations*, pp. 49–51.

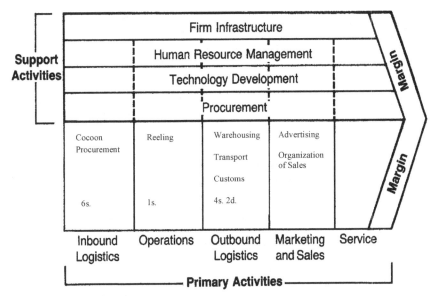

Figure 5.3　Value chain in Bengal silk production

Source: Michael E. Porter, 'Changing Patterns of International Competition', *California Management Review* 28 (2), 1986, p. 13. Costs are for the inputs necessary for producing 1 sm. lb. of raw silk or for warehousing and transporting 1 sm. lb.

their control over global commodity chains. The decisions taken by transnational companies about the locations of their business operations are based on factor endowments.[32] Decisions are often influenced by the 'visible hand' of managers as well as by governments' actions.[33] Since commodity chains are internalised within the organisational boundaries of vertically integrated firms, the governance structure of these corporations has a decisive role in allocating business activities to different geographical areas of a chain.[34] In the case of silk production in Bengal, it was the Court of Directors that represented the 'visible hand', who had decisive influence on the development of the industry.

From the point of view of commodity-chain and value-chain theory, the adoption of a centralised system in the production of raw silk in Bengal does

---

[32]　However, this is not always to the same extent that the theory would predict. Pankaj Ghemawat, 'Competition and Business Strategy in Historical Perspective', *Business History Review* 76 (1), 2002, pp. 38–40.

[33]　Alfred D. Chandler Jr, *The Visible Hand: The Managerial Revolution in American Business* (Cambridge, MA: Harvard University Press, 1977), pp. 1–13; Atul Kohli, *State-Directed Development: Political Power and Industrialization in the Global Periphery* (Cambridge: Cambridge University Press, 2004), pp. 8–9, 12–16.

[34]　Alfred D. Chandler Jr, *Scale and Scope: The Dynamics of Industrial Capitalism* (Cambridge, MA: Harvard University Press, 1990), pp. 3–47.

not seem misguided. The EEIC found that substantial changes in reeling practices were needed if the quality of Bengal raw silk was to improve and that measures of quality improvement were impossible to implement under the existing putting-out system. Improvements were possible only by attaining higher levels of control over the production process. Thus, even though the adoption of a type of factory system in eighteenth-century India has been considered premature, the actual circumstances of the silk industry present a case in which this adoption was rational. Silk reeling, however, remained a labour-intensive industry relying on cheap labour. By integrating reeling into the value chain, the EEIC strengthened its position vis-à-vis its competitors on the local market and gained higher levels of control over the quality of Bengal raw silk.[35]

Prices of Inputs, Costs of Production and the Effectiveness of the Transfer

This section analyses the costs of production of Bengal filature silk and factor endowments in the Bengal silk industry and compares them to Piedmont. The EEIC did not possess estimates of the prospective costs of producing filature-reeled silk in Bengal or the actual estimates for Piedmont. The expectation that the adoption of the filature system would be profitable was based on the fact that labour costs in Bengal were significantly lower than in Piedmont. My analysis shows that it was not only labour that was cheaper in Bengal than in Europe, but especially the cost of cocoons that made raw silk production in Bengal profitable.

Several documents allow us to consider the costs of filature silk production.[36] Table 5.1 shows the breakdown of production costs and reveals that cocoons were the most expensive input in filature silk, accounting for over 85 per cent of total production costs. All other items of production expenditure were therefore small and comprised charges for fuel, reelers' wages and sundry petty charges. Labour costs represented a low share of the total costs. Similarly, the cost of the wood needed as fuel for the furnaces which heated the water in the basins was modest. Overall, producing 1 sm. lb. of reeled silk in Bengal cost the Company 7s. It is not evident whether the EEIC included costs such as the wages of overseers, silk specialists and directors of filatures under sundry petty charges.[37] However, such inclusions would not dramatically change the overall costs incurred. Additional costs included freight,

---

35   Roberto Davini points out that the EEIC faced competition from local merchants in silk procurement throughout the eighteenth and nineteenth centuries. Davini, 'Una Conquista Incerta', pp. 10–54.

36   IOR/E/4/630, 12 April 1786, p. 390; IOR/E/4/637, 6 May 1791, p. 429.

37   It is not entirely clear what was in the category 'sundry petty charges', but it can be expected that it included the wages of non-reelers and the costs of running filatures.

Table 5.1   The cost of producing 1 sm. lb. of filature silk, 1786

Production costs		Total production cost (%)
Cocoons	6s.	85.7
Wages of reelers	6.8d.	8.1
Wood	3.7d.	4.4
Sundry petty charges	1.5d.	1.8
Total production costs	7s.	100.0
Additional costs		**Overall cost (%)**
Customs	3s.	26.9
Freight	7d.	5.2
Charges on merchandise	7d.	5.2
Total additional costs	4s. 2d.	37.3
Overall costs	11s. 2d.	

Source: IOR/E/4/630, 12 April 1786, p. 390; IOR/E/4/637, 6 May 1791, p. 429.

Table 5.2   Cost of inputs in Piedmont and Bengal, 1780s

	Piedmont		Bengal	
	d.	**Total (%)**	**d.**	**Total (%)**
Cost of cocoons (1 sm. lb.)	13.0	90.3	4.0	81.6
Cost of reeling 1 sm. lb. of cocoons (reeler wage)	1.4	9.7	0.9	18.4
Costs of reeling 1 sm. lb. of cocoons (reeler wage + cocoons)	14.4	100.0	4.9	100.0

Source: IOR/E/4/630, 12 April 1786, p. 390; Giuseppe Chicco, *La Seta in Piemonte 1650–1800: Un Sistema Industriale D'Ancien Régime* (Milan: Franco Angeli, 1995), pp. 212–13, 264.

customs and other charges such as warehousing (Table 5.1). Hence, the total costs of producing 1 sm. lb. of silk, before it could be sold on the British market, amounted to 11s. 2d.

It is important to compare these costs with the costs of producing reeled silk in Piedmont. Table 5.2 shows that cocoons were approximately three times more expensive in Piedmont than in Bengal. Similarly, the daily wages of reelers were approximately three times higher in Piedmont (9d.) than in Bengal (3d.). However, such data does not tell us much about labour productivity. From a comparison of the costs of reeling 1 sm. lb. of cocoons into filature-reeled silk, it is apparent that significantly more labour was needed in Bengal than in Piedmont (Table 5.2). Labour represented a higher share of the total cost of reeling in Bengal (18.4 per cent versus 9.7 per cent in Piedmont); however, the lower cost of cocoons was an important factor that offset lower labour productivity. Therefore, the reeling of 1 sm. lb. of filature silk – when both reelers' wages and costs related to cocoons are included – was still almost three times cheaper in Bengal than in Piedmont.

Overall, the data shows that if one considers the prices of inputs, Bengal had favourable conditions for silk thread production. Bengal's advantage came not only from cheap labour but also, and more importantly, the price of cocoons. Although the Court of Directors and the Board of Trade complained on several occasions about the rising cost of cocoons, their price never undermined the profitability of silk reeling. Cocoon prices remained relatively stable in the second half of the eighteenth century; the real issue was instead their supply and their quality.[38] This does not mean, however, that access to cocoons was never a problem for the Company, as bad weather and natural disasters reduced the supply of cocoons on several occasions.[39]

Moreover, such events also had an impact on the price of cocoons on

[38] It has been argued by Roberto Davini that main problem the EEIC faced was inadequate access to cocoons and their high price. In his thesis, Davini cites several examples of the complaints lodged by the Board of Trade about the expense and rising prices of cocoons. Quantitative evidence, however, shows that the price of cocoons was in reality very favourable. The complaints should not be considered as proof of the high price of cocoons but instead as evidence that the Company tried to procure cocoons at the lowest price possible. Davini, 'Una Conquista Incerta', pp. 129–35.

[39] According to Davini, external events such as the famine in Bengal in 1769–70 and the Maratha raids of the 1740s and 1750s significantly changed factor supply conditions. Both of these events led to a depopulation of Bengal. Although these events indisputably had a negative effect on the amount of labour available, a shortage of labour was not considered by the Court to be a long-term problem. Depopulation and natural disasters curtailed the supply of cocoons on several occasions and did have a negative impact on the quantity of Bengal raw silk imported into Britain. Roberto Davini, 'The History of Bengali Raw Silk as Interplay between the Company Bahadur, the Bengali Local Economy and Society, and the Universal Italian Model, c.1750–c.1830', *Commodities of Empire Working Paper* 6 (2008), p. 8; Roberto Davini, 'Bengali Raw Silk, the East India Company and the European Global Market, 1770–1833', *Journal of Global History* 4 (1), 2009, pp. 63–6; Davini. 'Una Conquista Incerta', pp. 33–4, 53. However, trade data does not support the supposition that such events had a long-term effect on the silk trade. In addition, the reports of silk specialists sent from Bengal to London imply that labour shortages were neither a long-term issue nor that they had a negative impact on reeling. Rather than complaining about a shortage of labour, the silk specialists pointed instead to the benefits of the new system of reeling: 'After the great mortality in Bengal in the year 1770 it was impossible for the Company to form any hopes of augmenting their investment in Silks. This augmentation however took place by the introduction of spinning after the Italian method.' Goldsmiths' Library (hereafter GL), 1795 fol. 16280, *Reports of the Committee of Warehouses of the East-India Company relative to Extending the Trade on Bengal Raw-Silk* (London: n.p., 1795), p. 18; IOR/E/1/61, fols 486–487v: 18 November 1777: 'Letter 240 James Wiss in London to the Court Outlining the Advantages of the Italian Method of Spinning Silk in Bengal', p. 487; IOR/E/4/630, 21 July 1786, p. 549; IOR/E/4/640, 25 June 1793, p. 512.

the local market. However, apart from the occasional surge of prices due to natural disasters, the price of cocoons did not change significantly in the 1770s or the 1780s, and oscillated around 5 Sicca Rupees and 6 Annas (11s. 8d.) per Seer (1.88 sm. lbs.). The Court in London observed that 'the price of Cocoons may be affected from accidental causes such as a scarcity of Crop, but we understand it has not undergone any very essential alteration for some years past'.[40] The EEIC also tried to facilitate an increase in the supply of cocoons by decreasing taxation on land under mulberry cultivation.[41] The principal problem was the system of cocoon procurement because it depended on agents called Pykars. These intermediaries often sold cocoons to the Company's filatures at much higher prices than they bought them from peasants.[42] Pykars often forced peasants to sell the cocoons at a price that was below the market value.[43] Although the sums lost in this way were not high enough to have a considerable impact on filature production, the behaviour of Pykars undermined the peasants' interest in selling cocoons to the Company.

Wood and labour were also important inputs, but they were not considered scarce or expensive. The Court was concerned more about the quality and availability of wood than its price.[44] Several silk districts of Bengal lacked access to adequate supplies of wood, which undermined the production capacity of filatures. Moreover, green wood was used with detrimental effects on the quality of the produced silk.[45] Similarly labour costs were never considered to be excessive by the Court, its sole concerns being the quality of reeling and the supply of reelers.[46]

It is very probable that the Company would not have been able to procure raw silk at cheaper prices than it was able to produce it. Table 5.3 shows the prices at which the EEIC bought raw silk in 1765–71 before the adoption of the Piedmontese system. If the average prices at which the EEIC bought

---

[40] IOR/E/4/630, 21 July 1786, p. 549.

[41] IOR/E/4/619: 'Cultivation of Mulberry, 17 March 1769', p. 334; IOR/E/4/623: 'Growth of Mulberry Plantations Encouraged, 24 December 1776', p. 286.

[42] Occasionally the prices would increase due to a shortage of cocoons caused by natural disasters. IOR/E/4/630, 21 July 1786, p. 548.

[43] Ibid., pp. 548–50.

[44] Green wood did not produce enough heat to warm the water basins to the temperature necessary for reeling. IOR/E/4/625, 9 April 1777, pp. 187–9.

[45] Some of the silk districts did not have access to as much wood as was needed during the reeling season. The problem was most serious in filatures in the districts of Kasimbazar, Ragnagatti and Boalia; the filatures in Kasimbazar and Boalia even competed with each other for wood. Davini, 'Una Conquista Incerta', pp. 237–41.

[46] The directors of filatures frequently complained about the limited supply and fluctuations in the number of reelers, and the need to retrain them at the beginning of each season. However, similar complaints were not uncommon in the early days of the factory system. Moreover, the Company never considerably increased the wages of reelers, and was still able to attract sufficient labour. For complaints from manufacturers, see: Pollard, *Genesis of Modern Management*, pp. 160–240.

Table 5.3   Comparative view of the prices at which the EEIC bought raw silk, 1765–71

	In shillings and pence for sm. lbs. of reeled silk						
Region	**1765**	**1766**	**1767**	**1768**	**1769**	**1770**	**1771**
Guzerat	9s. 6d.	9s. 2d.	8s. 2d.	9s. 2d.	9s. 6d.	11s. 4d.	11s. 6d.
Tannah	9s. 6d.	9s. 2d.		8s. 7d.	10s. 7d.	11s. 6d.	11s. 11d.
Poddapor	7s. 11d.	8s. 1d.	7s. 9d.	8s. 5d.	8s. 8d.	11s. 4d.	11s. 6d.
Commercolly	6s. 7d.	7s. 5d.	6s. 8d.	6s. 7d.	7s. 3d.	11s.	11s. 2d.
Rungpore	6s. 9d.	10s. 1d.	5s. 9d.	8s. 7d.	9s. 2d.	10s. 11d.	11s. 1d.
Jungepore			11s. 6d.	11s. 9d.	12s. 5d.	11s. 4d.	11s. 6d.
Mean price	8s.	8s. 9d.	5s. 8d.	8s. 10d.	9s. 7d.	11s. 3d.	11s. 5d.
Mean price of 1 sm. lb. of reeled silk, 1765–71 9s. 10d.							
Wound from pod		19s. 6d.	19s. 6d.	19s. 6d.	19s. 6d.	12s. 11d.	

Source: IOR/E/4/630, 21 July 1786, p. 561. Before the adoption of the filature system, 'raw silk wound from Pod' was a term used to describe raw silk reeled in the Company's facilities and under their supervision. It was only an experimental production. IOR/E/4/616: 'Bengal Raw Silk to be Investigated by Richard Wilder, Bengal Supplement 25 March 1757', pp. 656–7.

1 sm. lb. of silk from intermediary merchants are compared with the cost of producing 1 sm. lb. in filatures, it is apparent that the EEIC was able to produce silk more cheaply. Whereas the cost of producing silk in filatures in the 1780s was 7s., the Company had to pay on average 9s. 10d. for 1 sm. lb. of reeled silk when procuring it from intermediary merchants in the period 1765–71.

The case presented here shows that the adoption of a type of factory production system in the Bengal silk industry in the eighteenth century was not detrimental to the EEIC's silk trade. According to data presented by William Milburn, in the period 1786–1803 the prime cost of silk production amounted to £4,779,268 and generated net profits of £616,781 (Table 5.4). The manufacturing of Bengal raw silk continued to be profitable until the 1830s. According to the Company's statistics in the 1830s, 1 begah (⅓ acre) of mulberry land through its capacity to produce raw silk created a profit of 34 Rupees and 4 Annas (£3 8s. 6d.).[47] Even in the period 1834–39 when the EEIC was no longer in charge of raw silk manufacturing, it still made a profit of £1,042,679.[48] This evidence contrasts with findings for the Indian cotton

[47]   LSE Archives, W7204, East India Company, *Reports and Documents Connected with the Proceedings of the East-India Company in regard to the Culture and Manufacture of Cotton-wool, Raw Silk, and Indigo in India* (London: J. L. Cox, 1836), p. 171.

[48]   House of Lords, *Report from the Select Committee of the House of Lords Appointed to Consider of the Petition of the East India Company for Relief* (London: n.p., 1840), pp. iv, 8.

Table 5.4   Profits of the English East India Company generated by imports of
Bengal raw silk to Britain, 1786–1803

Year	Prime cost including freight and charges (£)	Profit (£)	Loss (£)
1786	192,898	5,609	0
1787	133,795	11,917	0
1788	212,357	9,531	0
1789	268,790	12,539	0
1790	274,553	34,203	0
1791	290,419	30,236	0
1792	378,512	13,415	0
1793	335,315	0	53,224
1794	290,419	19,324	0
1795	378,512	2,873	0
1796	335,315	0	7,888
1797	262,917	0	4,273
1798	277,990	44,883	0
1799	324,460	65,689	0
1800	208,969	88,676	0
1801	262,428	132,982	0
1802	156,502	112,747	0
1803	195,117	97,542	0
Total	4,779,268	682,166	65,385
Average	265,515	37,898	3,633
Net profit			**616,781**

Source: William Milburn, *Oriental Commerce* (London: Black, Perry & Co., 1813), vol. 2,
p. 257. The total numbers were calculated as the original totals counted by Milburn
contain errors.

industry, which show that the factory system did not emerge there because the
system could not cope with unfavourable factor endowments.[49] The evidence
presented here shows that the situation was different for silk reeling and that
the factor endowments did not play against a type of factory organisation.
Even the analysis of returns on investment shows that the investment was
profitable (see Appendix C, which indicates that the Internal Rate of Return
(IRR) on profit streams in the period 1772–79 reached 55 per cent). Overall,

---

[49]   Broadberry and Gupta, 'Lancashire, India', p. 300; Irfan Habib, 'The Technology and
Economy of Mughal India', *Indian Economic and Social Review* 17 (1), 1980, pp. 32–4.

centralisation of reeling and the adoption of filatures in Bengal silk reeling had undeniable benefits. First, the quality of Bengal raw silk improved and second, productivity increased. Quality improvement was the most significant benefit of the centralised system of organisation.

The English East India Company and Learning-by-Doing in the Silk Industry

Learning-by-doing has been considered as an important factor for increasing productivity by economic, business and development studies literature. Kenneth Arrow argued that 'technical change in general can be ascribed to experience, that it is the very activity of production which gives rise to problems for which favourable responses are selected over time'.[50] Experience, learning curves and progress ratios play an important role in increasing efficiency within organisations. Organisational learning was divided by Louis E. Yelle into two categories: labour learning (where learning is embodied in the workers) and organisational learning (where learning is embodied in the organisation).[51] In reality, both categories of organisational learning usually occur simultaneously. In the case of the EEIC the efficiency of reelers increased with experience and the capabilities of the Company's employees to manage silk production also improved.[52] Yet, this type of labour learning was curtailed by the turnover of both reelers and EEIC employees. Thus, the key became organisational learning, which was embodied in the system of guidelines and rules produced by the Court in London and transferred to Bengal. These encompassed 'best practices' in silk manufacturing, guidelines about technology upgrading, and analysis of cost efficiency in production. Second, experiments with silk-reeling practices led to several innovations that decreased production costs. Third, rules of management control of inter-mediaries (Pykars) involved in cocoon procurement also evolved thanks to experience in the nineteenth century.

Since the 1770s the Company had put an emphasis on the transmission of carefully gathered knowledge of 'best practices' in, for example, reeling, cocoon storage and warehousing, to improve the quality of Bengal raw silk. Silk specialists employed by the Company formulated guidelines that were to be applied universally in Bengalese silk filatures in order to produce silk of a quality that corresponded with the Italian product. These guidelines, together

---

[50]   Kenneth J. Arrow, 'The Economic Implications of Learning by Doing', *Review of Economic Studies* 29 (3), 1962, p. 156.

[51]   Louis E. Yelle, 'The Learning Curve: Historical Review and Comprehensive Survey', *Decision Sciences* 10, 1979, pp. 302–28.

[52]   IOR/E/1/61, fols 486–487v: 'Letter 240 James Wiss in London to the Court Outlining the Advantages of the Italian Method of Spinning Silk in Bengal', 18 November 1777, p. 487.

with additional instructions formulated by the Court in London, were transmitted at least once a year to the Board of Trade in Bengal.

Correspondence from London shows that the Company understood that the lack of knowledge of the best practices in Bengal was one of the reasons for the production of raw silk of an inadequate quality for the European market. Therefore, the Court in London believed that its employees in Bengal needed instructions about the methods of silk production, as it claimed:

> for want of sufficient knowledge and experience [our servants in Bengal], may not be able to instruct the Spinners in every point necessary for obtaining the desired improvements, we now transmit you such regulations as have been suggested by Mr Wiss for that purpose, and direct that our Board of Trade fail not to have them carried into execution.[53]

Apart from noting the underlying lack of knowledge, this quotation highlights that its approach was based on silk specialists creating instructions in London which were sent to Bengal to be implemented in the filatures. These instructions addressed not only the issue of quality but also the trade in raw silk, and the cost of production of filature-reeled silk.

The guidelines prepared by James Wiss in 1777 according to the experience and information he gathered in Bengal became the essential source of information for the improvement of the quality of filature silk. Abiding by his rules was supposed to guarantee production of a standard quality of raw silk. As the Court in London put it, 'by due attention to proper rules, and to the various means of improvement herein suggested, the greatest degrees of perfection will soon be attained'.[54] These guidelines were cited several times in the following years and they continued to be mentioned as the essential source of best practice for raw silk production in EEIC publications as late as 1836.[55]

The original version of the Wiss guidelines of 1777 and the version published in 1807 are extensive and provide precise directives for the directors of filatures and overseers.[56] The directors of the filatures were required to have supplies of clear water and dry wood already prepared, because clean water was essential for the brilliance of the silk and dry wood for keeping the water in the basins boiling steadily. The directors were also given directions on how best to store cocoons before reeling, and were strongly requested to separate cocoons that were damaged and cocoons undergoing fermentation from the rest. Moreover, they were directed to use ovens to kill the moths inside the cocoons. The guidelines also specified the number of cocoons that were to be

---

53 IOR/E/4/625, 9 April 1777, p. 172.
54 IOR/E/4/625, 'Mr. Wiss Superintendent of Silk Trade, 9 September 1777', p. 198.
55 IOR/E/4/626, 5 July 1780, p. 206; LSE Archives, W7204, *Reports and Documents*, p. 16.
56 IOR/E/4/625, 9 April 1777, pp. 171–216; LSE Archives, W7204, *Reports and Documents*, pp. 16–26.

used for reeling in each bund or rearing period. The quality of cocoons differed over the rearing season, with the best reared in March and November.[57]

The overseers were directed not 'to insist on more work being done in a day than is found practicable'.[58] Slow reelers were not to be penalised as this would lead them to favour quantity over quality. The overseer was, on the other hand, directed to ensure that reelers worked efficiently. At the beginning of each season, all of the overseers and the director of the factory were to observe the most capable reelers in producing a sample of the season's production.[59] They needed to ensure that the sample would be of a very high quality and that everyone involved in overseeing production would be aware of the quality expected. The guidelines also demanded all silk was to be labelled with the name of the overseer and the director of the filature, in order to guarantee direct responsibility for the quality of the produced silk.

In spite of having detailed knowledge about 'best practices' as well as the methods to rectify problems, it is necessary to point out that production of substandard-quality silk did not cease to be an issue. This was due to the fact that the Court in London lacked the mechanisms to ensure that guidelines were enforced. Moreover, especially in the initial years, the Company's employees in Bengal were not sufficiently familiar with production techniques to effectively implement such guidelines. Yet, three factors need to be taken into account when evaluating improvements in the quality of Bengal raw silk. First, issues with substandard quality did not affect Bengal raw silk exclusively, as evidence shows that the problem was widespread in the late eighteenth and early nineteenth centuries. For instance, low-quality raw silk was also reeled by households in Provence in France.[60] It can be expected that these problems also affected raw silk imported from the Mediterranean region. Second, the fact that silks from Aleppo, Valentia, Naples, Calabria and other places in the Mediterranean were driven out of the market by Bengal raw silk shows that it was competitive among silks of middling quality.[61] Third, British manufacturers demanded silk of middling quality. A government report from 1832 stated that Bengal silk was used for the 'manufacturing of coarser goods; principally for bandannas, sewing silks and stockings, hosiery, and a variety of things of that sort'.[62] At the same time, silk manufacturing in Britain started to focus on production of the 'coarser goods'.[63] Moreover, thanks to both labour and organisational learning, issues with the quality of Bengal raw silk became

---

[57]   IOR/E/4/625, 9 April 1777, pp. 173–205.
[58]   Ibid., p. 206.
[59]   Ibid., p. 208.
[60]   Archives Nationales, Paris: Serie F12, F12 677A.
[61]   LSE Archives, W7204, *Reports and Documents*, p. xxiv.
[62]   House of Commons, *Report from Select Committee on the Silk Trade with Minutes of Evidence, Appendix and Index* (London: n.p., 1832), p. 359.
[63]   Ibid., pp. 247–8.

less rife throughout the early nineteenth century as both the Company's employees in Bengal and the Company itself gained experience with silk production and management. The contention that the Company's servants in Bengal employed in the silk trade started to pay attention to silk reeling can be supported by evidence about the number of experiments carried out in silk filatures in the nineteenth century, as I will discuss.

Claudio Zanier has argued that apart from the large-scale changes to the system of production implemented in the 1760s and 1770s, the system of silk manufacturing was not further innovated. Yet the adaptations of the Piedmontese system to the Bengal environmental and socio-economic conditions implemented from the 1770s to the 1800s were far reaching. Moreover, the period after 1800 was characterised by small-scale innovations and experiments. The next phase of technology upgrading came in the 1820s and 1830s, a period which saw an increase in experimentation with both production practices and management.[64] In sericulture, the focus of these experiments was on upgrading the silkworm and mulberry varieties as described in the previous chapter. This continued into the nineteenth century and Italian silkworms and cuttings from Italian white mulberry trees were sent to Bengal with the aim of improving the quality of the silkworm breed and local mulberries.[65] However, such experiments from both the late eighteenth and early nineteenth centuries did not work well and did not have a long-lasting legacy. On the other hand, experiments in silk reeling were carried out on larger scale, were based on experience and everyday management of silk reeling, were more successful, and resulted in innovations in the system of reeling.

The majority of experiments focused on the technological issues of raw silk reeling. Commercial Residents from the Radanagore, Commercolly, and Gonatea factories developed new methods of constructing basins and furnaces for filatures. It was decided by the Bengal government that these methods were to be implemented as they enabled the 'saving of fuel and labour, [exhibited] superiority over the old filatures in the mode of supplying the basins with water, a greater degree of cleanliness in the interior of the filatures by the exclusion of smoke, and cheapness as well in their original construction and adaptation'.[66] Experimental filatures were established in Howrah and Gonatea. Their experiments brought merit especially in the case of the Gonatea filature where Colin Shakespear, the Commercial Resident there, developed a system of building furnaces and basins which he called pottery ghye. It was decided by the Bengal government that pottery ghye should be used as the standard 'to be substituted on all occasions of renewing basins, and should be forthwith constructed in place of those previously in use

---

64   LSE Archives, W7204, *Reports and Documents*, pp. xl–xlii.
65   Ibid.
66   Ibid., p. xl.

in all factories, where there might appear advantage in carrying the alteration into immediate effect'.[67]

As shown by experiments carried out in the Howrah filature, the energy efficiency of pottery ghye basins and furnaces was supposed to lead to fuel savings of approximately 70 per cent, as well as an improvement in silk quality.[68] Pottery ghyes were not the only innovation to emerge in the 1820s. Somerville furnaces, the Somerville reel, and quad basins and reel by Messrs. Heathcoate & Co. of Tiverton, Devon appeared at the same time. All these innovations were created either by Commercial Residents in different filatures or by English companies with the aim of decreasing production costs (especially to reduce the quantity of fuel required as wood was in short supply), expand production capacity, and improve the quality of reeled silk.[69] The Company diligently studied these innovations, considered the cost of their construction and adoption, their effect on the quality of the silk produced and the potential savings in production costs.[70] Only after these calculations had been done did the Company recommend the adoption of pottery ghyes and Somerville reels, which complemented each other and led to the greatest savings.[71] It has been calculated that the introduction of Shakespear's pottery ghye enabled manufacturing costs to be reduced by 50 per cent to 1s. 4d. per sm. lb. for the key March 'bund' or rearing season (Table 5.5).[72] The key advantages were savings on fuel (and to an extent also on sundry charges).[73] Moreover, these savings were realised despite the fact that the experimental filature paid its reelers 12–15 per cent more than the Cattorah filature. A comparison of manufacturing costs of 1 sm. lb. of raw silk in 1786 with those in the Cattorah filature for 1832 shows that these costs more than doubled. Charges for wood increased by a factor of three and wages increased from 6.8d. to 2s (average for reelers and spinners) (Appendix D).

Innovations were not restricted to silk technologies, as innovations in the system of cocoon procurement were also adopted. Prior to the 1810s the Company was not very successful in managing cocoon suppliers, relying on intermediary merchants called Pykars to deliver cocoons from sericulturalists.[74]

---

[67]   Ibid., p. xli.

[68]   Extract from a Letter from Bengal Board of Trade to the Honourable Vice-President in Council, 20 August 1832, in ibid., pp. 186–8, 196.

[69]   The reel made by Messrs. Heathcoate & Co. of Tiverton, Devon did not prove to be a success in improving the quality of the reeled silk.

[70]   LSE Archives, W7204, *Reports and Documents*, p. 197.

[71]   Ibid., pp. 199–201, 202–4.

[72]   The March bund was of major importance to the Cattorah filature in the Hurripaul district, as it was the season when the best quality as well as the largest quantity of cocoons were produced.

[73]   LSE Archives, W7204, *Reports and Documents*, pp. 207–11.

[74]   Direct dealing with growers of cocoons was less common. Ibid., p. xxxvi.

Table 5.5 Development of manufacturing costs of Bengal Raw Silk, 1786–1832[1]

Year	Filature	Bund[2]	Manufacturing costs per sm. lb.
1786	Not specified	Average/year	1s.
1832	Experimental	March	1s. 2d.[3]
		Average/year	1s. 6d.
	Cattorah	March	2s. 8d.
		March/April (rainy)	2s. 11d.
		October/November	4s. 11d.

Source: Calculated from LSE Archives, W7204, East India Company, *Reports and Documents Connected with the Proceedings of the East-India Company in regard to the Culture and Manufacture of Cotton-wool, Raw Silk, and Indigo in India* (London: J. L. Cox, 1836), pp. 208–9; IOR/E/4/630, 12 April 1786, p. 390.

[1] Excludes cost of cocoons.
[2] Quality and quantity of cocoons differed between bunds depending on the weather and the type of silkworm yielding cocoons.
[3] A year later the costs were brought down to 1s.

The price of cocoons increased from 1817, and this incentivised management experiments. Before 1827,

> it was the custom to make a settlement with the Pykars for each bund, respectively, but not until all the cocoons of the bund had been wound into silk, when the Resident proposed such price as he judged reasonable, and after the approval of the Board of Trade, the account was arranged, without reference to the prices paid at the other factories for silk of the same bund.[75]

This system was amended in 1827, when silk districts were divided into silk circles and all the factories in one circle started to pay a predetermined price for cocoons. In 1831 the system was further modified, when the Board of Trade decided that Pykars would be notified before each rearing season about the maximum price that they would be paid for cocoons.[76] This last measure finally helped to stop the rise in the price of cocoons, and from 1832 prices started to decrease to their former level as reflected in invoice costs (Table 5.6). Overall, innovations in production techniques and management of intermediary suppliers of cocoons helped to reduce the costs of silk production. Experiments continued to be carried out until 1833, when they came to a sudden halt as the EEIC was forced to cease its economic activities by the 1833 Charter Act.

The last channel through which the EEIC attempted to create favourable

[75] Ibid., p. xxxvii.
[76] Ibid.

Table 5.6   Invoice costs of the Company's Bengal raw silk, 1817–1835

Year	per sm. lb.		Year	per sm. lb.	
	s.	**d.**		**s.**	**d.**
1817	12	10	1827	16	4
1818	13	5	1828	15	2
1819	14	2	1829	14	0
1820	14	10	1830	13	5
1821	15	11	1831	13	0
1822	15	8	1832	12	6
1823	15	8	1833	12	2
1824	15	10	1834	11	10
1825	16	4	1835	11	10
1826	15	10			

Source: Calculated from LSE Archives, W7204, East India Company, *Reports and Documents Connected with the Proceedings of the East-India Company in regard to the Culture and Manufacture of Cotton-wool, Raw Silk, and Indigo in India* (London: J. L. Cox, 1836), p. 95.

* The Company's documents show that up to the 1830s prices paid for cocoons were strongly determined by their quality. The highest prices were generally paid for the March bund of cocoons produced by the annual worm.

conditions for its silk manufacturing is related to the Company's political power in Bengal, which it used to promote mulberry cultivation. In 1769, the Court ordered that rents on land planted with mulberries were to be reduced so as to make mulberry cultivation more profitable for the landowners and peasants. The Court also encouraged the Board to find other measures which would promote mulberry cultivation.[77] The order to find new policies to promote cultivation was repeated on several other occasions, as for instance in 1776, when the Court suggested that wastelands should be cleaned up and turned into mulberry plantations.[78]

---

[77] IOR/E/4/618, 16 March 1768, p. 919; IOR/E/4/619, 17 March 1769, p. 334. The Court also attempted to improve the practices of mulberry cultivation. The Company's silk specialists sent guidelines about the best practices of mulberry cultivation and they also attempted to introduce Chinese varieties of mulberry trees. However, their efforts did not have a decisive impact because it was difficult to enforce new practices and the introduction of Chinese mulberry trees did not spread beyond the experimental stage. WBSA, BoT (Comm) Prcds 29 May 1789, Letter from Maldah 7 April 1789, as cited in Davini, 'Una Conquista Incerta', p. 68; WBSA, BoT (Comm) Prcds 29 May 1789, Letter from Radanagore 21 March 1789, as cited in ibid., p. 69. WBSA, BoT (Comm) Prcds 29 May 1789, Letter from Commercolly 14 February 1789, as cited in ibid.

[78] IOR/E/4/623, 24 December 1776, pp. 284–6. The Court was keen to promote mulberry

Conclusion

Differences in factor prices are currently used as the major determinants of technological paths. Factor-price theory can shed light on why some technology transfers fail. However, the theory is unable to capture all technology changes or explain technological paths. Factor-price theory postulates that India was unable to switch to the factory system in the eighteenth century as the system did not fit its factor-supply conditions.

The transfer of Piedmontese silk-reeling technology contradicts these predictions. Despite adopting a hierarchical organisation of labour and advanced machinery, the Piedmontese system of reeling does not represent an example of capital-intensive, labour-saving technology. The cost of producing silk in filatures was lower than the cost of procuring it from intermediary merchants. The new technology entailed high initial costs, but analysis of the return on investment shows that it was a highly profitable venture. This can be explained by several factors specific to the Bengal silk industry. First, the Bengal silk industry, in contrast with the cotton industry, did not develop superior knowledge and expertise in raw silk production which would set it apart from its competitors but lagged behind technologically. Second, efforts to improve the quality of Bengal raw silk necessitated both technical and organisational innovations.[79] Mere increases in labour intensity could not be a substitute for technology and labour organisation.

Most importantly, the adoption of the Piedmontese technologies enabled the EEIC to capture a further stage of the raw silk commodity chain. The Company was thus able to build a business model that relied on adaptations of the quantity and fineness of produced silk according to the information gathered on sales. Furthermore, the business model also relied on economies of scale for first, increasing bargaining power vis-à-vis producers of inputs such as cocoons, and second, in implementing cost-saving technologies. These factors were crucial for making the Company's venture profitable. Moreover, learning-by-doing during the late eighteenth and early nineteenth centuries helped the EEIC to innovate silk-reeling technologies and gather a pool of 'best practices'. Most importantly, thanks to learning-by-doing, the EEIC was able to overcome some of its problems in management and in particular the successful reform of the system of cocoon procurement.

cultivation on wastelands and in this regard the plan was influenced by mercantilist thinking. IOR/E/1/61, fols 486–487v: 'Letter 240 James Wiss in London to the Court Outlining the Advantages of the Italian Method of Spinning Silk in Bengal, 18 November 1777', p. 487.

79   Strict discipline, attention to detail and minute regulation were as important as the adoption of the Piedmontese reeling machine for the production of high-quality raw silk. Zanier, 'Pre-Modern European Silk Technology and East Asia', p. 114.

Chapter 6

THE BENGAL SILK INDUSTRY AND BRITISH LAISSEZ-FAIRE POLICIES

Nineteenth-century textile production was characterised by innovations in technology and management. Europe led the way in cotton and silk production – Britain in cotton, Italy and France in silk – and aspiring textile producers were importing new technologies and adapting them. In the second part of the nineteenth century, raw silk production spread to new areas, most importantly to Japan but also to Egypt. These new producers could not rely solely on cheap labour as standardisation of the quality of raw silk was becoming increasingly important, especially with the rise of mechanised silk weaving in the USA. Importation of advanced technologies of silk reeling was thus a necessity. The most successful newcomer to raw silk production was Japan. It was one of the leaders in catching up with the major producers of both cotton and silk, and it relied on imported technologies as well as on domestic innovations and adaptations.[1] Technological upgrading in Japan was assisted by the state as well as large entrepreneurs. Both the state and large producers provided entrepreneurial guidance about new technologies, best practices in production and management, and information about faraway markets.[2] Merchant networks and domestic banks were instrumental in the provision of credit.[3]

---

1 Debin Ma, 'Why Japan, Not China, Was the First to Develop in East Asia: Lessons from Sericulture, 1850–1937', *Economic Development and Cultural Change* 52 (2), 2004, pp. 374–6, 383; Motoshige Itoh and Masayuki Tanimoto, 'Rural Entrepreneurs in the Cotton-Weaving Industry of Japan', in Yujiro Hayami (ed.), *Toward the Rural-Based Development of Commerce and Industry: Selected Experiences from East Asia* (Washington: World Bank, 1998), pp. 61–3.

2 See for instance: Eugene Choi, 'Entrepreneurial Leadership in the Meiji Cotton Spinners' Early Conceptualisation of Global Competition', *Business History* 51 (6), 2009, pp. 930–2; Itoh and Tanimoto, 'Rural Entrepreneurs', pp. 61–3; Toshihiko Kawagoe, 'Technical and Institutional Innovations in Rice Marketing in Japan', in Hayami (ed.), *Toward the Rural-Based Development of Commerce and Industry*, pp. 37–43; Shin'ichi Yonekawa, 'University Graduates in Japanese Enterprises Before the Second World War', *Business History* 26 (2), 1984, pp. 193–218.

3 Debin Ma, 'Between Cottage and Factory: The Evolution of Chinese and Japanese

At the time when Japan started to import silk technologies, Bengal was some steps in front as it already possessed a system of filatures producing raw silk with the use of European technologies adapted to local conditions. Yet instead of surging further ahead, Bengal raw silk production fell behind its competitors, and by the end of the nineteenth century it had lost its position in European silk weaving. Bengal raw silk as a share of total imports of raw silk to Britain declined from around 40 per cent in the period from the 1790s to the 1810s to around 13 per cent in the 1860s. To explain this shift we need to look at changes in the political economy in Britain and consider the role of the English East India Company in silk manufacturing in the period from the 1770s to the 1830s.

The beginning of the nineteenth century marked a change from mercantilism to laissez-faire policies in the British political economy. Laissez-faire policies were promoted by a number of economists, pamphleteers and politicians, most notably by David Ricardo, an MP at the time (1818–23). As previously with mercantilism, laissez-faire policies were to be exported to colonies administered by Britain. The repercussions of this shift in political economy on the EEIC's venture into Bengal silk manufacturing, and on the Bengal silk industry in general, were to have a long legacy. The Company had to sell its silk filatures to private entrepreneurs as its direct involvement in silk manufacturing was to end in 1835. This led to a dramatic reduction in raw silk exports to the British market as British entrepreneurs were reluctant to get involved in Bengal silk manufacturing. Although this can be partially explained by the misleading perception that raw silk manufacturing was not profitable, the key factor that dampened the interest of entrepreneurs seems to be the lack of capital. In silk reeling, capital was necessary for advance payments to cocoon producers, for running filatures and for technological upgrading, as the nineteenth century saw increasing adoption of inanimate power and new machinery. The evidence shows that private entrepreneurs had very limited knowledge of the prices and quality of raw silk on the global markets, and of the new technologies employed in the leading silk regions. Previously, this information was supplied by the EEIC, which also had access to capital for technological upgrading. In addition, the scale of production enabled the EEIC to reduce the transmission costs of technology transfer.[4] Therefore, to understand why private entrepreneurs did not carry on producing Bengal raw silk for exports, it is necessary to consider the changes in the organisation of the silk industry in Bengal and the scale of production. Moreover, it is necessary to consider the role of entrepreneurial guidance as this factor has been considered key for the textile industries in Japan catching up and surging

Silk-Reeling Industries in the Latter Half of the Nineteenth Century', *Journal of the Asia Pacific Economy* 10 (2), 2005, p. 209.

4   Karolina Hutková, 'Technology Transfers and Organization: The English East India Company and the Transfer of Piedmontese Silk Reeling Technology to Bengal, 1750s–1790s', *Enterprise & Society* 18 (4), 2017, pp. 921–51.

ahead. This chapter argues that capital and entrepreneurial guidance before 1833 was provided by the EEIC and was vital for the development of the sector. After privatisation, entrepreneurial guidance was lost and the sector became fragmented. Agency houses – new forms of business organisation that emerged in India in the nineteenth century – had no interest in raw silk production as they gave preference to low-skilled and low-capital-intensive ventures.[5] Silk filatures were thus sold to a large number of small firms that did not co-ordinate among themselves, and so technological upgrading started to dwindle.

From Mercantilism to Laissez-Faire Policies

The nineteenth century in Britain saw a gradual shift from mercantilism to laissez-faire policies. Yet, a perception of the nineteenth century as a heyday for laissez-faire approaches to governance would be misleading.[6] Recent research has questioned the extent to which we can perceive the period as one free of state intervention. Rather, the second part of the nineteenth century is best characterised by 'interventionist free trade'.[7] Contemporary government policies did not put an end to state intervention in social and economic policies. Liberalisation was applied particularly to trade policies as Britain shifted to free trade.

Economic liberalisation was championed by contemporary economists and by merchants with an interest in international trade. Monopolies in particular came under attack from political economists, manufacturing and commercial interests, especially in the outposts and the northern industrial towns, and also increasingly from government officials.[8] Pamphleteers had criticised the Company since the second part of the seventeenth century.[9] Among the most prominent critics were Adam Smith, Josiah Tucker, Thomas Mun, James

---

5   According to Stanley Chapman, agency houses and their later form the managing agency system functioned as investment groups rather than managing agents. Initially the firms were interested especially in exporting textiles, indigo and tea. In order to carry out the trade they needed a high degree of financial liquidity and were therefore unable to set up factory enterprises or buy shares in them. S. D. Chapman, 'The Agency Houses: British Mercantile Enterprise in the Far East c.1780–1920', *Textile History* 19 (2), 1988, pp. 239, 244–5.

6   See for instance: Norman Gash, *Aristocracy and People: Britain 1815–1865* (London: E. Arnold, 1979), pp. 1–9.

7   Ron Harris, *Industrializing English Law: Entrepreneurship and Business Organization, 1720–1844* (Cambridge: Cambridge University Press, 2000), p. 285.

8   Harris, *Industrializing English Law*, p. 206; Anthony Webster, 'The Political Economy of Trade Liberalization: The East India Company Charter Act of 1813', *Economic History Review* 43 (3), 1990, pp. 404–9; D. J. Moss, 'Birmingham and the Campaigns against the Orders-in-Council and East India Company Charter, 1812–13', *Canadian Journal of History*, 11 (2), 1976, pp. 173–88.

9   Emily Erikson, *Between Monopoly and Free Trade: The English East India Company, 1600–1757* (Princeton: Princeton University Press, 2014), pp. 1–3.

Steuart, James Mill, John Stuart Mill and David Ricardo. Although Smith and Tucker, for instance, saw a justification for the creation of the EEIC's monopoly in the early seventeenth century when long-distance traders faced precarious conditions and uncertainty due to the state of transportation, lack of information about markets and political instability abroad, they argued that by the late seventeenth century the Company was no longer beneficial for trade with Asia.[10] By the nineteenth century the EEIC was the only remaining trading company with a monopoly.[11] After an extensive lobbying campaign carried out by the Company as well as its opponents, the EEIC finally lost its monopoly on Indian trade with the 1813 Charter.[12] The 1833 Charter abolished the Company's monopoly on Chinese trade and forbade the EEIC from pursuing economic activity.

It is necessary to perceive the abolition of the EEIC's monopoly as part of a more general push for trade liberalisation in the nineteenth century. One of the key petitions requesting the removal of commercial restrictions was put forward by the Merchants of London in 1820 claiming:

> That foreign commerce is eminently conducive to the wealth and prosperity of the country, by enabling it to import the commodities for the production of which the soil, climate, capital, and industry of other countries are best calculated, and to export in payment those articles for which its own situation is better adapted; that freedom from restraint is calculated to give the utmost extension in foreign trade, and the best direction to the capital and industry of the country; that the maxim of buying in the cheapest market, and selling in the dearest, which regulates every merchant in his individual dealings, is strictly applicable, as the best rule for the trade of the whole nation; that a policy, founded on these principles, would render the commerce of the world an interchange of mutual advantages, and diffuse an increase of wealth and enjoyments among the inhabitants of each State; that, unfortunately, a policy, the very reverse of this, has been, and is more or less adopted and acted upon by the Government of this and of every other country; each trying to exclude the production of other countries, with the specious and well-meant design of encouraging its own productions; thus inflicting on the bulk of its subjects, who are consumers, the necessity of submitting to privations in the quantity or quality of commodities.[13]

[10]   Hoh-cheung Mui and Lorna H. Mui, *The Management of Monopoly: A Study of the East India Company's Conduct of its Tea Trade, 1784–1833* (Vancouver: University of British Columbia Press, 1984); K. N. Chaudhuri, *The Trading World of Asia and the English East India Company, 1660–1760* (Cambridge: Cambridge University Press, 1978).

[11]   The only other monopolies left in the nineteenth century were the Marine Insurance Corporate Monopoly and the Bank of England.

[12]   Webster argues that the changes in government policy were motivated economically. India was seen as an important source of raw materials for British producers, and by opening up trade the government aimed to combat domestic economic problems. Webster, 'The Political Economy of Trade Liberalization', pp. 404–5.

[13]   Hansard's Historical Parliamentary Debates, 'Petition of the Merchants of London Respecting Commercial Restrictions', *House of Commons Debate 8 May 1820*, vol. 1, pp. 165–7.

The government responded to these demands gradually. Although the Prime Minister, Lord Liverpool, proclaimed himself a supporter of free-trade policies, his Tory government had already been in office for thirteen years when free-trade policies started to be implemented. William R. Brock argued that it was the 1822 appointments of Frederick John Robinson and William Huskisson into the Cabinet that led to the shift in government policies from 'reactionary Toryism' to 'liberal Toryism'.[14] Barry Gordon explained the 1820s rise of liberal trade policies as the outcome of the growing influence of Ricardo and his writing on economics.[15] The growing influence of Ricardian economics is also noticeable in the petition of the Merchants of London. Norman Gash argued that the growth of liberal Toryism was a response to the rise of the middle classes and the relative decline of landed classes.[16] Boyd Hilton, on the other hand, saw the increase in the liberal economic policies of the Tories as an attempt to prevent large-scale social and economic change through widening of food and employment provision for the growing population.[17] Whatever the motivation of the Liverpool government, the outcome was a reduction in duties and taxation, liberalisation of navigation laws and the removal of many of trade restrictions, such as the simplification of tariffs and the opening of duty-free warehouses to foreign ships.[18]

Contemporary opinion held that unrestricted access to trade increased the prosperity of a country and that private entrepreneurs were more efficient at carrying out business activity. These two principles were emphasised as the rationale behind the Company's loss of monopoly, and most notably as the reason why it was prevented from pursuing economic activities in 1833. Private entrepreneurs were thought of as individual merchants/small firms/family firms/partnerships, not as joint-stock companies, since joint-stocks were perceived unfavourably due to their long-term association with monopoly. Such confusion was perpetuated even by Adam Smith who argued that the East India Company

> upon the redemption of their funds, and the expiration of their exclusive privilege, have a right, by act of parliament, to continue a corporation with joint-stock, and to trade in their corporate capacity to the East Indies in common with the rest of their fellow-subjects. But in this situation, the superior

---

14 William R. Brock, *Lord Liverpool and Liberal Toryism, 1820 to 1827* (Cambridge: Cambridge University Press, 1940), pp. 121–77.

15 Barry Gordon, *Political Economy in Parliament, 1819–1823* (Basingstoke: Macmillan Press Ltd, 1976), pp. 1–16.

16 Gash, *Aristocracy and People*, pp. 9–55.

17 Boyd Hilton, *Corn, Cash, Commerce: The Economic Policies of the Tory Government, 1815–1830* (Oxford: Oxford University Press, 1977), pp, 300–6.

18 Harris, *Industrializing English Law*, p. 251.

vigilance and attention of private adventurers would, in all probability, soon make them weary of the trade.[19]

This led Ron Harris to conclude that Smith perceived the EEIC and joint-stock in general as inferior to individual merchants.[20] Such reasoning was also behind the 1833 sale of the EEIC's silk factories to private entrepreneurs.

The 1813 Charter had no major effect on the Company's silk venture as the EEIC was allowed to continue manufacturing and trading in raw silk. The 1813 Charter compelled the Company to include private and privilege silk on board its ships. However, the EEIC procured silk from private manufacturers as well as transporting privately made raw silk to London for sale before 1813. The key impact on the Company's Bengal silk venture came with the 1833 Charter. It was considered that if the EEIC had any positive effect on trade and wealth creation, that by the nineteenth century it had petered out. Private entrepreneurs were unanimously seen as more efficient in carrying out trade and this policy extended also to manufacturing. Yet, even though such organisation of business might have fitted Anglo-Indian trade in general, it was not ideal for raw silk production.

It is true that in Japan and China raw silk production was carried out by large as well as small-scale manufacturers. In China technological upgrading was carried out by European manufacturers. One of East Asia's most powerful trading firms, Jardine, Matheson & Co., the US trading firm Russell & Co., as well as Chinese merchants, were all instrumental in transferring European silk-reeling technologies to China.[21] Although the adoption of innovative sericultural and silk-reeling technologies in China is considered as being delayed, in comparison with Bengal this was still a success story. In Japan the adoption and adaptation of European sericultural and silk-reeling technologies was actively promoted by the Meiji government as well as by large trading companies. The Japanese government was instrumental in facilitating the development of sericulture by fostering scientific research. The key innovations – the F1 variety of silkworms, the autumn crop of silkworms – to come from this research, increased the quality of Japanese cocoons and the productivity of Japanese sericulture.[22] In silk reeling, innovations in the systems of management and entrepreneurial leadership ensured the proliferation of innovative technologies and quality improvement. In

---

[19]   Adam Smith, *An Inquiry into the Wealth and Poverty of Nations* (State College, PA: University of Pennsylvania, 2005), p. 713.

[20]   Harris, *Industrializing English Law*, p. 205.

[21]   The proliferation of innovative silk-reeling technologies and the setting up of factories in China was slowed down by political conditions, especially by geographically limited extra-territorial protection to foreign entrepreneurs, and the adverse stance of local officials. Ma, 'Between Cottage and Factory', pp. 200–5.

[22]   Debin Ma, 'The Modern Silk Road: The Global Raw-Silk Market, 1850–1930', *Journal of Economic History* 56 (2), 1996, pp. 339–42.

the initial period of filature-based silk reeling in the 1870s and 1880s, silk reeling was carried out in small-scale family-based filatures. To ensure standardisation these filatures were organised into co-operatives called sha, which co-ordinated the purchase of cocoons and hiring of labour. The system was abandoned only in the 1890s when filatures grew in size.[23] In silk weaving, trade associations in silk districts, together with the government, facilitated the establishment of educational institutes to enhance the capacity for absorbing new technologies and knowledge.[24] The transfer of European silk technologies did not occur under a single system of business organisation and, as evidence shows, the joint-stock type of business organisation was not a necessary precondition. However, manufacturers needed access to credit, since capital was essential for the adoption of new technologies, Furthermore they needed information about technological and market trends in order to make raw silk of the quality required on the global market. In Japan credit was provided by merchant networks and domestic banks, in China by foreign and domestic banks, and trading firms; in both regions, information was supplied by trading firms and merchant groups.[25] The question to ask, then, is whether individual merchants or small merchant firms in Bengal in the 1830s to the 1850s were in an ideal position to obtain access to credit networks and information about global silk markets?

Ideal Business Forms and Entrepreneurial Guidance in the Bengal Raw Silk Industry

Business history literature defines the ideal form of business organisation as that ideally suited for a particular industry, one that allows organisational, technological and financial challenges to be overcome and allows the venture to thrive in the long term. Past success stories are the key source of information about ideal business forms.[26] It is also necessary to acknowledge that

---

23   Ma, 'Between Cottage and Factory', pp. 206–8.
24   Tomoko Hashino, 'Institutionalising Technical Education: The Case of Weaving Districts in Meiji Japan', *Australian Economic History Review* 52 (1), 2012, pp. 25–7. This can be seen as a variation of the entrepreneurial leadership provided by the Mitsui Trading Company together with the Osaka Spinning Company to the nascent cotton spinning industry, which was competing against established British manufacturers. Choi, 'Entrepreneurial Leadership', pp. 930–2.
25   Mathias Hoffmann and Toshihiro Okubo, '"By a Silken Thread": Regional Banking Integration and Pathways to Financial Development in Japan's Great Recession', *Center for Economic Studies & ifo Institute Working Paper* No. 4090, 2013, pp. 27–34; Ma, 'Between Cottage and Factory', pp. 208–11.
26   As pointed out by Leslie Hannah, this led to a tendency of overemphasising successes, whereas failures are little studied. Leslie Hannah, 'Marshall's "Trees" and the Global "Forest": Were "Giant Redwoods" Different?', in Naomi R. Lamoreaux, Daniel M. G. Raff and Peter Temin

the development of business organisation did not happen in a vacuum, as political economy thought and the development of the legal system shaped the path of business organisation.[27] The development of the legal system and business law historically lagged behind economic development; moreover, the prevailing system of political economy thought could preclude certain types of business organisation from emerging. Research on business institutions and their relationship to national economic performance focused principally on western Europe and the USA. Less is known about other regions and industries beyond manufacturing. This chapter takes a micro-perspective and points to distinctive requirements with regard to technology and management in the Bengal silk industry.

Mark Casson has argued that economic organisation is a 'rational response to the social need to economize on information costs'.[28] Firms are specialised intermediators. Firms 'create markets by innovating new products. They engage in arbitrage and speculation, integrating markets over time and space.'[29] This is a step away from the neoclassical perception of a firm whose strategic decisions are limited to responding to changes in factor and product prices through alterations in inputs and outputs. Instead Casson's view of a firm proposes giving businesses a much more strategic role. Historical case studies have shown that, through information sharing, firms could play an important role in economic development. In this way a firm can provide entrepreneurial leadership and vision for the whole sector or industry.[30] 'Planned co-ordination of economic activity, not only within dominant enterprises but also within the industry as a whole', was found to be essential for the rapid development of the Japanese cotton industry in the late nineteenth century.[31] Lars G. Sandberg, William Mass and William Lazonick, and Eugene Choi emphasised especially the role of entrepreneurial co-ordination for the emerging textile industry.[32] It was a case of vertical integration and

(eds), *Learning by Doing in Markets, Firms, and Countries* (Chicago: University of Chicago Press, 1999), p. 254.

[27] It has been pointed out by Ron Harris that the dominance of the joint-stock limited corporation since the late nineteenth century was not inevitable from the 1500–1800 perspective. Harris, *Industrializing English Law*, pp. 1–14.

[28] Mark Casson, *Information and Organization: A New Perspective on the Theory of the Firm* (Oxford: Oxford University Press, 1997), p. 3.

[29] Ibid., p. 5.

[30] Entrepreneurial guidance has been discussed by Alexander Gerschenkron, *Economic Backwardness in Historical Perspective: A Book of Essays* (Boston, MA: Harvard University Press, 1962). However, in his view special institutions are necessary for providing capital and entrepreneurial guidance. Choi, 'Entrepreneurial Leadership', pp. 930–2.

[31] William Mass and William Lazonick, 'The British Cotton Industry and International Competitive Advantage: The State of the Debates', *Business History* 32 (4), 1990, Special Issue on International Competition and Strategic Response in the Textile Industries since 1870, p. 48.

[32] Lars G. Sandberg, *Lancashire in Decline: A Study in Entrepreneurship, Technology, and International*

industry-level leadership. Leadership was taken up by the dominant spinning and trading companies that, as in the case of Mitsui Trading Company and Osaka Cotton Spinning Company, co-operated to reduce the costs of obtaining information about technical and commercial trends on the world markets.[33] This was a crucial advantage in the phase of late industrialisation for which technological and managerial guidance was essential.

Not all business forms are equally suited to give entrepreneurial guidance, as economies of scale and scope decrease transaction and transmission costs of information. Business historians generally attribute advanced technical, organisational and marketing capabilities to joint-stocks.[34] On the other hand, post-Chandlerian research has called attention to the fact that co-operatives and partnerships can often resolve organisational, information and management problems more effectively than joint-stocks.[35] The key factor to consider is that partnerships and co-operatives also built their success on intermediation of information and risk, and on access to capital. Overall, partnerships, co-operatives and joint-stocks possess technical, organisational, managerial and financial advantages not accessible to individual entrepreneurs. These advantages may be decisive for the success or failure of a business venture, especially if the venture is capital intensive or relies on the transfer of advanced technology. Although this conclusion is not surprising, it would not find much support in the mainstream political economy thought of the beginning of the nineteenth century. Efficiency was equated with private entrepreneurs, as individuals and organisational forms such as partnerships and trusts were viewed with distrust. The greatest suspicion was reserved for joint-stocks due to their long-term association with monopoly. Moreover, features of modern business organisation, such as legal personality, managerial hierarchy and limitation of liability, were not easily accessible to firms in the early nineteenth century.

Changes in political economy have impacts on the organisation of business and make certain business forms more beneficial than others. It is both the political and socio-economic environments that champion certain business

---

Trade (Columbus, OH: Ohio University Press, 1974); Mass and Lazonick, 'British Cotton Industry', pp. 37–48; Choi, 'Entrepreneurial Leadership' pp. 927–58.

33 Choi, 'Entrepreneurial Leadership', pp. 930–2.

34 Alfred Chandler, *Scale and Scope: The Dynamics of Industrial Capitalism* (Cambridge, MA: Harvard University Press, 1994); William Lazonick, *Business Organization and the Myth of the Market Economy* (Cambridge: Cambridge University Press, 1991).

35 Eric Hilt found that in the American whaling industry the joint-stock form was less productive than unincorporated form of business, as diffuse ownership reduced the stake of the manager in a whaling voyage. Eric Hilt, 'Incentives in Corporations: Evidence from the American Whaling Industry', *Journal of Law and Economics* 49 (1), 2006, p. 202. This illustrates that specific conditions such as higher susceptibility to agency problems make certain organisational forms a better solution.

forms as ideal.[36] In Britain the period between the sixteenth and nineteenth centuries saw the rise of business forms such as the family firm, unincorporated company, partnership, trust and joint-stock company.[37] The fact that by the middle of the nineteenth century the joint-stock company became the ideal form for doing business should not be taken as inevitable, but as a development conditioned by changes in moral sentiments towards business, changes in the law, economic development and the rise of new industries, and changes in political economy thought. It was argued by scholars such as Ron Harris that the centuries-long association of the joint-stock company with monopoly slowed down the dominance of this business form. Moreover, even features of modern business organisation were perceived with distrust and their legal existence came into force only gradually. Until the late nineteenth century, unincorporated companies – that is, companies without explicit state permission – were the common form of business organisation. Unincorporated companies had several limitations, most importantly that they were not legal entities and thus had no legal personality, which created problems with governance and made their standing in court litigation problematic. Moreover, these companies had unlimited liability and limited longevity.[38] In Britain companies could gain incorporation by specific act or charter to become joint-stocks.[39] Throughout the eighteenth century, the incorporated joint-stock form of business increased in popularity. Ron Harris estimated that between 1740 and 1810 the total capital of the joint-stock type of business in England increased from £18–19 million to more than £90 million, an increase of 500 per cent.[40] Yet, access to incorporation remained limited until the nineteenth century, and the process was often

---

[36] Under mercantilism the relationship between merchants and the state was built on protection and dependence. In return for exclusive trade rights merchants provided governments with loans, gifts and dividends. In this way, large chartered companies such as the EEIC were not only the ideal solution for expanding trade with Asia but vessels for building the fiscal military state and the Empire. For a discussion of the role of joint-stocks in trade see: Chaudhuri, *Trading World of Asia*, pp. 1–22; Charles Wilson, *England's Apprenticeship 1603–1763* (London: Longmans, Green & Co., 1971), p. 173; Ralph Davis, *England's Overseas Trade, 1500–1700* (London: Macmillan, 1973), p. 43; Ann M. Carlos and Stephen Nicholas, 'Giants of an Earlier Capitalism: The Chartered Companies as Modern Multinationals', *Business History Review* 62 (3), 1988, pp. 399–402. For discussion of the role of the EEIC in domestic political economy see, for instance, Huw Bowen, *Business of Empire: The East India Company and Imperial Britain, 1756–1833* (Cambridge: Cambridge University Press, 2006), pp. 29–52.

[37] Reforms favoured business types such as co-operatives, limited partnerships and friendly societies and failed to recognise the benefits of limited liability companies. Christine E. Amsler, Robin L. Bartlett, and Craig J. Bolton, 'Thoughts of Some British Economists on Early Limited Liability and Corporate Legislation', *History of Political Economy* 13 (4), 1981, p. 775.

[38] Harris, *Industrializing English Law*, pp. 141–5.

[39] Ibid., pp. 132–6, Amsler, Bartlett, and Bolton, 'Thoughts', pp. 776–7.

[40] Harris, *Industrializing English Law*, p. 194.

costly and prolonged.[41] Many companies therefore started as unincorporated with the view of later incorporation. The difficulties inherent in this approach to doing business became apparent after a series of court verdicts that refused to recognise the legal standing of unincorporated companies.[42] Only the repeal of the Bubble Act in 1825 and the General Incorporation Act of 1844 reduced transaction costs and regularised free incorporation by registration, and provided companies with a legal entity and transferable shares.[43] Limited liability was introduced as an integral feature of the incorporated company in 1856.[44]

Indian Company law mirrored British law, and in 1850 the Registration of Joint-Stock Companies Act was enacted in India based on the British 1844 Joint-Stock Companies Act. In 1857 the Joint-Stock Companies Act that introduced limited liability was passed in India. Yet adopting this legislation did not mean immediate expansion of the joint-stock type of business. The abolition of the EEIC's monopoly in 1813 and the opening up of Indian trade to British firms led to the reorganisation of Anglo-Indian business. The managing agency – a specifically hybrid form of ownership – emerged as a solution to high agency costs that arose due to the geographical distance between owners and managers. The form also enabled access to fixed capital.[45] Michael Aldous has argued that the joint-stock form fitted well with the growing capital requirements of the nascent industries. However, the governance structure of joint-stock was not ideal in dealing with high agency costs that arose due to the long distance between Britain and India, and also the distance between production sites within India. A modification of the joint-stock form – the so-called managing agency – emerged as a result. Managing agents had the capacity to access the information and resources needed to reduce the agency costs of doing business.[46] Managing agencies

---

41 Amsler, Bartlett, and Bolton, 'Thoughts', pp. 774–93.

42 The judiciary of the early nineteenth century was of gentlemanly origin and isolated from the business community. They viewed the rise in speculation on the financial markets in the beginning of the nineteenth century with suspicion. A stream of litigation cases such as King v. Dodd and Buck v. Buck that argued for the applicability of the Bubble Act and questioned the legal status of unincorporated companies gave them the opportunity to express their conservative views. The judges decided against the companies in many of the litigations and proclaimed them to be without legal standing. Such an approach to the legality of incorporated companies made them obsolete as business forms and led to an increased interest in incorporation. The government therefore needed to address the difficulties companies faced when attempting to achieve incorporation. Harris, *Industrializing English Law*, pp. 230–49.

43 The Bubble Act of 1720 'allowed the formation of joint-stock corporations only by specific authorisation of the State while outlawing other forms of joint-stock association'. Ibid., p. 1.

44 Ibid., pp. 287–93.

45 Michael Aldous, 'Avoiding Negligence and Profusion: The Failure of the Joint-Stock Form in the Anglo-Indian Tea Trade, 1840–1870', *Enterprise & Society* 16 (3), 2015, p. 649.

46 Aldous, 'Avoiding Negligence', pp. 680–2.

developed from trading partnerships and enabled the expansion and interna-
tionalisation of industries such as the Indian indigo industry.[47]

The managing agencies, however, expressed little interest in manufacturing, in capital-intensive types of production or in industries dependent
on the adoption of advanced technologies, innovations and a high level of
skills. The key sector in which managing agencies were active was indigo
production, which required little technological innovation and was managed
on a system similar to putting-out. Since relatively little capital was necessary
to enter the sector and profits could be made quickly, indigo production drew
large numbers of Europeans and hundreds of small factories were established.[48] The capital intensity of the Bengal silk industry seems to explain
the lack of interest on the part of the managing agencies, whose capital
stocks were limited.[49] In addition, the financial crisis of 1833 did not create
beneficial conditions for managing agencies to invest in new ventures.[50]

Tea became another industry that took off in the nineteenth century. Tea,
in contrast with indigo, was considered a capital-intensive industry as building
tea gardens, land clearances and construction of transport infrastructure
required significant capital outlays.[51] Moreover, specialised knowledge was
also necessary for the development of the nascent industry. The EEIC was
the first to experiment with tea production, and the Company started to
set up tea gardens in the late 1830s in Assam with the prospect of opening
the sector to private enterprise. The high prices paid for the Assam tea on
the London market spurred interest in tea production in both London and
Calcutta, and two companies were formed: the Bengal Tea Association of
Calcutta and the Assam Company of London. Both were interested in taking
over the Company's experimental gardens.[52] In 1839 the Assam Company,
a joint-stock company formed by a merger between the two companies, was

---

47 Ibid., p. 682.
48 Indrajit Ray, *Bengal Industries and the British Industrial Revolution (1757–1857)* (New York:
    Routledge, 2011), pp. 223–7.
49 Chapman, 'The Agency Houses', p. 244; Radhe Shyam Rungta, *The Rise of Business
    Corporations in India, 1851–1900* (Cambridge: Cambridge University Press, 1970), p. 22.
50 The withdrawal of the EEIC from export trade shook the old agency houses and led to their
    destruction. Agency houses in Calcutta, Bombay and Madras provided the EEIC with services
    such deposit banking, issuing paper money, financing indigo production, shipping and urban
    investment. Since their business activities were closely linked with the EEIC, the Company
    withdrawal led to their demise. Although new agency houses emerged almost immediately
    to connect peasant producers to the Western market, the demise of the old agency houses
    was still accompanied by a credit crisis and economic depression from 1830 to 1833. K. N.
    Chaudhuri, 'India's Foreign Trade and the Cessation of the East India Company's Trading
    Activities, 1828–40', *Economic History Review* 19 (2), 1966, p. 346; Anthony Webster, *The
    Twilight of the East India Company: The Evolution of Anglo-Asian Commerce and Politics, 1790–1860*
    (Woodbridge: Boydell Press, 2009).
51 Aldous, 'Avoiding Negligence', p. 665.
52 Rungta, *Rise of Business Corporations*, pp. 95–6.

formed and obtained two-thirds of the EEIC's tea gardens.[53] Michael Aldous emphasised that the fact that entrepreneurs adopted the joint-stock form to meet the capital requirements in the tea industry shows that entrepreneurs were aware that different types of business form brought distinctive benefits.[54]

This begs the question why the joint-stock form was not used in the silk industry. First, it seems that at least some private manufacturers considered raw silk unprofitable. Second, raw silk production necessitated very specialised knowledge, access to information about global silk markets and a labour force skilled in reeling.[55] Third, capital intensity in the Bengal raw silk industry was significantly higher than in tea. The expenditure of the Assam Company in 1840 was £50,000, whereas the average prime costs of raw silk production incurred annually by the EEIC in the period 1786–1803 were over £260,000 (see Table 5.4). Lastly, none of the various *Reports* or other documents show awareness of the benefits of the joint-stock form for Bengal raw silk production on the part of the EEIC, the House of Commons, Parliament or entrepreneurs. Thus, the Bengal silk industry was to follow the path preferred by contemporary political economists and the government, and become dominated by individual merchants, family firms and small partnerships.

Laissez-Faire Policies and the Effectiveness of the Business Model of Bengal Raw Silk Production after 1833

On 23 July 1833 the Bengal government was informed by the Court in London that, according to a new Bill debated by Parliament, the Company's trade with India and China was to cease. The EEIC was to stop its economic activities by 1834, or as quickly as possible without creating a negative impact on economic activity in India and on those British manufacturers depending on Asian imports.[56] For Bengal raw silk manufacturing this meant that the EEIC was to continue buying raw silk for exports for an interim period, as well as manufacturing raw silk in the filatures still owned by the Company. The sale of the silk filatures started in 1833, and the Court in London advised that it should be done as fast as possible yet at the same time with 'prudence'. The Court in its letter to the government in Bengal stated:

53 H. A. Antrobus, *The History of the Assam Company 1839–1953* (Edinburgh: Constable Ltd, 1957), p. 40.

54 Aldous, 'Avoiding Negligence', pp. 666–7.

55 The high mortality rates of tea workers in Assam illustrates that human capital and fluctuation of workers was not considered an issue. Silk reelers needed training and supervision, which implies investment, and their wages were also significantly higher.

56 LSE Archives, W7204, East India Company, *Reports and Documents Connected with the Proceedings of the East-India Company in regard to the Culture and Manufacture of Cotton-wool, Raw Silk, and Indigo in India* (London: J. L. Cox, 1836), p. xli.

the Injunction to use prudence being understood to refer less to the pecuniary gain or loss of the Company, than to the interests of the people and to the keeping up the supply of silk for this country, it was declared the silk-growers should not suddenly be deserted, unless there were capitalists ready to carry on the filatures, even though some loss should be incurred in protecting them.[57]

Initially the EEIC reported that neither the quality nor the quantity of the Bengal raw silk exported to the British market declined. This is also supported by quantitative data which shows that in the years following the sale of the filatures the quantities remained stable at around 1.4–1.5 million lbs. per year. The decline was relative: whereas from 1842 to 1849 the quantity of Bengal raw silk as a share of total imports of raw silk to Britain surpassed 30 per cent, in the 1850s the relative decline accelerated and from 1853 to 1856 the share decreased to less than 10 per cent to then increase to over 13 per cent in the 1860s (Tables 6.1 and 6.2).[58] We can find several explanations for this development. First, private entrepreneurs never expressed a great interest in Bengal silk manufacturing. Second, the EEIC supported private silk entrepreneurs by providing services until the end of the 1830s, and the expansion of imports from China and new silk regions such as Japan and Egypt to Britain took place only from the 1840s onwards. Third, entrepreneurs in Bengal were less successful in their efforts to modernise silk production than their counterparts in Europe, Japan and China.

Private manufacturers never expressed a huge interest in raw silk production, in spite of support from the EEIC, and only 26 per cent of Bengal raw silk imported to Britain in the period 1792–1835 was produced in private filatures.[59] Moreover, the silk from private filatures sold for lower prices than the Company's silk, on average 19 per cent lower in the period 1829–32.[60] Private merchants were interested instead in the so-called 'new articles' of Indian trade: sugar, indigo and coffee.[61] It is true that private

---

[57]   Ibid., p. xlii.

[58]   *East India Products, Part II: Reports on the Silk Industry in India and on the Supply of Timber in the Burmah Markets* (London: George Edward Eyre and William Spottiswoode, 1874), p. 28.

[59]   Robert Gordon, *East India Company, India and China Trade* (House of Commons, 1833), p. 4.

[60]   Ibid.

[61]   Bowen, *Business of Empire*, p. 245. Peter Marshall pointed to the fact that the EEIC relied on private initiative to supply new commodities such as sugar and indigo to European markets rather than becoming directly involved in their production. He argued that it was a mutually profitable arrangement: 'private European enterprise also profited by the Company's policy of entering into contracts for building, shipping, or supplies in Bengal, rather than undertaking these services itself'. Peter Marshall, 'Private British Investment in Eighteenth-Century Bengal', in Patrick Tuck (ed.), *The East India Company, 1600–1858* (London: Routledge, 1998), vol. 4, p. 130. It is necessary to remember that the production of sugar or indigo was less technologically advanced than the production of raw silk; it also required less specialised knowledge, and therefore it seems that there were fewer barriers to entry in the sugar and indigo industries for private manufacturers.

Table 6.1   Quantity of Bengal raw silk as a percentage of total imports of silk into Britain, 1842–56

Year	Imports of Bengal raw silk	Total average annual imports of raw silk	Quantity of Bengal raw silk as % of total
1842	1,359,599	3,951,773	34.4
1843	1,195,433	3,476,313	34.4
1844	1,669,133	4,149,932	40.2
1845	1,721,517	4,354,696	39.5
1846	1,415,325	4,407,264	32.1
1847	1,083,198	4,133,302	26.2
1848	772,152	4,471,735	17.3
1849	1,804,327	4,991,472	36.2
1850	1,569,995	4,942,407	31.8
1851	1,198,871	4,608,336	26.0
1852	1,335,486	5,832,551	22.9
1853	538,502	6,480,724	8.3
1854	696,728	7,535,407	9.3
1855	884,004	6,618,862	13.4
1856	610,422	7,383,672	8.3
Average	1,190,313	5,155,896	25.3

Source: Hadfield, *A Return of the Quantities of Silk of the Various Kinds Imported into the United Kingdom from various Countries, from 1842–56, Both Inclusive, Distinguishing Each Year's Importation, and the Countries from Whence they Came* (London: n.p., 1857), pp. 2–3.

Table 6.2   Quantity of Bengal raw silk as a percentage of total imports of silk into Britain, 1861–66

Year	Total average annual imports of Bengal raw silk	Total average annual imports of raw silk	Quantity of Bengal raw silk as % of total
1861–66	1,485,763	11,095,068	13.4

Source: Annual Statement of the Trade and Navigation of the United Kingdom with Foreign Countries and British Possessions in the Year 1868 (London: George Edward Eyre and William Spottiswoode, 1869), p. 16; *Annual Statement of the Trade and Navigation of the United Kingdom with Foreign Countries and British Possessions in the Year 1861* (London: George Edward Eyre and William Spottiswoode, 1869), p. 12; *East India Products, Part II: Reports on the Silk Industry in India and on the Supply of Timber in the Burmah Markets* (London: George Edward Eyre and William Spottiswoode, 1874), p. 28.

entrepreneurs frequently complained about the Company's monopoly in silk, and in particular that the EEIC interfered with the trade by giving advances to cocoon suppliers and binding them to sell their cocoons to the Company.[62] It seems that especially in districts such as Commercolly, Jungypore, Malda and Surdah where competition for silk was high, the Company's agents in the 1820s even resorted to threats.[63] In the districts of Bauleah, Hurripaul, Radanagore and Kasimbazar, on the other hand, private entrepreneurship was not restricted in the 1820s.[64] To understand the relationship between private manufacturers and the Company it is necessary to consider it in the framework of competition and principal–agent problems.[65] In the period 1770s–90s the EEIC encouraged the establishment of private filatures and often rented the Company's filatures to private entrepreneurs.[66] However, the low quality of silk from private filatures and the collusion among private entrepreneurs and the Company's Bengal agents which made the EEIC buy overpriced silk, threatened the venture and led to the Company's decision to increase its direct involvement in silk reeling.[67] Yet the policy of the Court of Directors was not to discourage private enterprise, though the way the official policy was implemented in Bengal depended on the local agents. In the face of fierce competition with local traders the Company's agents often struggled to secure enough cocoons and the entry of private entrepreneurs only amplified the problem. The Court of Directors' policy was to provide services and guidance to private filatures, and the testimonies of several entrepreneurs bear this out.

Prior to 1833 the Company provided private entrepreneurs, who set up their own filatures or hired the Company's, with a range of services: warehousing, transport, sales, marketing and entrepreneurial guidance. The Company provided private filatures with guidelines about best practices in reeling, innovations in reeling and machinery, and in filature construction. The EEIC also sent its European silk specialists to the private filatures to share best practices and to assist in mitigating problems.[68] Among the most

---

62 House of Commons, *Minutes of Evidence Taken before the Select Committee on the Affairs of the East India Company in the Last Session of Parliament and also the Accounts and Papers Laid before the Said Committee* (London: n.p., 1831), p. 108.

63 Ibid., p. 109.

64 Ibid., p. 172.

65 The principal–agent problem denotes the dilemma of how to motivate an agent to act in the best interest of the principal. It arises from asymmetries of information or conflict between the interests of principals and agents. See Sanford J. Grossman and Oliver D. Hart, 'An Analysis of the Principal–Agent Problem', *Econometrica* 51 (1), 1983, pp. 7–46; Ray Rees, 'The Theory of Principal and Agent, Part I', *Bulletin of Economic Research* 37 (1), 1985, pp. 3–26.

66 IOR/E/4/618, 24 December 1765, p. 97; IOR/E/4/638, 30 May 1792, p. 470; IOR/E/4/621, 7 April 1773, p. 506; IOR/E/4/623, 5 April 1776, pp. 269–76. IOR/E/4/628, 16 March 1784, pp. 261–5. IOR/E/4/628, 11 April 1785, p. 555.

67 IOR/E/4/630, 12 April 1786, pp. 390–2.

68 IOR/E/4/625, 14 July 1779, pp. 484–6.

important services offered to private merchants by the Company was the possibility of withdrawing their silk from sale if prices offered at this sale did not reach an agreed minimum price.[69] In this way the Company provided merchants with a level of security highly appreciated by some of them, as can be seen from this statement made in front of the Select Committee on the Silk Trade by a silk merchant:

> I think the East India Company are nothing more than servants of the public; suppose I have a shipment of silk comes into the St. Katherine's Docks, I try to make a sale, and if I cannot effect a sale a few days before the Company's sale comes on, I desire this silk to be removed from St. Katherine's Dock to the Company's warehouses; they are bound to take it in and to print it in the catalogue with that of the Company; then the day before the declared sale comes on, they may say to the Company, I withdraw that, though it is printed in your catalogue, and send it back from the Company's warehouses to St. Katherine's Dock; when the Company put up the sale it is put up at a certain price, and it is sold if it sells for a penny above that price.[70]

The Company also provided manufacturers in Bengal with information about developments on the European markets and the changes in European demand.

In the transitional period of 1833–35 the majority of the EEIC's filatures were sold off. From the names mentioned in the Company's documents it seems that they were bought up mostly by European merchants and less often by Indian merchants.[71] During the 1830s the new system of silk manufacturing for exports still resembled the pre-1833 arrangement, only now the entrepreneurs bought the filatures instead of hiring them from the EEIC. The Company still held a position of co-ordinator of silk manufacturing for exports. In 1838 the Court reported with satisfaction that the sale of filatures had not 'occasioned a falling off in the quantity of Silk forwarded to Europe in the last three years, and advert to the Export Warehouse Keeper's favourable report on the quality of some of the Private Silk in those consignments'.[72] This favourable situation was a reflection of the Company's continued involvement in silk exports. In 1835 the Court of Directors ordered that 'any filature in the Company's possession should be used for investment' and this policy remained in practice until 1838.[73] The Company continued to provide

---

69   House of Commons, *Report from Select Committee on the Silk Trade with Minutes of Evidence, Appendix and Index* (London: n.p., 1832), pp. 698–9.
70   Ibid., p. 699.
71   See IOR/E/4/741, 1834, pp. 708, 716, 720; IOR/E/4/757, 25 September 1838, pp. 509–10; IOR/E/4/758, 6 March 1839, pp. 917–23.
72   IOR/E/4/754, 10 April 1838, p. 749.
73   Ibid., p. 747.

Table 6.3   Imports of Bengal raw silk by the EEIC and private manufacturers to London, 1792–1835

Year	EEIC imports (sm. lbs.)	Private imports (sm. lbs.)	Total (sm. lbs.)
1792	372,553	28,892	401,445
1793	677,988	91,885	769,873
1794	494,487	0	494,487
1795	379,543	12,984	392,527
1796	340,060	21,046	361,106
1797	88,219	0	88,219
1798	352,780	0	352,780
1799	643,803	1,618	645,421
1800	454,600	0	454,600
1801	310,368	0	310,368
1802	78,950	35,794	114,744
1803	336,189	68,904	405,093
1804	415,917	205,793	621,710
1805	460,303	375,601	835,904
1806	235,215	173,308	408,523
1807	225,984	2,677,601	2,903,585
1808	325,243	53,225	378,468
1809	116,124	46,623	162,747
1810	373,598	211,120	584,718
1811	258,953	145,803	404,756
1812	558,862	423,565	982,427
1813	831,891	252,459	1,084,350
1814	722,727	114,239	836,966
1815	522,810	279,476	802,286
1816	381,215	398,549	779,764
1817	373,459	128,876	502,335
1818	758,116	402,860	1,160,976
1819	553,105	197,235	750,340
1820	811,875	259,572	1,071,447
1821	817,625	172,838	990,463
1822	845,382	197,235	1,042,617
1823	850,668	310,518	1,161,186
1824	660,012	271,637	931,649

Year	EEIC imports (sm. lbs.)	Private imports (sm. lbs.)	Total (sm. lbs.)
1825	699,230	220,206	919,436
1826	898,388	338,635	1,237,023
1827	926,678	99,361	1,026,039
1828	1,039,623	96,686	1,136,309
1829	1,129,710	258,044	1,387,754
1830	1,096,071	90,092	1,186,163
1831	1,030,280	64,597	1,094,877
1832	750,828	205,625	956,453
1833	698,851	52,129	750,980
1834	757,517	53,124	810,641
1835	721,509	6,025	727,534
Total	25,377,309	9,043,780	34,421,089
Average	576,757	205,540	782,297
Average % of total	73.7	26.3	

Source: LSE Archives, W7204, East India Company, *Reports and Documents Connected with the Proceedings of the East-India Company in regard to the Culture and Manufacture of Cotton-wool, Raw Silk, and Indigo in India* (London: J. L. Cox, 1836), pp. 3–4.

services to the now privately owned filatures.[74] Most importantly, it continued to provide guidance on profitability when it reported that:

> 226 Bales or 427 Maunds [32,025 sm. lbs.] of the Investment 1836 had been valued at 302,650 Gov. Rupees [£30,265] giving an average of 1,417½ Rupees [£141 15s.] per Bale of 2 Maunds [150 sm. lbs.]. This cost is evidently too high to afford a profitable remittance, according to the best estimate which can be made of the prospects of the home Market for the present year.[75]

Considering the remaining EEIC's filatures, the Court pointed out that silk manufacturing 'must cease altogether, unless Silk can be provided at a cost not exceeding over [one] thousand Gov. Rupees per Bale [£100 per 150 sm. lbs.], including Indian Charges'.[76]

Until 1839 the EEIC was still involved in the sale of Bengal raw silk on the London market, to smooth out the transition process and to accrue profits.

---

[74] Ibid., p. 748.
[75] Ibid., p. 751. This means that the production costs of 1 sm. lb. were 18s. 11d.
[76] Ibid., p. 754. This means that the production costs of 1 sm. lb. should not surpass 13s. 4d.

Table 6.4   Profits made by the East India Company in the Bengal raw silk trade, 1834–39

Year	Profit (£)
1834–35	513,000
1835–36	284,516
1836–37	56,292
1837–38	122,038
1838–39	66,833
Total	1,042,679

Source: House of Lords, *Report from the Select Committee of the House of Lords Appointed to Consider of the Petition of the East India Company for Relief* (London: n.p., 1840), pp. iv, 8.

The Company relied on the raw silk trade for profits, as can be seen from Table 6.4. It bought part of the Bengal raw silk production from the Bengal government and sold it in London. These profits were used in Britain to cover 'home expenditure' – dividends and payments payable in Britain. In the 1830s, home expenditures made up to £3,200,000 annually and were covered from Bills on India, Advances in China, Advances in India and Silk Sales.[77] The Company was slowly abandoning the silk trade as directed by the 1833 Charter, yet from 1834 to 1839 over £1 million of profits still came from silk sales. For the period 1835–39 sales of silk constituted 3.6 per cent of remittances to Britain, which illustrates that for the Company the raw silk trade was not a loss-making business that should be discouraging private entrepreneurs.

Considering the profitability of the trade, it might seem baffling that raw silk production went into decline and by the 1870s was considered negligible.[78] One important factor seems to be the misleading perception about the lack of profitability, which was a notion subscribed to by the managing houses as well as by many European entrepreneurs. For instance, one of the houses considered that silk filatures 'are far too expensive and in many respects useless, and a system not to be upheld by the private merchant'.[79] This was based on calculations of production costs for which data was obtained from a 'friend'.[80] In addtion, many British silk manufacturers had an unfavourable view of venturing into Bengal silk manufacturing. The British government perceived that private manufacturers would be more efficient in producing

[77] House of Lords, *Report from the Select Committee of the House of Lords Appointed to Consider of the Petition of the East India Company for Relief* (London: n.p., 1840), pp. iv, 1–8.
[78] *East India Products*, pp. 28–30.
[79] Baring Archive Series HC6.3.1, Letter 11, 1833.
[80] The key problem was considered to be the advances to intermediaries (Pykars) who, as it was supposed, often failed to abide by the contract and supply cocoons for which they took advances. It is true that this happened but in the 1810s the Company improved the system of management of Pykars. LSE Archives, W7204, *Reports and Documents*, p. 95.

silk in Bengal, yet many of them – including large-scale operations such as Grout, Baylis & Co. – were often wary about the Company's withdrawal from raw silk manufacturing in Bengal and some even warned against it. Private entrepreneurs heard in the 1830s by the Select Committee on the Silk Trade – a Parliamentary committee inquiring into silk manufacturing and trade – did not uniformly champion the withdrawal of the EEIC because, as some of them argued, the Company was able to produce silk more cheaply. Joseph Grout, a manufacturer of silk crape of Grout, Baylis & Co., argued in front of the Select Committee that the price at which he was buying the EEIC's Bengal raw silk was 6 per cent lower than the cost of producing raw silk in Bengal on his own. Grout drew attention to the fact that his business partner who managed the venture in Bengal had over ten years' experience with silk production. He also pointed out that the high chances of dying due to the epidemiological and climatic conditions in India led to less interest in doing business there.[81]

Grout ended his comments on the role of the EEIC in importation of silk to the British market by claiming that: 'I should be exceedingly sorry, as a large consumer of Bengal silk, to see the Company decline the raising of it, for I am sure if it gets into the hands of individuals, we shall have very little raw silk imported into this country from India in future.'[82] Grout's perception was based on his own experiments with silk manufacturing in Bengal and on his conviction that 'the Company put up their silk below the cost price'.[83] However, William Milburn's analysis of 1813, the Company's own statistics and return on investment analysis all show that this was not the case.[84] Instead, the key advantages that enabled the Company to produce silk profitably were access to capital, the knowledge of 'best practices' of silk reeling gained thanks to learning-by-doing, management practices developed through learning-by-doing, access to silk specialists, an existing network of employees that could be deployed to the silk industry, networks of intermediary merchants dealing with silk cocoon producers, and economies of scale in cocoon procurement, reeling, advertising, warehousing and sales.

By 1840 European entrepreneurship in Bengal raw silk was limited to small-scale ventures. Among the largest producers were Alexander Rogers, a silk and indigo manufacturer, and Messrs Watson & Co., who had filatures in several districts.[85] European capital had been only partially directed to raw

---

81 House of Commons, *Report from Select Committee on the Silk Trade*, p. 697.
82 Ibid.
83 Ibid., p. 699.
84 William Milburn, *Oriental Commerce* (London: Black, Perry & Co., 1813), vol. 2, p. 257; LSE Archives, W7204, *Reports and Documents*, p. 171; Appendix C.
85 House of Commons, *Report from the Select Committee on East India Produce together with Minutes of Evidence, an Appendix, and Index* (London: n.p., 1840), pp. 307–8. Messrs Watson & Co. were among the key producers of raw silk in the 1870s.

silk production, with some raw silk filatures converted into sugar refineries, as happened at Gonatea in particular.[86] The overall state of raw silk production in Bengal in 1840 was not flourishing. Although the relative decline of raw silk imports to the British market set in only in the late 1840s, quality had started to decline a decade earlier. According to information presented to the Select Committee on East India Produce, the average price of Bengal raw silk on the London market in the late 1830s was 16s. per 1 sm. lb., whereas Chinese silk sold on average for 22s. This situation did not change and in the 1860s Bengal raw silk sold for prices lower than Chinese or Italian silk, and even Japanese silk – the newest competitor on the global market with raw silk – sold for higher prices.[87] The obvious reason was the quality of Bengal raw silk. Although several manufacturers – Alexander Rogers, Messrs Watson & Co., and Haldumand & Co. – were able to produce raw silk of fine quality in Bengal, on the whole Bengal raw silk was coarse and of non-standard quality.[88] As this was an issue both during the Company's time in charge and later on, the key aspect to look at is the trend in Bengal raw silk quality. A deterioration in quality was observed by Bengal silk manufacturer Alexander Rogers, Secretary to the East India Company James Cosmo Melvill, as well as Spitalfields silk weaver John Poyton; that is, by all the individuals questioned by the Select Committee on East India Produce on the subject of raw silk quality in 1840.

The key reason for the declining quality and quantity of Bengal raw silk as a percentage of total imports of raw silk to Britain was the lack of capital. This testimony in front of the Select Committee on East India Produce illustrates the issues in 1840: 'the failure of the large agency houses, to the amount of 20 millions of money, disturbed the whole capital of the country; the whole cultivation of silk is now thrown upon private individuals, who have not sufficient capital'.[89] Agency houses were not interested in investing in silk manufacturing even after they overcame the financial crisis of 1833. The government of India offered neither capital nor assistance to silk manufacturers as raw silk production had 'been thought to possess sufficient vitality to stand alone'.[90] This is not to say that the government did not support experimentation with sericulture in new regions, but these were small-scale projects.[91] The lack of government support should be seen as one of the key

---

[86] Ibid., pp. 129–30.
[87] *East India Products*, p. 28.
[88] House of Commons, *Report from the Select Committee on East India Produce*, pp. 307–8.
[89] Ibid., p. 307. Rogers also argued that the Company 'interfered' with the silk trade and that private entrepreneurs had not yet had time to apply their capital to silk manufacturing.
[90] *East India Products*, p. 25.
[91] For details see: L. Liotard, *Memorandum on Silk in India, Part 1* (Calcutta: Superintendent of Government Printing, 1883), pp. 25–30; House of Commons, *Report from the Select Committee on East India Produce*, pp. 27, 34–5, 49–50.

differences between the silk industries of Japan and Bengal, as in Japan the Meiji state was instrumental in the expansion and innovation of sericulture.[92] Without the capital necessary for the adoption of new technologies, mechanisation did not expand, and without mechanisation, standardising the quality of Bengal raw silk was impossible.

Besides having capital to invest in raw silk manufacturing, particularly for upgrading technology, the Company also had a vast knowledge of the global trade in raw silk. From the evidence presented to the Select Committee on East India Produce it becomes clear that even successful Bengal silk manufacturers, such as Alexander Rogers, had a very limited grasp of the qualities and prices of Turkish, Chinese and Italian silks, and no acquaintance with the modes of sericulture or reeling in any of these regions.[93] This should be seen as a serious handicap in a market that was becoming increasingly more integrated and where technological upgrading had played an essential role since early modern times. A lack of awareness about prices and modes of reeling, the unavailability of capital, together with the opportunity for European brokers to buy Indian silk handkerchiefs cheaply, explains the growth in exports of finished silks and the decline in raw silk. The end of the prohibition of imports of finished silks into the British market in 1826 opened a new avenue for European merchants and brokers. In the 1830s and 1840s, corahs, bandanas and other types of Indian silk handkerchief found a ready market in Europe.[94] Moreover, silk handkerchiefs made from unreeled silk were cheap and easily procured on the Indian market.[95] Indian corahs and bandanas were popular in spite of being coarse or so-called heavy items, meaning they contained large quantities of roughly processed silk. The fact to note is that they were cheaper on the British market than the raw silk they contained.[96] Yet although the same weight of raw silk would sell for a higher price than Indian handkerchiefs, merchants still preferred to import handkerchiefs instead of raw silk. Even though the trade in Indian silk handkerchiefs proved to be short-lived and the demand for Indian bandanas and corahs started to decline in the 1860s and 1870s as their production was taken up in Britain, merchants and manufacturers still did not shift to raw silk.[97]

Further explanation of the relative decline of raw silk exports from Bengal to Europe can be found in the changes in the commodity and value chains

---

92 Ma, 'Why Japan not China', p. 370; Lillian M. Li, 'Silks by Sea: Trade, Technology, and Enterprise in China and Japan, *Business History Review* 56 (2), 1982, p. 193.

93 House of Commons, *Report from the Select Committee on East India Produce*, pp. 308–10.

94 Ibid., p. 127.

95 Ibid., p. 169.

96 Ibid., pp. 469–70.

97 *East India Produce*, pp. 28–9. In the first phase from the 1830s to the 1840s, British silk manufacturers bought grey, plain Indian silk handkerchiefs for printing. House of Commons, *Report from the Select Committee on East India Produce*, pp. 421–2.

of raw silk production. Unfortunately, information about the breakdown of costs of silk production for private entrepreneurs is not available. However, from analysis of the changes in the commodity chain of raw silk production (Figure 6.1) is clear that in comparison with the Company, private entrepreneurs had less economic power vis-à-vis peasants due to the fact that they had less market power and had to compete for cocoons with other entrepreneurs, European as well as domestic, especially handkerchief producers. This needs to be seen as a serious setback, because it was only after the Company's system of cocoon procurement was reformed in 1831, and prices for cocoons started to be set centrally in a co-ordinated fashion, that cocoon prices stopped increasing.

Private entrepreneurs also had less control over the secondary stage of the chain since they had no administrative power over land and could not, for instance, attempt to promote silk production through the lowering of land taxes as the Company had done.[98] Moreover, they arguably also had less power over reelers as argued by Alexander Rogers:

> if you go back to the Company's time, I would agree that the quality has deteriorated, for this reason, that the natives are now independent silk reelers, whereas formerly they were not allowed to reel for themselves separately; they were obliged to pass it through the Company's filatures, or to sell it to the East India Company.[99]

There is no evidence that wages increased sufficiently to become a concern for the entrepreneurs.[100] However, what did matter was that the quality of silk decreased. The increasing market integration and competition from Chinese (and later Japanese) silk was driving down prices.[101] Considering the fact that

---

[98] IOR/E/4/619, 'Cultivation of Mulberry, 17 March 1769', p. 334; IOR/E/4/623, 'Growth of Mulberry Plantations Encouraged, 24 December 1776', p. 286.

[99] House of Commons, *Report from the Select Committee on East India Produce*, p. 307.

[100] None of the government reports and none of the entrepreneurs mentioned that wages would be an issue. On the contrary, wages in India were considered to be low. On the other hand, labour should not be considered as being cheap because productivity was very low (see Table 5.2) and this cancelled out the advantage that low wages might represent. Indrajit Ray pointed to the fact that the monthly wage rates of reelers increased considerably between 1791 and 1815. Indrajit Ray, 'Long Waves Of Silk Prices In Bengal During 17th–18th Centuries' (paper presented at the conference 'Global Economic History Network Conference: Cotton Textiles', Pune, December 2005), pp. 29–30. Yet, from the point of profitability the key issues to consider are labour productivity and quality of output. An increase in wages spiked by an enhanced productivity of reelers and/or an improved quality of reeled silk could easily boost profits if translated into higher prices on the buyers' market and/or a decrease in manufacturing costs.

[101] Reduction of tariffs on Chinese raw silk and the opening up of China to international trade after the Opium Wars played a crucial role in expanding the quantity of Chinese raw silk exported to the British market in the 1830s. More detail on raw silk import duties is shown in Table 7.1.

Table 6.1   Commodity chain in raw silk production in Bengal, after 1833

Primary stage	Secondary stage	Tertiary stage
Controlled by peasants	Controlled by entrepreneurs	Controlled by entrepreneurs
Inputs: Silkworm eggs, mulberry leaves, water, peasant labour, land for mulberry cultivation and cocooneries.	**Inputs:** Land for filatures, filatures, labour of reelers, supervision, cocoons, wood.	**Inputs:** Freight, customs, charges for warehouses, etc.

Difference with the previous period		
Primary stage	**Secondary stage**	**Tertiary stage**
Less economic power vis-à-vis peasants, no co-ordination	No economies of scale, less control over inputs such as land due to lack of administrative power	No economies of scale

marginal profits were always moderate – in the range of shillings per sm. lb. of raw silk – quality improvement was essential as it yielded higher profits. Moreover, access to cheaper cocoons and efforts to reduce manufacturing costs became even more essential under falling prices. Without innovations in the production process, quality improvement and reduction of manufacturing costs turned out to be difficult. Entrepreneurs could not take advantage of economies of scale and the proliferation of innovations in silk-reeling technologies was stunted. The Company relied on economies of scale from the 1770s to the 1830s when investing in innovations of technology and sending European silk specialists to implement best practice.[102] During the Company's time, European silk specialists were regularly sent to consult with all the silk filatures (often also the private ones) as it decreased the unit costs of the consultation process. Similarly, the Company used to send models of machinery from London to Calcutta where copies were made and then sent to the Company's filatures.[103] This decreased the unit cost of technology transfer, and this is without taking into account the cost of collecting information about up-to-date technologies. An important factor that is not considered in the calculations of production costs in chapter 5 is the cost of information. The Company had communication channels and also personnel – the Inspector of Raw Silk in London and Superintendent General in Calcutta – who gathered information at sales from British manufacturers as well as information about technologies, and these were transferred to Bengal. Again, the Company had

---

[102] Hutková, 'Technology Transfers and Organization', pp. 934–6.
[103] IOR/E/4/625, 14 July 1779, pp. 485–6.

the advantage that this information was transferred to all filatures. Another factor was knowledge of the Bengal environment. As pointed out by private manufacturers such as Grant, in the pre-1833 period the entrepreneurs newly arrived to Bengal relied on the Company for information and assistance, such as provision of architects for building their filatures.[104]

Economies of scale were also beneficial for the reason that harvests often failed due to adverse weather conditions; having filatures in all silk districts was beneficial as it enabled the EEIC to spread the risk. Likewise, the weather determined the outcome of silkworm breeding with each silk district producing a raw silk with distinct characteristics, depending on the type of silkworm raised there (see Appendix F). The fact that entrepreneurs could not rely on economies of scale in the tertiary stage might not have been such an obstacle, especially considering the substantial reduction of custom duties from 3s. 1d. to 1d. in 1826.[105] This should have been of considerable advantage to the entrepreneurs. There is no evidence that costs of transportation, warehousing, advertising and organisation of sales were prohibitive for the private silk manufacturers. The Company necessarily had an advantage in this respect as it had large warehousing capacities and a system of regular biannual sales. However, this does not seem to be a decisive factor in explaining the reason why private entrepreneurs should have only a limited interest in raw silk production in Bengal.

Overall, although development of silk manufacturing in the post-1833 period was less well documented, three facts still stand out. First, mulberry cultivation in Bengal was undergoing a contraction and by the 1870s raw silk was no longer produced in the silk districts of Dinegapur, Rungpur, Bogra and Pubna.[106] A decline in raw silk production for exports was accompanied by an increase in production of silk for domestic markets.[107] Attempts to expand raw silk cultivation and manufacturing to new regions in India also followed. Yet even exports of silk textiles to Europe were declining over the nineteenth century.[108] Second, the nineteenth century saw an increased interest in wild varieties of silk. Such silks did not gain large markets in Europe due to their lower quality, and interest in them was driven mostly by ethnographic factors.[109] Third, private entrepreneurs in Bengal were less successful in modernising silk production and in adopting scientific methods than their competitors in Japan and China. Government reports at the time

104 House of Commons, *Report from Select Committee on the Silk Trade*, p. 697.
105 Donald C. Coleman, *Courtaulds: An Economic and Social History*, vol. 1: *The Nineteenth Century Silk and Crape* (Oxford: Clarendon Press, 1969), p. 66.
106 *East India Products*, p. 29.
107 Ibid., pp. 28–30.
108 Ibid.
109 Thomas Wardle played an essential role in popularising the wild silks of India. Thomas Wardle, *The Wild Silks of India, Principally Tusser* (London: n.p., 1880).

Bengal silk, as well as contemporary writings by Liotard and Mukherji, show that experimentation with sericulture and silk reeling continued even after the Company withdrew.[110] The majority of these experiments seemed to focus on sericulture, and attempts were made in particular to adopt European and Japanese varieties of mulberries and silkworms in Bengal as well as in new regions such as Bombay, Madras and Assam. Although none of these experiments were successful, what they do indicate is the lack of knowledge of silk production and lack of management skills on the part of private individuals as well as the governments of respective residencies. The attempts resembled the EEIC's trial-and-error type of experimentation in the 1750s.[111] Innovations in reeling were implemented principally by Mr Basford, superintendent of the filatures of Messrs Watson & Co., who was awarded a gold medal from the Society of Arts for the silk he produced according to his new reeling methods. However, the overall quality of Bengal silk did not increase in the 1840s–1860s.

Conclusion

Bengal raw silk production was a profitable venture for the East India Company, and economies of scale played a key role as they allowed it to set up a successful business model. The EEIC relied on up-to-date information about the raw silk market to set rules about the quality of silk to be produced, on technological innovation to reduce production costs and on management strategy to limit the rise of the price of cocoons. Economies of scale allowed the EEIC to become an agent of change and facilitate large-scale alteration in the mode of raw silk production. Yet contemporary political economy theorists and politicians remained blind to the positive role of the EEIC in raw silk manufacturing in Bengal, and expected the trade in raw silk to flourish after the privatisation of the Company's filatures. Even EEIC officials seemed unaware of the benefits derived from economies of scale. This might seem to be a bewildering paradox, yet changes in political economy provide a ready answer.

If we perceive firms as specialised intermediators that integrate markets and whose strategic role is to mediate information, risk and access to capital, it becomes clear that firms have a strategic role in economic development.[112] However, not all forms of business are ideal for trading under all circumstances, as different sectors often have different needs. Therefore, forms of

110 N. G. Mukherji, *A Monograph on the Silk Fabrics of Bengal* (Calcutta: Bengal Secretariat Press, 1903), p. 62; Liotard, *Memorandum on Silk in India*.
111 See Liotard, *Memorandum on Silk in India*, pp. 25–30, 77–83.
112 Casson, *Information and Organization*, pp. 3–5.

business favoured by political economy or the legal system may diverge from those that are ideal for trading in a specific sector of the economy. Since information costs differ among societies and are especially high in economies with high communication costs and low levels of market integration, different forms of business and organisation of production become beneficial. Access to capital is another major concern, and not all business forms may have access to credit, especially if credit networks are underdeveloped and information is imperfect.

By the end of the seventeenth century the English East India Company was viewed as being no longer beneficial for trade with Asia. Due to the long-term association of monopoly with joint-ventures, and large-scale business in general, political economy thinkers championed individual merchants, small-scale partnerships and family firms as the most efficient business forms. Unfortunately for the Bengal silk industry in the period from the 1830s to the 1850s, these forms of business had limited access to capital and equally limited knowledge about global silk markets and the technologies of silk production. Transportation and communications were still underdeveloped and managing agencies, hybrid business forms that emerged after the abolition of the EEIC's monopoly and the opening of the Indian trade to British firms, had no interest in raw silk manufacturing.[113] There were no 'investment groups' or free-standing firms – a form of foreign direct investment typical in the late nineteenth century – ready to provide capital and information intermediation that were interested in the Bengal raw silk industry.[114] Thus, the quality and (relative) quantity of Bengal raw silk exported to foreign markets started to decline and a formerly profitable sector of industry eventually disappeared.

[113] The main inventions in transportation and communications, such as the transcontinental telegraph, steamships and the opening of the Suez Canal, came only in the second part of the nineteenth century.

[114] A free-standing company was a form of foreign investment. These were firms owned by British expatriates that accessed the financial markets in London for capital. They were very successful in raising capital and acquiring information on trading conditions, yet their manufacturing experience developed only gradually. Mira Wilkins, 'The Free-Standing Company, 1870–1914: An Important Type of British Foreign Direct Investment', *Economic History Review* 41 (2), 1988, pp. 277–9. Investment groups were a spin-off from merchant houses. They emerged after the Napoleonic wars and had a particularly strong presence in India and the Far East, although they were active globally. They had strong ties with the City of London, which gave them access to capital. Stanley D. Chapman, 'British-Based Investment Groups before 1914', *Economic History Review* 38 (2), 1985, pp. 231–5.

Chapter 7

BENGAL RAW SILK AND BRITISH DEMAND IN THE NINETEENTH CENTURY

> So that those districts in England principally employed in making the coarse description of commodity we have been making for the last few years may be in a state of prosperity, while Spitalfields, where you are used to consume Italian silks in making velvets and figured articles, may not be in a state of prosperity?[1]

The above excerpt from an inquiry into the state of the silk industry carried out in 1832 by the House of Commons Select Committee on the Silk Trade is a fitting depiction of the state of British silk weaving in the middle of the nineteenth century. Producers of crape, ribbons and other smaller silk items of middling quality were able to make profits, whereas producers of high-quality, broad silk weaves were facing difficulties. Since this book is concerned not only with raw silk production in Bengal but also with the link between the British and Bengal silk industries, it is important to explore the development of the British silk industry in the nineteenth century. This is crucial, particularly in assessing whether demand for Bengal raw silk was stable or diminishing. Research into the nineteenth-century silk industry has shown a high degree of complementarity between raw silk-producing regions and weaving centres – China and France, and Japan and the USA.[2] As the previous chapters have shown, the British and Bengal silk industries had a strong connection in the eighteenth century. It is essential to assess whether the political economy changes of the post-mercantilist era weakened this link and if the structural changes to the British silk industry decreased the demand for Bengal raw silk.

In the nineteenth century the British silk industry became one of the targets of critics of mercantilism. It was argued that mercantilist regulation was to blame for the stagnation of the British silk industry and that only

---

[1] House of Commons, *Report from Select Committee on the Silk Trade with Minutes of Evidence, Appendix and Index* (London: n.p., 1832), p. 361.
[2] Debin Ma, 'The Modern Silk Road: The Global Raw-Silk Market, 1850–1930', *Journal of Economic History* 56 (2), 1996, pp. 346–7.

the disbanding of protective measures and a reduction of import duties on finished silks could revive the industry.[3] The whole debate was conceptualised as one focused on labour, the poverty and destitution of weavers and throwsters, a debate on the role of Spitalfields, and competition with France or Continental Europe in general. The advocates of laissez-faire policies, whose arguments triumphed, viewed liberalisation as a force that would reinvigorate both production and employment in the silk industry.

The chapter first looks at nineteenth-century changes to regulation of the British silk industry and on the political economy debates that guided those changes. Second, the chapter considers technology, labour and the product mix of the British silk industry. Finally, it examines the raw silk inputs in British silk weaving, paying attention to the suitability of Bengal raw silk.

Nineteenth-Century Political Economy and the British Silk Industry

The early nineteenth century became a critical period for the British silk industry. Until then the silk industry was protected and to a large extent also regulated by the government. The 1766 Act prohibited imports of all foreign silks and velvets, and moreover silk manufacturing in London was regulated by the 1773 Spitalfields Acts which mediated piece wages and competition among weavers. Their gradual revocation in the 1820s and 1830s had unintended far-reaching effects as increased competition led to the demise of high-end production and favoured the manufacture of mid- to lower-end quality goods.

The seventeenth and eighteenth centuries had seen a rise in measures to protect the English silk industry. Imports of Asian silk textiles were prohibited by legislation in 1699, 1702 and 1720, and French finished silks were the subject of high tariffs, yet English silk manufacturers nevertheless appealed for the general prohibition of their importation. In 1766 this appeal was granted and imports of foreign silks and velvets were banned.[4] Initially the prohibition was to last only for five years but in the end remained in place for sixty years. Further legislation intended to protect the industry were the Spitalfields Acts of 1773, 1792 and 1811, the first of which came into force at a time when London silk weavers, particularly journeymen, were

---

3   David Ricardo, 'Spitalfields Acts, 9th May 1823', in *The Works and Correspondence of David Ricardo. Volume 5 Speeches and Evidence 1815–1823*, ed. P. Sraffa and M. H. Dobb (Indianapolis: Liberty Fund, 1951), pp. 291–5.

4   Donald C. Coleman, *Courtaulds: An Economic and Social History*, vol. 1: *The Nineteenth Century Silk and Crape* (Oxford: Clarendon Press, 1969), p. 18; William Page, 'Industries: Silk-weaving', in William Page (ed.), *A History of the County of Middlesex: Volume 2, General; Ashford, East Bedfont With Hatton, Feltham, Hampton With Hampton Wick, Hanworth, Laleham, Littleton* (London: Victoria County History, 1911), pp. 132–7.

experiencing distress. The Acts were preceded by several years of intermittent rioting by journeymen.[5] The Spitalfields Act of 1773 gave Justices of the Peace of the City of London, Westminster, the Tower Liberty and Middlesex the authority to 'settle, regulate and declare' the piece wages of silk weavers in their respective areas. The piece rates were discussed and agreed upon jointly with committees of masters and journeymen.[6] Besides wages, the Acts also impacted the organisation of silk weaving by limiting the number of apprentices to two per weaver, and by allowing masters to employ only people resident in their areas.[7] The purpose of the Acts was to regulate the conditions of journeymen rather than to help the expansion of the industry.

Though from a current viewpoint the Acts necessarily seem to be hostile to economic activity, contemporaries did not uniformly oppose them. As J. H. Clapham concluded in his influential 1916 analysis of the Spitalfields Acts:

> the small men thought in Spitalfields terms, clung to the Acts as the bulwark of their district against pauperism, and – being mainly in the staple trade – did not worry much about outside competition. The big men, who made experiments and had knowledge of the new commercial and industrial world, thought the Acts a relic of barbarism, an interference with capital and political economy, and a nursery of combination.[8]

This was not unknown to contemporary politicians as a similar view was presented, for instance, by William Hale, silk manufacturer of Christchurch, Spitalfields, to the House of Lords: 'I suppose I can name one individual who has signed the petition, whose fortune would amount to the whole of those who wish to have the Spitalfields Acts continued'.[9] The consequences of these differing views on the Acts reverberated into business strategies. Whereas the small producers were in favour of expanding the Acts beyond London, the large manufacturers either switched their production outside of London or ran workshops both in London and outside.[10]

By the beginning of the nineteenth century these measures started to be perceived by a growing proportion of economists, manufacturers and also finally MPs as a brake on the development and competitiveness of the industry. The most prominent critic was David Ricardo, whose position as an MP gave him ample opportunity to channel his opposition to the Spitalfields Acts and demand their repeal. The debate about the merit of the Spitalfields Acts was spurred by an 1821 report presented to Parliament

5   Ibid.
6   J. H. Clapham, 'The Spitalfields Acts, 1773–1824', *Economic Journal* 26 (104), 1916, pp. 460–1.
7   Ibid., p. 461.
8   Ibid., p. 464.
9   House of Lords, *The Sessional Papers, 1801–1833*, vol. 156, 1823, p. 31.
10 It was illegal for a London manufacturer to put out work to other areas, but this rule was frequently evaded. Clapham, 'Spitalfields Acts', p. 462.

advocating for their total abolishment.[11] The pamphlet stated that: 'the duty on the raw material being great, the wages of labour high, and the pressure of taxation heavy, the manufactured commodity is necessarily very much enhanced in price'.[12] The manufacturers argued that the regulation imposed on them by the Acts made their product uncompetitive at home and abroad as 'the London silk manufacturer is threatened with the loss of the domestic trade also, through the competition of manufactories recently established at Macclesfield, Manchester, Reading, and other places'.[13] The manufacturers' petition was built on two main propositions. First, that the Acts facilitated wage rigidity by not allowing higher wages to be paid in good times. Second, the Acts were said to thwart technological change as they prevented skilled labour from being rewarded with higher wages and created no incentive to employ new technologies as manufacturers would not be able to change wages even after the implementation of such labour-saving technologies.[14] These views were reflected by David Ricardo who, in a debate in Parliament, expressed his astonishment that:

> in the year 1823, those acts should be existing and in force. They were not merely an interference with the freedom of trade, but they cramped the freedom of labour itself. Such was their operation, that a man who was disposed to embark in the trade could not employ his capital in it in London; and, as it might be inconvenient, in many instances to carry that capital out of London, the trade was necessarily cramped and fettered.[15]

Ricardo further questioned the fact that the silk industry should be regulated at all when other industries were not: 'Why should he [the magistrate] have the power to fix the price of labour, more than the price of bread, meat, or beer?'[16] Ricardo's observation begs a further question: was the silk industry fundamentally different from the industries he mentioned? In a recent addition to the sparse literature on the Spitalfields Acts, Simon Hupfel argued that it is necessary to consider them in the wider framework of the organisation of the London silk industry. According to Hupfel it is essential to make a distinction between industries producing fashionable and

---

11 The report was published in 1822 as *Observations on the Ruinous Tendency of the Spitalfields Act to the Silk Manufacture of London* (London: John and Arthur Arch, 1822). The petition was discussed by Parliament in 1823. Hansard's Historical Parliamentary Debates, 'Spitalfields Silk Manufacture Acts – Petition for the Repeal Thereof', *House of Commons Debate 9 May 1823*, vol. 9, pp. 143–50.

12 *Ruinous Tendency of the Spitalfields Act*, p. 1.

13 Ibid., p. 2.

14 Simon Hupfel, 'The Spitalfields Acts and the Classics: Ricardo, J. S. Mill, Bowring, and Senior on the London Silk Industry, 1823 to 1841', *European Journal of the History of Economic Thought* 19 (2), 2012, p. 169.

15 Hansard's Historical Parliamentary Debates, 'Spitalfields Silk Manufacture Acts', p. 149.

16 Ricardo, *Works and Correspondence*, p. 296.

luxurious products and those making more mundane ones. Hupfel argued that 'regulated prices were above all an indirect means to enforce incomplete contracts in a highly unstable subcontracting economy'.[17] This instability was due to the technical and labour demands of silk cloth production, the complex system of contracts connecting merchants and weavers, and the variation in demand for luxury products such as silk cloths. Hupfel maintained that collective regulation of wages served to protect the interests of weavers in a situation in which they had lower bargaining powers than merchants.[18] Nevertheless, Hupfel admitted that the Spitalfields Acts on their own could not promote the production of fashionable silks with complicated designs.[19] It is necessary to consider that new designs necessitated the adoption of new looms or new settings of looms, as well as an investment in skills, and this constituted a considerable source of risk. From this point of view, a set wage represented a form of insurance. At the same time, decreasing prices of English silk cloths by reducing wages did not make them more appealing to those English consumers interested in fashionable luxury goods.[20] Lastly, it is necessary to keep in mind that originally the Spitalfields Acts were tools of social reconciliation rather than an industrial policy.

The Spitalfields Acts are the most discussed in the literature, yet their effects on the industry as a whole were much more limited than the liberalisation of imports of finished silks to the British market. The 1824 Resolution of the House of Commons ended the prohibition of the importation of silk manufactures from 5 July 1826 and instead imposed a tariff of £30 on every 100 lbs. of manufactured silk imported to Britain. The Resolution also ended export tariffs on manufactured silk and rearranged tariffs on raw and thrown silk imports.[21] The aim was to discourage smuggling as well as open up the

---

17   Hupfel, 'Spitalfields Acts', pp. 170–1. Here he draws on a scholarship that shows the model of dispersed manufacturing remained competitive and in many cases the source of competitive advantage for producers in semi-luxuries. See for example: Maxine Berg, 'Small Producer Capitalism in Eighteenth-Century England', *Business History* 35 (1), 1993, pp. 17–39; Pierre Claude Reynard, 'Manufacturing Strategies in the Eighteenth Century: Subcontracting for Growth among Papermakers in the Auvergne', *Journal of Economic History* 58 (1), 1998, pp. 155–82; Giorgio Riello, 'Strategies and Boundaries: Subcontracting and the London Trades in the Long Eighteenth Century', *Enterprise & Society* 9 (2), 2008, pp. 243–80; Alain Cottereau, 'The Fate of Collective Manufactures in the Industrial World: The Silk Industries of Lyons and London, 1800–1850', in Charles F. Sabel and Jonathan Zeitlin (eds), *World of Possibilities: Flexibility and Mass Production in Western Industrialization* (Cambridge: Cambridge University Press, 1997), pp. 75–152.

18   Hupfel, 'Spitalfields Acts', p. 171.

19   At the same time Hupfel pointed out that the history of the European silk industry shows that uncertainty about wages drove weavers into producing less intricate products.

20   Brenda M. King, *Silk and Empire: Studies in Imperialism* (Manchester: Manchester University Press, 2005), p. 16; Hupfel, 'Spitalfields Acts', pp. 189–93.

21   Parliamentary Papers, *Accounts and Papers Relating to Customs and Excise, Imports and Exports, Shipping and Trade, Volume 34, Session 6 December 1831 – 16 August 1832* (London: n.p., 1832), pp. 12–13.

Table 7.1   Silk import duties (per sm. lb. of 16 oz), 1817–29

	Raw			**Thrown**		
	China	**Bengal**	**Italy**	**Organzine and crape**	**Tram**	**Singles**
1817–23	5s. 6d.	3s. 6d.	5s. 6d.	14s. 8d.	14s. 8d.	14s. 8d.
1824	3d.	3d.	3d.	7s. 6d.	7s. 6d.	7s. 6d.
1825	3d.	3d.	3d.	5s.	5s.	5s.
1826	1d.	1d.	1d.	5s.	3s.	3s.
1829	1s. (per cwt.)	1s. (per cwt.)	1s. (per cwt.)	3s. 6d.	2s.	1s. 6d.

Source: Donald C. Coleman, *Courtaulds: An Economic and Social History*, vol. 1: *The Nineteenth Century Silk and Crape* (Oxford: Clarendon Press, 1969), p. 66.

market to competition, as this was supposed to give a new impetus to British silk manufacturers.[22] The intention was to establish *ad valorem* duties of 30 per cent on average but, in practice, duties by 1832 were as high as 35 per cent. A further reduction came in 1845, when rates were reduced to an average of 15 per cent *ad valorem*. These rates remained in place until 1860, when the Gladstone government removed tariffs on silk manufactures altogether.[23] In addition, duties on thrown silk were reduced (Table 7.1), which increased the pressure on silk throwsters to increase efficiency. According to Coleman, the main effect of trade liberalisation was to speed up the process already under way: mechanisation, economies of scale, and specialisation on simpler and cheaper fabrics.[24]

The debate that encompassed the liberalisation of the British silk industry was regarded in the scholarship from three main viewpoints. Scholars such as Hertz found liberalisation of the silk industry was a welcomed policy, alleviating the inefficiencies of the medieval economic order.[25] The second group of scholars focused on the social effects of liberalisation, with several therefore viewing the disbanding of the silk industry guild regulations and the opening of the market to foreign competition as a negative step.[26] The

---

22   Coleman, *Courtaulds: An Economic and Social History*, p. 66; Ricardo, *Works and Correspondence*, pp. 295–7, 306–9.

23   Coleman, *Courtaulds: An Economic and Social History*, p. 66.

24   Ibid., pp. 67–9.

25   Gerald B. Hertz, 'The English Silk Industry in the Eighteenth Century', *English Historical Review* 24 (96), 1909, pp. 722–7.

26   Frank Warner, *The Silk Industry of the United Kingdom: Its Origin and Development* (London: Drane's, 1921), pp. 88–90. Clapham also emphasised the social impacts of the repeal of the Acts. Clapham, 'Spitalfields Acts', pp. 459–71. The very acute distress of Spitalfields weavers provoked the interest of policymakers, and the employment situation and poverty of Spitalfields silk weavers was discussed in several Reports, including House of Commons,

third and newest strand of scholarship, represented by Hupfel, offers a more balanced view. Hupfel emphasised the wider political context, drawing attention to the fact that the liberalisation of the silk industry was part of a new approach to industrial policy which started to favour heavy industry and factory organisation. Hupfel argued that such a policy disadvantaged traditional industry centres such as Spitalfields.[27] He recognised that Spitalfields silk production was lagging behind France in design and fashion, but did not blame this on the Spitalfields Acts as had the nineteenth-century economists. Rather, Hupfel perceived the Acts as an imperfect institutional device for settling industrial disputes in a manufacturing system that was based on subcontracting. Hupfel drew a parallel between functioning subcontracting economies in the production of fashionable wares in London and Spitalfields silk weaving.[28] Yet, it is problematic to compare Spitalfields silk weaving with the production of other luxury and fashionable wares, as the key issue was that Spitalfields products were not fashionable and were of a lower quality than Lyon silks. Customers both at home and abroad were willing to pay a higher price for more expensive but fashionable and high-quality Lyon silks.[29]

The major limitation of the scholarship focusing on the changes in political economy regulating the British silk industry is the narrow focus on Spitalfields. All three of the views discussed above put a disproportionate emphasis on Spitalfields broad weaving, which they essentially equate with the British silk industry. Yet Spitalfields broad weaving, although the most well-known segment of the British silk industry, never achieved the quantitative importance of haberdashery, which represented the majority of British silk products.[30] The golden era of the Spitalfields silk industry came with the Seven Years War (1756–63), when conflict disrupted the French silk trade and English silk manufacturers increased their exports at the expense of the French. Yet, this state of affairs did not last beyond the end of the war.[31] Spitalfields-made silk cloths were not in high demand on the global

Report from Select Committee on the Silk Trade. According to Cottereau the repeal of the Acts was one of the main reasons for the decline of the Spitalfields industry: Cottereau, 'The Fate of Collective Manufactures', pp. 128–30.

27 Hupfel, 'The Spitalfields Acts', pp. 191–2.

28 Ibid., p. 171.

29 King, *Silk and Empire*, p. 16.

30 Spitalfields' reputation was created thanks to the accomplished work of designers such as Joseph Dandridge, John Vansommer, Christopher Baudouin, James Leman and Anna Maria Garthwaite, but it only remained at the forefront of silk weaving and design from the 1730s to the 1760s. Natalie Rothstein, *Spitalfields Silks* (London: Stationery Office, 1975), pp. 1–2. See also: Warner, *Silk Industry of the United Kingdom*, p. 42; Natalie Rothstein, 'The Silk Industry in London, 1702–1766' (unpublished M.A. thesis, University College London, 1961); Natalie Rothstein, *Silk Designs of the Eighteenth Century: In the Collection of the Victoria and Albert Museum, London* (London: Thames and Hudson, 1990); and Gail Malmgreen, *Silk Town: Industry and Culture in Macclesfield 1750–1835* (Hull: Hull University Press, 1985), p. 8.

31 Coleman, *Courtaulds: An Economic and Social History*, p. 18.

market and were sold predominantly in Britain while haberdashery was sold on the domestic market as well as being exported.[32] Yet even contemporary economists and politicians focused in their debates on whether the policies of liberalisation would bring a revival to Spitalfields, scholars evaluated the effects of these policies on Spitalfields, and both groups ignored the economic reality of the British silk industry. By the nineteenth century on a global level, the silk industry was moving towards mechanisation and production for the middle strata of society such as occurred in the silk industry in the USA. A more artisanal type of production remained longest in that segment of silk industry that focused on the production of luxury textiles. The best example is the French silk industry, which retained its focus on the production of luxury silks. The luxury segment of the industry also faced competitive pressures: the French silk industry needed to set fashion trends and be able to change designs rapidly to compete in the more globalised market. The British silk industry, which was never involved in producing high-end luxury goods, could hardly compete and it thus needed to focus on the more mechanised and larger-scale production of medium-quality items. This focus was facilitated in particular by comparatively higher wages in the British silk industry than in the French.[33] D. C. Coleman pointed out that the essence of the nineteenth-century development of the English silk industry was the expansion of simpler and plainer silk fabrics, and its move from London out to Lancashire, Cheshire and Norwich.[34] Overall, the nineteenth-century history of the British silk industry is one of factor endowments; reallocation of resources into less-sophisticated products such as bandanas, sewing silks, stockings, hosiery and silk mixes; mechanisation of weaving; and entrepreneurship and new approaches to production such as spinning waste silk. It is a switch from artisanal towards mechanised industrial production using power looms. From this point of view, an industrial policy favouring factory production does not seem harmful.

Technology, Labour and Product Mix in the British Silk Industry

In order to accurately evaluate the effects of the changes in British political economy on the silk industry, it becomes necessary to distinguish between silk throwing and the two main branches of silk weaving: broad weaving and the production of ribbons, smaller items and haberdashery. The amount of labour and type of technology in silk throwing depended on the characteristics of the raw silk and the fineness that the thrown yarn was supposed to

---

[32]   British-made silk cloths and haberdashery were sold in Continental Europe and in the Americas but struggled against competition when trade opened.

[33]   For a detailed discussion of wages in France and Britain see: House of Commons, *Report from Select Committee on the Silk Trade*, especially pp. 243–4, 258–9.

[34]   Coleman, *Courtaulds: An Economic and Social History*, p. 23.

achieve. The technology and labour employed in silk weaving depended on the product mix. Simpler and plainer weaves demanded less labour. Products requiring a high level of skill were manufactured in London, whereas products relying on cheap labour and prone to mechanisation were made outside the capital. In addition, the organisation of silk weaving differed depending on whether it was located in London or not. Consequently, the artisanal workshops of London and the larger-scale and more mechanised production outside the capital were differentially affected by nineteenth-century legislation. Efficient silk manufacturers with large-scale production and up-to-date technology producing standardised textiles remained competitive, while small-scale producers relying on handwork and producing 'fancy' textiles were driven out of the market.[35]

S. R. H. Jones argued that the British silk industry was the world's first modern factory industry.[36] This seems to be a great overstatement, considering that the Italian silk industry started to mechanise throwing from the thirteenth century and silk reeling from as early as the seventeenth century.[37] Moreover, in Britain the process of mechanisation proceeded at a slow pace even in the eighteenth and nineteenth centuries, and largely focused on silk throwing. In the early eighteenth century the processes of winding, throwing and weaving were done predominantly by hand under the putting-out system. Especially in the case of silk winding, handwork persisted late into the nineteenth century as it was among the worst-paid industrial jobs and similarly, silk throwing was done by 'women and children, and the poorest of the poor'.[38] In silk throwing, hand-operated silk-throwing mills were used up to the early nineteenth century. Their operation necessitated large amounts of unskilled labour and required experienced supervision.[39] Bigger throwsters employed predominantly women and children in their workshops. Hand throwing persisted into the nineteenth century in spite of the impetus generated by industrial espionage of the Lombe brothers in the early eighteenth century.

In 1718 Thomas Lombe, with assistance of his brother John Lombe, built a water-powered silk-throwing mill in Derby according to Italian designs, which he obtained illegally. Notwithstanding the fact that this became one of the best-known cases of premodern industrial espionage, Lombe's mill

---

35   D. C. Coleman, *Myth, History and the Industrial Revolution* (London: Hambledon Press, 1992), p. 100.

36   S. R. H. Jones, 'Technology, Transaction Costs, and the Transition to Factory Production in the British Silk Industry, 1700–1870', *Journal of Economic History*, 47 (1), 1987, p. 75.

37   Richard Hills, 'From Cocoon to Cloth: The Technology of Silk Production', in Simonetta Cavaciocchi (ed.), *La Seta in Europa Secc. XIII–XX* (Prato: Istituto Internazionale di Storia Economica, 1993), p. 70.

38   Coleman, *Courtaulds: An Economic and Social History*, p. 13. Winding is a process of transferring raw silk kept in a skein onto a bobbin.

39   Ibid.

became the first power-operated textile factory in Britain.[40] Throwing mills enabled the equivalent labour of several hundred hand-throwsters to be saved, as operators were needed only to join the threads and replace the spools and reels.[41] Yet the progress of the technology was slow, one of the reasons being the quality of raw silk imported to Britain. After the King of Savoy banned exports of Piedmontese raw silk to Britain in 1724 in retaliation for the Lombe's industrial espionage, there was no appropriate source of raw silk. Italian silk mills used raw silk made in Italy of a very high quality – of a precise fineness and made from a standard quality of threads – to produce organzine. Using this technology in England, without adaptation, to throw lower-quality silk threads created problems: silk threads frequently broke and caused work in the mill to stop.[42] Overall, mechanised silk throwing did not initially achieve commercial success and in 1765 only one-ninth of the organzine used by the British silk industry was thrown in the country.[43]

More mechanisation, again predominantly in silk throwing, started to be employed only from the 1750s when the industry overcame a period of stagnation.[44] Further impetus for silk throwing came with the engagement of the EEIC in the trade from the 1770s.[45] The EEIC experimented with throwing Bengal raw silk in Britain between 1794 and 1815 but without major success.[46] Table 7.2 shows that the Company was able to throw on average only around 20,000 sm. lbs. per year in this period, which was well below the target of 300,000 sm. lbs. that the Company set for itself. Overall imports of thrown silk in 1794–1815 were on average 385,636 sm. lbs. per year. This means that the silk thrown by the EEIC accounted for only 5.5 per cent of total imports of thrown silk. The Company faced technical issues as it was unsuccessfully attempting to throw Bengal raw silk into fine organzine.[47] The quality of the thrown silk was sufficient only for use in the ribbon industry. Moreover, the

[40] Goldsmiths' Library (hereafter GL), 1795 fol. 16280, *Reports of the Committee of Warehouses of the East-India Company relative to Extending the Trade on Bengal Raw-Silk* (London: n.p., 1795), p. 2; Dionysius Lardner, *A Treatise on the Origin, Progressive Improvement, and Present State of the Silk Manufacture* (Philadelphia: Carey & Lea, 1832), p. 62; Jones, 'Technology, Transaction Costs', pp. 75–7; Giuseppe Chicco, *La Seta in Piemonte 1650–1800: Un Sistema Industriale d'Ancien Régime* (Milan: Franco Angeli, 1995), pp. 71–96.

[41] Robert Patterson, 'Spinning and Weaving', in Charles Singer (ed.) *A History of Technology II: The Mediterranean Civilizations and the Middle Ages, c.700 BC – c.AD 1500* (Oxford: Clarendon Press, 1956), p. 207; Hills, 'From Cocoon to Cloth', p. 72. According to Patterson only two to three operators were needed but he does not give an indication of the capacity of the mill.

[42] IOR/E/4/627, 12 July 1782, p. 351; IOR/E/4/625, 9 April 1777, p. 175.

[43] Coleman, *Courtaulds: An Economic and Social History*, p. 17.

[44] Ibid., p. 14.

[45] Ibid., p. 17; GL, 1795 fol. 16280, *Reports of the Committee of Warehouses of the East-India Company*, pp. 1–2, 4.

[46] IOR/E/4/643, 3 July 1795, p. 586.

[47] RSA/SC/EL/2/31, *Third Report of the Committee of Warehouses of the East-India Company relative to Extending the Trade on Bengal Raw-Silk* (London: n.p., 1795), pp. 6–7, 11–14.

Table 7.2 Comparison of the quantity of raw silk thrown into organzine by the EEIC and the quantity of thrown silk imported to Britain, 1796–1815

Year	Thrown on account of EEIC (lbs.)	Imported (lbs.)	EEIC thrown silk as % of imported thrown silk
1796	25,948	399,000	6.5
1797	19,961	402,000	5.0
1798	9,085	403,000	2.3
1799	16,426	468,000	3.5
1800	20,511	335,000	6.1
1801	32,691	275,000	11.9
1802	29,717	396,000	7.5
1803	25,618	385,000	6.7
1804	45,407	449,000	10.1
1805	27,492	433,000	6.3
1806	51,847	515,000	10.1
1807	40,620	346,000	11.7
1808	29,452	415,000	7.1
1809	11,485	502,000	2.3
1810	13,869	451,000	3.1
1811	13,547	20,000	67.7
1812	10,883	618,000	1.8
1813	4,380	0	100.0
1814	10,796	646,000	1.7
1815	6,434	358,000	1.8
Total	468,715	8,484,000	5.5
Mean	21,296	385,636	5.5
Median	19,047	400,500	4.8

Source: LSE Archives, W7204, East India Company, *Reports and Documents Connected with the Proceedings of the East-India Company in regard to the Culture and Manufacture of Cotton-wool, Raw Silk, and Indigo in India* (London: J. L. Cox, 1836), p. 7; B. R. Mitchell, *British Historical Statistics* (Cambridge: Cambridge University Press, 1988), p. 344

Table 7.3   Silk mills in the UK, 1835

Country	County	Parish	No. of Mills
England	Somerset		8
	Wiltshire		2
	Gloucestershire		2
	Worcestershire		8
	Warwickshire		5
	Lancashire	Manchester	15
		Eccles	3
		Cockerham	1
		Lancaster	1
		Leigh	1
		Ashton-under-Lyne	1
		Melling	1
		Stockport	1
		Cheadle	1
	Cheshire	Sandbach	7
		Middlewich	1
		Astbury	37
		Prestbury	40
		Wilmslow	1
	Derbyshire	Glossop	1
	Staffordshire	Leek	6
		Keele	1
		Newcastle	2
		Stoke-on-Trent	1
		St. Mary's, Stafford	1
	West Riding of Yorkshire	Almondbury	2
		Dewsbury	1
		Halifax	4
		Leeds	1
Scotland	Lanark		3
	Renfrew		3
Ireland			1
		Total	**163**

Source: Compiled from House of Commons, *Return of the Number of Persons Employed in Cotton, Woollen, Worsted, Flax and Silk Factories* (London: n.p., 1836).

Table 7.4   Mechanisation in silk mills, 1835

County	No. of mills (in operation)	No. of mills (out of work)	No. of steam engines	No. of water-wheels
Lancashire and Cheshire	110	26	97	32
Staffordshire	11	0	10	1
Derbyshire	1	0	0	1
West Riding of Yorkshire	8	0	8	7
Somerset	7	0		
Wiltshire	1	0		
Gloucestershire	2	0		
Worcestershire	8	0		
Warwickshire	5	0		

Source: Compiled from House of Commons, *Return of the Number of Persons Employed in Cotton, Woollen, Worsted, Flax and Silk Factories* (London: n.p., 1836).

EEIC was making losses in silk throwing.[48] The Company had to admit that the venture was far from successful and by 1808 was ready to abandon it.[49]

Unfortunately, data on silk-throwing output is not available for this period so it is not possible to compare the total domestic production of thrown silk with imports. As a matter of fact, statistics for domestic silk throwing are not available for most of the nineteenth century. Data does exist, however, concerning the number, geographical location and sometimes even the type of power used in silk factories in the UK. Table 7.3 is based on data from the 1835 Returns of the Factory Commissioners, which examined employment in British textile industries.[50] Although the report did not distinguish whether these mills were involved in silk throwing or weaving, we can assume that most of the 163 mills operating in Britain were engaged in silk throwing as mechanisation went faster in that sector of the industry than it did in weaving. The table shows that mechanised silk production was located outside London and that silk production in Scotland and Ireland was negligible. The key centres were to be found in Lancashire and Cheshire, in the parishes of Astbury and Prestbury, and also in Manchester. Table 7.4 shows that Lancashire and

48   IOR/E/4/640, 25 June 1793, pp. 513–14; IOR/E/4/643, 3 July 1795, p. 597; IOR/E/4/645A, 27 July 1796, p. 330; RSA/SC/EL/2/31, *Third Report of the Committee of Warehouses*, pp. 4–5.

49   LSE Archives, W7204, East India Company, *Reports and Documents Connected with the Proceedings of the East-India Company in regard to the Culture and Manufacture of Cotton-wool, Raw Silk, and Indigo in India* (London: J. L. Cox, 1836), p. xxix.

50   House of Commons, *Return of the Number of Persons Employed in Cotton, Woollen, Worsted, Flax and Silk Factories* (London: n.p., 1836).

Table 7.5   Power looms used in silk weaving, 1835

County	Parish	No. of power looms	% of power looms
Lancashire	Manchester	306	17.6
	Middleton	60	3.4
Cheshire		414	23.8
Staffordshire		119	6.9
Derbyshire		166	9.6
Devonshire		80	4.6
Essex		106	6.1
Norfolk		300	17.3
Somersetshire		156	9.0
Worcestershire		7	0.4
Warwickshire*		22	1.3
Total		1,736	100.0

Source: Compiled from House of Commons, *Return of the Number of Power Looms used in Factories, in the Manufacture of Woollen, Cotton, Silk and Linen* (London: n.p., 1836).

* estimate made by the Superintendent of the County

Cheshire used the highest number of steam engines and waterwheels but the amount used in Staffordshire and the West Riding are also significant, especially since they are employed in a smaller number of mills. Data for the number of steam engines and waterwheels used in Somerset, Wiltshire, Gloucestershire, Worcestershire and Warwickshire is not available. Yet it is safe to assume that, as in the case of the cotton industry, northern England was the leader in the adoption of inanimate energy. These conclusions are also supported also by the data on geographical distribution of power looms in Britain. From Table 7.5 it is apparent that 44.8 per cent of these looms were located in Lancashire and Cheshire; Norfolk, with 17.3 per cent, was the only other centre of mechanised silk weaving.

When we compare mechanisation in the silk industry in 1835 with that in 1856, for which another detailed report by the Factory Commissioners exists, progress is undeniable as the total number of silk factories increased by almost a factor of three from 163 to 460. The number of power looms increased more than fivefold. Out of the 460 factories, 255 engaged in silk throwing, 129 in silk weaving, 36 factories in both silk throwing and weaving, and for the remaining 40 silk factories the Commissioners did not distinguish which sector they engaged in. The industry was predominantly located in England and employed over 56,000 people (Table 7.6 and 7.8–7.11 show a detailed breakdown for England, Scotland and Ireland). It is clear from Table 7.7 that

Table 7.6 Mechanisation in silk industry in the UK, 1856

Total silk factories	No. of factories	No. of spindles	No. of power looms	Moving power: steam (in horse-power)	Moving power: water (in horse-power)	No. of employees
England	454	1,063,555	9,260	4,238	816	55,300
Scotland	6	30,244		122		837
Ireland						
Total	460	1,093,799	9,260	4,360	816	56,137

Source: House of Commons, *Return of the Number of Cotton, Woollen, Worsted, Flax, and Silk Factories* (London: n.p., 1857), p. 22.

Table 7.7 Mechanisation and employment in the British silk industry, 1856

Type of factory	No. of factories	No. of spindles	No. of power looms	% of total moving power (horse-power)	% of total no. of employees
Silk throwing	255	839,999 (77%)		64.2	55.1
Silk weaving	129		5,719 (62%)	14.5	20.0
Silk throwing and weaving	36	253,800 (23%)	3,536 (38%)	18.4	22.3
Silk throwing and/or weaving	40		5	2.9	2.6
Silk industry total	460	1,093,799	9,260	100.0	100.0

Source: Compiled from House of Commons, *Return of the Number of Cotton, Woollen, Worsted, Flax, and Silk Factories* (London: n.p., 1857), p. 22.

Table 7.8   Silk throwing in the UK, 1856

Throwing	No. of factories	No. of spindles	No. of power looms	Moving power: steam (in horse-power)	Moving power: water (in horse-power)	No. of employees
England	249	809,755		2,545	654	30,076
Scotland	6	30,244		122		837
Ireland						
Total	255	839,999		2,667	654	30,913

Source: House of Commons, *Return of the Number of Cotton, Woollen, Worsted, Flax, and Silk Factories* (London: n.p., 1857), p. 22.

Table 7.9   Silk weaving in the United Kingdom, 1856

Weaving	No. of factories	No. of power looms	Moving power: steam (in horse-power)	Moving power: water (in horse-power)	No. of employees
England	129	5,719	734	20	11,176
Scotland					
Ireland					
Total	129	5,719	734	20	11,176

Source: House of Commons, *Return of the Number of Cotton, Woollen, Worsted, Flax, and Silk Factories* (London: n.p., 1857), p. 22.

Table 7.10 Silk throwing and weaving in the UK, 1856

Throwing and weaving	No. of factories	No. of spindles	No. of power looms	Moving power: steam (in horse-power)	Moving power: water (in horse-power)	No. of employees
England	36	253,800	3,536	838	112	12,478
Scotland						
Ireland						
Total	36	253,800	3,536	838	112	12,478

Source: House of Commons, *Return of the Number of Cotton, Woollen, Worsted, Flax, and Silk Factories* (London: n.p., 1857), p. 22.

Table 7.11 Silk throwing and/or weaving in the UK, 1856

Throwing and/or weaving	No. of factories	No. of spindles	No. of power looms	Moving power: steam (in horse-power)	Moving power: water (in horse-power)	No. of employees
England	40		5	121	30	1,470
Scotland						
Ireland						
Total	40		5	121	30	1,470

Source: House of Commons, *Return of the Number of Cotton, Woollen, Worsted, Flax, and Silk Factories* (London: n.p., 1857), p. 22.

silk-throwing factories had the highest number of employees – 55 per cent of the people employed in the silk industry in Britain – and used 64 per cent of the horsepower of the whole industry, relying mostly on steam for moving power. Silk-weaving mills were much less mechanised as they used only 14.5 per cent of the aggregate moving power, yet employed 20 per cent of people engaged in the silk industry. Interestingly, the most heavily mechanised were the factories involved in both silk weaving and throwing, as they represented only 7.8 per cent of all factories but employed 23 per cent of all spindles, 38 per cent of power looms and 18.4 per cent of the aggregate moving power. Also, over 22 per cent of the employees in the silk industry worked in these mills. It is useful to look at the geographical breakdown of the data. Appendix E shows that silk throwing was located in Cheshire (27.5 per cent of spindles), with other major centres in the West Riding of Yorkshire (14.5 per cent), Essex (10.2 per cent) and Derbyshire (9.2 per cent). Several factories – accounting for 18 per cent of the total – were located in Worcestershire, Gloucestershire, Lancashire and Staffordshire, but they were smaller and only accounted for 13 per cent of the total number of spindles. The key region for silk weaving was Lancashire with 43.8 per cent of power looms, followed by Warwickshire with 30.5 per cent and Cheshire with 16.7 per cent. Those factories with the highest capacity involved in both throwing and weaving were located in Lancashire (28.5 per cent of spindles and 35.7 per cent of power looms), Norfolk (31 per cent and 18.5 per cent), Essex (10 per cent and 16.1 per cent) and Derbyshire (9 per cent and 11 per cent).

Overall, the data from the 1835 and 1856 reports shows progress in mechanisation and indicates that the major centres of the silk industry were located in northern and south-eastern England. Comparison between data in Tables 7.4–7.5 and Appendix E discloses that Lancashire, Cheshire and Norfolk retained their position as leading centres of both silk throwing and weaving. Essex saw a rapid rise in mechanisation in both throwing and weaving, Warwickshire started to specialise in silk weaving, and the progress of mechanisation between 1835 and 1856 was especially fast considering the low initial numbers of power looms. Derbyshire retained its relative position in silk throwing and weaving, Yorkshire continued to be one of the key centres of mechanised silk throwing but the relative importance of Staffordshire, on the other hand, declined. The data does not suggest an absolute decline in the British silk industry after the 1826 liberalisation, but to get a better under-standing of the changes in the industry it is necessary also to consider the testimonies of silk manufacturers and weavers.

In 1832 a Select Committee of the House of Commons was appointed to examine the state of the British silk industry. It called in silk manufacturers and weavers to inquire about conditions in the industry. On the whole, according to the testimonies of manufacturers recorded in the *Report from Select Committee on the Silk Trade*, the level of mechanisation in the British silk industry in the 1830s was lower than that in Italy or France. Simple weaving was a semi-skilled task mostly carried out by women.[51] Hand weaving was widespread and mechanisation low. Women represented three-quarters of the single hand weavers in Staffordshire and Warwickshire as well as the majority of weavers in Macclesfield.[52] Only weaving of figured fabrics was a skilled task, for which a draw-loom was used and the work done by men.[53]

Technological backwardness was named by both broad silk and ribbon manufacturers as the reason for the lack of competitiveness. By volume, the production of haberdashery played a more significant role than broad weaving. Broad weaving was situated in London and, as the 1835 and 1856 reports and the testimonies of silk manufacturers suggest, mechanisation was very low and silk cloths for use in dressmaking were produced in small workshops. Haberdashery and smaller silk items, on the other hand, were produced outside London. Silk merchants and manufacturers pointed to the fact that by 1832 the finer kinds of goods were no longer produced at Spitalfields but imported from France.[54] This was ascribed to Spitalfields silks not being fashionable. The fact that Spitalfields silks could not compete against French ones had repercussions for the product mix made in London, and the Spitalfields weavers had to start competing against those operating outside the capital. Moreover, large producers often decided to switch their production away from London. The situation the Spitalfields weavers faced is well depicted in the question posed by a member of the Select Committee to silk manufacturer William Brunskill:

> The Spitalfields people did not care about the inferior fabrics made in the country; they had sufficient employment in making velvets, and other superior descriptions of silks; but having now lost that, they are struggling against Manchester, and other towns in the country, to gain back trade they did not care about formerly?[55]

The quotation also refers to the fact that, prior to the liberalisation of 1826, Spitalfields used to produce for a different type of customer than did Manchester. Before 1826, Manchester manufacturers used to copy patterns made in Spitalfields, apply them onto coarser textiles and sell them a few months later to customers of poorer means. After 1826, Manchester manufacturers started to follow the fashions in Lyon and offer contemporary fashionable patterns to their customers with a few months delay after Lyon's silks were sold to the wealthier classes. For Spitalfields the liberalisation of the silk trade meant that it had 'lost its trade in rich silks, especially fancy and figured silks, and in

51 Ibid., pp. 13–14.
52 Hertz, 'English Silk Industry', p. 724.
53 Coleman, *Courtaulds: An Economic and Social History*, p. 14.
54 House of Commons, *Report from Select Committee on the Silk Trade*, pp. 22–3.
55 Ibid., p. 39.

some instances it had adopted the low Manchester trade … hence a competition has arisen between those places'.[56] Silk merchants used to buy Spitalfields-made gros de Naples, twill sarsnets, satins, figured satins, velvets, figured velvets, cut figured gauzes, gold and silver tissues, figured gauze handkerchiefs, scarfs, plushes, Italian nets, figured plushes, poplins, figured poplins, and lustres but after 1826 they bought only gros de Naples, low satins, and low back velvets in Spitalfields.[57] The effects on the livelihoods of London weavers were intensified by the fact that they could not shift to the production of cottons, for instance, as was possible in cotton/silk districts such as Manchester.[58]

The Committee paid particular attention to the situation of Spitalfields weaving. However, the key branch of the British silk industry was haberdashery, especially ribbon production. The best-quality ribbons were made in Coventry, but in the 1830s the Coventry ribbon trade was in a similar state of distress as Spitalfields broad weaving. William Brunskill, broad silk manufacturer in Spitalfields and ribbon manufacturer in Coventry, when questioned by the Select Committee on the Silk Trade, ascribed the distress to foreign competition. The ribbon manufacturers were using less-innovative technology, their products were of lower quality due to technological backwardness, less skilled labour and the use of inferior quality silk, and, moreover, their products were not considered fashionable. Brunskill argued that the trade was in need of capital to buy the jacquard looms necessary to weave gauze ribbons.[59] Moreover, the British ribbon makers did not produce any special looms such as the 'la bar loom', a type of power loom used in St Etienne ribbon manufacturing.[60] Under such conditions, opening up to foreign competition resulted in a shift in demand in favour of foreign silks as consumer preferences were not driven primarily by prices but fashion. The Select Committee was surprised to have Brunskill agree that: 'in preference to English ribbons of any fashion, or any beauty, do you mean that French ribbons, however expensive, would sell in preference to English ribbons, however beautiful?'[61] Brunskill was able to substantiate this point with further information, as he also traded with foreign silks on the British market. He found French ribbons and German velvets to sell better in spite of their higher prices in Britain than domestically made ribbons and velvets.[62] Another major branch was crape production, which by the 1830s was also negatively affected by competition with European crape.[63]

---

[56] Ibid., p. 482.
[57] Ibid., p. 707.
[58] Ibid., p. 482.
[59] Ibid., p. 19.
[60] Ibid., p. 21.
[61] Ibid., p. 19.
[62] Ibid., p. 24.
[63] The term crape was first used for the black silk used for mourning dress; by the nineteenth century there were crapes of several colours. Ibid., p. 694.

The depressed demand for English ribbons and broad silks necessarily had negative effects on the employment of weavers. Furthermore, changes in the fashion of female dress in 1827–28 facilitated unemployment as the sarsnets that replaced gros de Naples in female wardrobes required considerably less labour but more silk yarn in production.[64] On the whole this meant that not all weavers were employed for the full year. Single-hand loom weavers were most affected by seasonal unemployment.[65] This implies that lack of advanced technology together with reduced demand reduced the earnings of the Coventry silk weavers. Not only was the employment of jacquard loom weavers the most stable, they also earned the highest wages at £2–£3 per week. However, it is necessary to acknowledge that they also worked longer hours. Handloom weavers earned only 4s. to 8s. per week and 3s. 6d. when producing narrow types of ribbon.[66] The question of wages was of prime importance to the Select Committee and all of the manufacturers were asked about the wages they paid their weavers. The Committee's conviction that single-hand loom weavers were paid significantly lower wages than engine weavers was uniformly supported by the manufacturers. Benjamin Poole, an engine weaver from Coventry, gave evidence about the development of wages of single-hand loom weavers in Coventry in the period 1804–31, stating that between 1804 and 1824 the wages of single-hand loom weavers decreased by 15 per cent and by a further 15 per cent between 1826 and 1829.[67] As wages were very low, the workforce consisted primarily of young or very young females, to a higher extent than in other textile industries. This is apparent in the 1830s as well as for the end of the nineteenth century.[68]

The Committee put much less emphasis on technology than on employment. Yet, it brought out one important aspect: the manufacturers questioned by the Committee were not overly willing to upgrade their technologies. They assumed that mechanisation would need large capital investment, whose costs would not be recovered.[69] Yet, the data from the 1850s shows that mechanisation progressed steadily. The 1845 reduction of import duties on finished silks to 15 per cent *ad valorem* intensified the competition that the British silk industry faced, and only silk-throwing and -weaving factories using up-to-date

---

64 House of Lords, *Report from the Select Committee of the House of Lords Appointed to Consider of the Petition of the East India Company for Relief* (London; n.p., 1840), p. 477.
65 House of Commons, *Report from Select Committee on the Silk Trade*, p. 27.
66 Ibid.
67 Ibid., p. 59.
68 The 1836 Report shows that silk industry employed a higher proportion of women than other textile industries and that its labour force was younger. See: House of Commons, *Return of the Number of Persons Employed*, p. 5. Moreover, data from factories owned by large-scale silk manufacturers supports this conclusion. In 1838 in the Halstead factory owned by Courtauld & Co., 83 per cent of the workforce was female, in 1886 it was 92 per cent and in 1899, 86 per cent. Coleman, *Courtaulds: An Economic and Social History*, p. 232.
69 House of Commons, *Report from Select Committee on the Silk Trade*, p. 26.

technologies survived.[70] Such conditions favoured large-scale producers such as the firms of Grout, Baylis & Co., Courtaulds & Co. in East Anglia and Brocklehurst at Macclesfield.[71] The rise of not only these large firms but also smaller ones such as Daniel Walters, Carter and Vavasseur, and T. F. Gibson of Spital Square, explain the growth of silk production in the Essex–Suffolk area. These firms shifted their production from the capital to traditional silk centres, as well as to counties in close proximity to London.[72]

The British silk industry was not the world's first modern industry, rather it was behind its global competitors. This became significant since the silk industry was one of the first sectors to experience market integration in the nineteenth century, as showed by Debin Ma.[73] Competition was fierce and it was necessary to employ modern methods such as mechanisation, economies of scale and scope, and to find a niche in the market. In this sense, liberalisation opened up the British market to foreign silks and the British silk industry to competitive pressure. Inevitably, the British silk industry was transformed from a traditional to a modern industrial sector. Large firms became successful if they were able to compete in globalised markets, follow trends, and – as in the case of Courtaulds & Co. and its venture into the production of artificial fibres – even to set trends.[74] On the other hand, traditional producers such as the Spitalfields weavers lost out and disappeared. Yet the decline of traditional silk producers in Britain cannot be perceived as a decline of luxury artisanal production wiped out by mass-produced textiles. Spitalfields was not Lyon: it did not produce high-quality, fashionable textiles, and did not have the skill set or technologies necessary to turn into an artisanal industrial district.

The Role of Bengal Raw Silk in British Weaving in the Nineteenth Century

The task of this chapter was to ascertain the effects on the demand for Bengal raw silk. The evidence from the *Report of the Select Committee* shows that the changes in the product mix and the push for mechanisation favoured the use of Bengal raw silk. In comparison to other types of silk, the use of Bengal raw silk provided the manufacturer with several advantages. First, its price was lower than that of the other raw silks. Second, its quality, though of the lowest

---

[70]   Coleman, *Courtaulds: An Economic and Social History*, pp. 100–2.

[71]   Ibid., pp. 100–4; Coleman, *Myth, History*, pp. 99–100.

[72]   Being in close proximity to London was useful in the first part of the nineteenth century when Spitalfields still consumed thrown silk. Ibid., pp. 99–104, especially p. 100.

[73]   Ma, 'Modern Silk Road', pp. 331–3.

[74]   The venture of Courtaulds & Co. into the manufacturing of artificial fibres was studied by, for instance: Donald C. Coleman, *Courtaulds: An Economic and Social History*, vol. 2: *Rayon* (Oxford: Clarendon Press, 1969); Geoffrey Owen, *The Rise and Fall of Great Companies: Courtaulds and the Reshaping of the Man-Made Fibres Industry* (Oxford: Oxford University Press, 2010).

Table 7.12   Imports of raw silk into Britain as % of total, 1830–40

Year	% East Indies and China, St Helena and the Cape of Good Hope	% Turkey	% Other[1]
1830	54.3	13.0	32.7
1831	53.3	13.0	33.7
1832	56.3	12.0	31.8
1833	48.9	12.6	38.5
1834	65.7	11.4	23.0
1835	51.3	15.8	32.8
1836	60.5	14.8	24.7
1837	74.5	6.0	19.4
1838	53.4	15.1	31.5
1839	48.9	14.2	37.0
1840	39.8	18.3	41.9
Average	55.2	13.3	31.5

Source: House of Commons, *An Account of all Raw and Waste Silk Imported and Entered for Home Consumption in Each Year, from 1814 to the 5th day of January 1842* (London: n.p., 1842), p. 296.

[1]   Other would in this case signify Europe and essentially Italy.

grade on the market, still sufficed for the production of the lower-quality and cheaper types of goods for which there was demand in Britain and abroad. Third, as a silk of coarser variety the process of throwing Bengal raw silk was less labour intensive and in some instances it could even be used in the raw form for the production of small items of haberdashery for which quality was not decisive. Thus, the switch towards the production of simpler and plainer silks created an environment favourable for importation of Bengal raw silk.

From 1830 to 1840, Italian, Chinese and Bengal silk comprised 80–90 per cent of the raw silk imported to the British market (see Table 7.12). Italian silk was used primarily in Spitalfields and Coventry for broad weaving and the production of superior grades of ribbons.[75] As a premium-quality raw silk, Italian silk was thrown into organzine of fine quality – 28 deniers on average. Silk cloths and other items made from Italian silk were destined for the domestic market. Chinese raw silk was used for throwing into organzine as well as into coarser sorts of yarn. Principally, after throwing, Chinese silk was used in weaving plain gros de Naples: a plain weave with corded effect.[76]

[75]   House of Commons, *Report from Select Committee on the Silk Trade*, pp. 17–18.
[76]   Ibid., p. 361.

There was considerable demand for Chinese silk on the British market and manufacturers welcomed the increased imports of the finest Chinese silk in the 1830s, especially as the price of Chinese silk decreased.[77] Yet, as pointed out by William Stone, a silk broker: 'the working of China silk is not so light as the working of Bengal; for instance, it occupies a great deal more machinery and time and expense to work Chinese than it does to work Bengal'.[78]

Bengal raw silk was used for the production of coarser goods, especially bandanas, sewing silks, stockings, hosiery and similar items that were intended principally for export. For the purposes of producing less sophisticated silk items the benefits of Bengal raw silk were indisputable. As pointed out by Alexis J. Doxat, London silk merchant, it could often be used in weaving without throwing:

> of late years large quantities of Bengal silks have been used in a raw state; that many of the low goods we make principally for export, are made of very coarse silk, only wound off, and the first operation of winding off coarse silk is very inconsiderable; in that state it gives extremely little employment.[79]

Even when thrown into yarn before weaving, throwing of Bengal silk required less labour as it was on average made into coarser 50 deniers yarn. Bengal silk was thrown predominantly in Manchester and Macclesfield, where it was used in waistcoating.[80] Although the best quality Bengal silk was used for throwing into the finest 28 deniers organzine, this amounted to a minor proportion of the silk imported from Bengal. Overall, the fact that Bengal raw silk was considerably coarser than Italian silk did not prevent its widespread use. William Stone, a partner in the house E. Durant & Company, silk brokers, considered 'Bengal silk to be extremely beneficial to our manufactures in this country' as it was 'much more suitable to some objects than the Italian'.[81] As pointed out by Stone, Bengal silk could not be a substitute for Italian silk but was often mixed with it. From the *Report of the Select Committee* it is not clear whether Bengal silk was used only as warp or also as weft when mixed with Italian silk. Stone argued that it was used as warp, yet Louis Schwabe, a Manchester silk manufacturer, showed the Committee samples in which Bengal thrown silk was used for both weft and warp in the production of gold-coloured figured damask, for weft in crimson and gold tissue damask, and also in a pattern of tissue satin.[82] This attests to the fact that, in Manchester, Bengal silk was also used for broad weaving.

[77]   Ibid., pp. 247, 360–1.
[78]   Ibid., p. 361.
[79]   Ibid., pp. 225–6.
[80]   Ibid., p. 360.
[81]   Ibid., p. 359.
[82]   Ibid., p. 639.

Table 7.13   Consumption of thrown silk according to fineness and origin, 1826–31

Country of origin	Quantity (per annum)	Fineness (in deniers, average)
Italy	1,471,000	30
Bengal and China	1,611,000	80
Turkey	365,000	100
Total	3,447,000	60*

Source: Compiled from House of Commons, *Report from Select Committee on the Silk Trade with Minutes of Evidence, Appendix and Index* (London: n.p., 1832), p. 224, * as estimated in the *Report*.

The different characteristics and prices of the Italian, Chinese and Bengal raw silks and the necessity to save on production costs led silk manufacturers to make concurrent use of all three types. For instance, Joseph Grout – a crape manufacturer with mills in Norwich, Great Yarmouth, Bungay and Mildenhall – stated that he was buying one-third each of Bengal, Italian and China raw silks.[83] Still, there was an undeniable increase in the amount of coarser sorts of raw silk – from Bengal, China and to a lesser extent Turkey – thrown in Britain. The key factors driving demand for thrown silk of coarser sorts was the fact that this silk was cheaper than finer varieties, as well as cheaper to use as it needed less labour. Furthermore, coarser yarn was suitable for weaving coarser silk goods.[84] Table 7.13 illustrates that Bengal and Chinese raw silk were the most consumed type of thrown silk. It is necessary to keep in mind that in the beginning of the nineteenth century the proportion of Bengal raw silk thrown in silk mills was negligible and, as the throwing experiment of the EEIC attests, Bengal raw silk was not favoured by throwsters. Although the manufacturers emphasised that the quality of Bengal raw silk did increase in years prior to the Select Committee's inquiry, they were not disinclined to use it.[85]

Conclusion

Policymakers and economists expected the liberalisation policies of the nineteenth century to revive the British silk industry – even its most traditional segment, Spitalfields silk weaving. As it turned out, several sectors of the British silk industry, most notably broad silk weaving but even some of the higher-quality ribbon and haberdashery production, never advanced

83   Ibid., p. 247.
84   Ibid., pp. 224–5.
85   Ibid., pp. 360, 697.

beyond the stage of an infant industry and were unable to withstand foreign competition. Therefore, the reduction of tariffs on imported silk textiles in the 1820s led to large-scale structural changes in silk throwing and weaving in Britain. Smaller producers of more luxurious items were eliminated and bigger producers switched to lower-quality silk products and mixes in which European competition was less intensive. Together with the adoption of the Jacquard loom and power loom, these changes resulted in structural unemployment. The organisational and technological changes that accompanied the structural shifts led to the expansion of less-sophisticated ribbon and crape production in the 1830s. Further reductions in tariffs in the 1850s reinforced the focus on production of lower-quality silk products and spinning waste silk. The changes necessarily meant an expanding demand for raw silk of the coarser variety, such as Bengal raw silk. Considering the fact that the volume of raw silk imports continued to expand in the 1840s and 1850s, and in 1856 surpassed 7 million lbs., the market situation was ideal for the importation of Bengal raw silk. Yet, although the market conditions should have benefited the manufacturers of Bengal raw silk, Bengal was overtaken by other producers of lower-quality raw silk such as Turkey, Egypt and China.

CONCLUSION

The early modern silk industry has received considerably less attention than other industries, such as cotton, linen and woollens, or ceramics and metalwares, which has in turn downplayed its importance in early modern economies. Yet, the silk industry pioneered new technologies and new systems of organisation of production that only took root in other sectors centuries later. Complex silk-reeling machines, for instance, were already in use for the production of silk threads in the early seventeenth century. In contrast, the celebrated machinery for spinning cotton was only invented in Europe in the late eighteenth century. Today, it is believed that cotton-spinning technologies heavily borrowed from mechanised silk reeling. Likewise, a centralised system of production was first adopted in textile manufacturing for the reeling of silk. Such early-seventeenth-century technological adoption was driven by demand rather than supply-side conditions: it was the demand for high- and standard-quality silk threads and yarns that led to major technological innovations. In the nineteenth century, the raw silk trade was one of the first to experience high levels of market integration. This was a further impetus for standardisation of quality, employing mechanisation and modernising the system of labour organisation and management.

The key innovations in technologies and systems of organisation emerged in Italy such that the north-western region of Piedmont became the leader in producing high-quality silk thread and yarn in Europe. Several other silk-producing regions in other countries attempted to emulate Piedmont and, in the course of the late seventeenth and eighteenth centuries, they adopted Italian machinery and the Piedmontese system of production. However, such ventures were never successful in the long term. This failure can be explained by lack of adaptations rather than by the incompatibility of the factor endowments of the country of origin and the country to which the technology was transferred.[1] Comparatively, the most successful transfer of Piedmontese technologies was carried out by the English East India Company.

---

[1]   This explanation has been particularly favoured by Yujiro Hayami and Vernon W. Ruttan, 'Factor Prices and Technical Change in Agricultural Development: The United States and Japan, 1880–1960', *Journal of Political Economy* 78 (5), 1970, pp. 1115–41; Stephen Broadberry and Bishnupriya Gupta, 'Lancashire, India, and Shifting Competitive Advantage in Cotton Textiles, 1700–1850: The Neglected Role of Factor Prices', *Economic History Review* 62 (2),

Although the EEIC did not achieve its goal of producing 'Bengal Italian raw silk' because the quality of its Bengal silk never matched the Italian quality, it succeeded in capturing more than 40 per cent of the raw silk import market in Britain from the 1790s to the 1830s. My analysis of the transfer of Piedmontese reeling technology to Bengal shows that the factor endowments of Bengal were not incompatible with the new technology. On the contrary, low labour costs and cheap cocoons represented competitive advantages. In addition, return on investment analysis shows that the investment in the new technology was highly profitable. It can seem puzzling, then, that the production of Bengal raw silk for exports went into decline in the second part of the nineteenth century with the amount of Bengal raw silk as a share of total raw silk imports to Britain plummeting to just 13 per cent in the 1860s.

Yet, when we consider the substantial advantages that the EEIC possessed the decline becomes easily understandable. The Company did not have a monopoly on raw silk production in Bengal but the scale of production it achieved thanks to its establishment of a network of filatures represented the key advantage. Economies of scale decreased the unit cost of technology transfer and consultation provided by silk specialists sent to Bengal, while scale also gave the Company better standing vis-à-vis its competitors on the Bengal market. Long-term involvement in silk production enabled the Company to accrue benefits from learning-by-doing. In particular, the EEIC improved its strategy of managing intermediaries and thus succeeded in controlling the growth of cocoon prices. Furthermore, the EEIC accumulated up-to-date information about the raw silk market to set rules about the quality of silk to be produced and promoted technological innovation to reduce production costs. Lastly, and most importantly, the EEIC had the capital necessary to invest in new technologies and to cover the prime cost of silk production, which on average surpassed £260,000 a year.

Private entrepreneurs who bought silk filatures from the EEIC after 1833 had none of these advantages. The firms they formed – family firms or partnerships – had limited longevity and unlimited liability, lacked access to capital, had limited knowledge of developments on the global raw silk markets and often had limited experience with silk production. In a competitive sector experiencing growing market integration, this was a serious disadvantage. Yet, neither the British government or Parliament nor the EEIC appreciated the benefits that economies of scale and the joint-stock form represented for technology upgrading and profitability. On the one hand this can be seen as a reflection of the fact that the public and the political agents were

2009, pp. 279–305; E. Rothbarth 'Causes of the Superior Efficiency of USA Industry as Compared with British Industry', *Economic Journal* 56 (223), 1946, pp. 383–90; Robert Allen, *The British Industrial Revolution in Global Perspective* (Cambridge: Cambridge University Press, 2009), *passim*.

growing tired of dealing with East Indian affairs.[2] On the other, this illustrates the legacies of the rise of classical economic thought, which generated a widespread perception that private individuals are under all circumstances the most efficient economic agents. Moreover, in the 1830s, joint-stock types of business were equated with monopoly and it took a further decade before the benefits of joint-stocks were recognised. In any case the message is clear: British political economy shaped the development of the Bengal silk industry at least to the same extent as did market fundamentals.

Political economy played a crucial role in two respects. First, the economic policies of the British government transformed incentives. Second, political economy shaped the institutional environments in which entrepreneurs operated. The British government's support of the domestic silk industry was the key reason for the Company to get involved in silk manufacturing in Bengal. Protectionist policies enabled the silk industry to remain one of Britain's seven most important export sectors until the nineteenth century.[3] This was a guarantee for the EEIC that a steady demand for raw silk in Britain would continue. Both the British government's support of the domestic silk industry and the EEIC's involvement in the Bengal silk industry had their roots in contemporary mercantilist thinking. It was perceived to be in the national interest to supply the British silk-weaving industry with raw material from dependent territories. The improvement and expansion of raw silk production in Bengal was presented by the EEIC as an extension of British policies beneficial to British manufactures. Moreover, the EEIC also applied mercantilist ideas to governing Bengal: silk production was supposed to allow the most efficient use of factors of production – labour and land. Finally, mercantilist policies supported the government's decision to grant the EEIC the monopoly on trade with Asia, as it was expected to aid British exports and create revenues for the British state. The right to trade with Asia also gave the EEIC the right to become a silk manufacturer in Bengal, and this remained in place until the 1833 Charter revoked the Company's trading privileges. Thus it was more than economic laws that fundamentally determined the success of the EEIC's involvement in raw silk production in Bengal.

2   Huw Bowen, *Business of Empire: The East India Company and Imperial Britain, 1756–1833* (Cambridge: Cambridge University Press, 2006), p. 296.
3   B. R. Mitchell, *British Historical Statistics* (Cambridge: Cambridge University Press, 1988), pp. 469–70.

APPENDIX A: DESCRIPTION OF THE PIEDMONTESE REELING MACHINE BY DIONYSIUS LARDNER

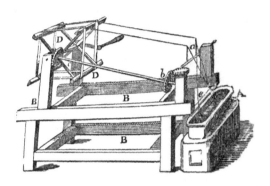

A is a copper boiler about 18 inches long, and six inches deep, set in brickwork, so as to admit of a charcoal fire being made beneath it: if other fuel be used, a small flue or chimney must be added to carry away the smoke. B is a stout wooden frame whereon the several working parts of the reel are supported. D represents the reel on which the silk is to be wound; *a* is the layer which directs the position of the threads in their passage to the reel; *b* and *c* is the wheel-work which gives motion to this layer. The reel D is merely a wooden spindle, turned by a crank handle at one end, and having four arms mortised at each end within the frame. These arms support the four battens or rails on which the silk is wound. The rails, which are parallel to the axis, are placed at such a distance from it, that they may produce a skein of proper size by the winding of the silk upon them. They are usually so disposed as to pass through the space of one yard at each revolution. One of each of the two sets of arms is made with hinges to fold in the middle of its length, in order that the rail which these two arms support may fall in or approach the centre as occasion may require: this, by diminishing the size of the reel, allows the skeins of silk to be readily slipped off when the winding is completed.

At the end opposite to the handle of the wooden spindle, and within the frame B, there is placed a wheel with twenty-two teeth, giving motion to another wheel *c*, which has about double that number of teeth, and is fixed on the end of the inclined axis *c b*; this, at the opposite end, has a wheel *b* of twenty-two teeth, which gives motion to a horizontal cog-wheel of thirty-five teeth. This last wheel turns upon a fixed pivot in the frame, and has, near to its periphery or outer rim, a pin, to which the wooden rail or layer *a* is attached. The opposite end of this rail plays in a mortise or opening made in the frame B. This layer is furnished at equal distances from the frame with two wire loops or eyes, through which the silk threads are passed in being wound. Now, if motion be given to the horizontal cog-wheel by means of the other wheels and inclined axis, when the handle of the reel is turned, it is evident that this will cause the layer likewise to move to and fro, directing the threads which pass through its wire eyes alternatively to the right and left, through a range equal to the diameter of the horizontal cog-wheel to which it is attached.

The iron bar *e*, which is fixed over the centre of the boiler, is pierced with two holes, through which the threads are led in their passage from the boiler to the layer.

If the thread of each cocoon were reeled separately, it would, from its extreme tenuity, be wholly unfit for the purpose of manufacture: several threads are therefore reeled together. The cocoons which are to be wound being put into water contained in the boiler A, the gummy matter which they possess is softened, so that the unwinding of their threads is facilitated, and at the same time the fibres, which are brought together in the reeling, adhere, and form one strong and smooth thread.[1]

---

[1]   Dionysius Lardner, *A Treatise on the Origin, Progressive Improvement, and Present State of the Silk Manufacture* (Philadelphia: Carey & Lea, 1832), pp. 155–6.

APPENDIX B: AVERAGE PRICES OF BENGAL RAW SILK ON THE BRITISH MARKET ACCORDING TO THE TYPE OF THE SILK, 1796–1856

| Year | Type 1 | | Type 2 | | Type 3 | | Type 4 | | Types 1–4 |
	Lowest average price s.	Highest average price s.	Lowest average price s.	Highest average price s.	Lowest average price s.	Highest average price s.	Lowest average price s.	Highest average price s.	Average s.
1796			6	30	9	27			18
1797			9	27	6	20			15.5
1798			6	20	12	22			15
1799	14	21	5	22			12.5	15	14.9
1800			12.5	16	11	23			15.6
1801			11	23	5	20			14.8
1802			5	30	11.5	25.5			18
1803	10.5	24.5	12	28.5			6	23	17.4
1804	6	22	3	20			6	25	13.7
1805			5	25	8	26			16
1806			9	21	6	20			14
1807			7	20	9	22			14.5
1808	9	23	18	45			14	34	23.8
1809			14	34	18	36			25.5
1810	18	36	20	39			21	36	28.3
1811			23	39	22	37			30.3
1812			22	37	12	30			25.3
1813	12	30	12	30			12	25	20.2

| Year | Type 1 | | Type 2 | | Type 3 | | Type 4 | | Types 1–4 |
	Lowest average price s.	Highest average price s.	Lowest average price s.	Highest average price s.	Lowest average price s.	Highest average price s.	Lowest average price s.	Highest average price s.	Average s.
1814			12	15	11	26.			16.0
1815			11	26	11	24.5			18.1
1816			11	24	8	24			16.8
1817	8	26	11	31			23	39	23
1818			23	39	16	20			24.5
1819	16	36	13	30			15	20	21.7
1820	18	26.2			16.1	23.3	17.1	24.5	20.9
1821	16.9	23.5	15.3	24.4	15.8	24	16.2	26.2	20.3
1822	15.3	24.2	15	25.1	16	27.9	17.2	28.8	21.2
1823	16.1	26.3	15.1	27.6	14.1	22.3	14.1	21.3	19.6
1824	14.3	19.5			14.1	20.3	14.1	23.7	17.6
1825	20.6	31			12.7	21.8	14.3	20.6	20.2
1826	13.1	19.1			11.5	18.4	11.8	19.9	15.6
1827	13.3	23.7			13.1	21.7	14.7	21.7	18
1828	15.5	23.5			15.7	22.7	15.2	22.9	19.2
1829	11.3	21.7			10.1	19.2	10.8	18.9	15.3
1830	10.5	16.4			11.6	18.1	12.6	18.3	14.6
1831	12.9	18.2			11.9	16.1	11.2	16.2	14.4

Year	Type 1 Lowest average price s.	Type 1 Highest average price s.	Type 2 Lowest average price s.	Type 2 Highest average price s.	Type 3 Lowest average price s.	Type 3 Highest average price s.	Type 4 Lowest average price s.	Type 4 Highest average price s.	Types 1–4 Average s.
1832	11.1	17			10.6	16.8	10.9	17.6	14
1833	11.3	18.1			12	18.9	15.8	22.5	16.4
1834	13.4	19.3			12.9	19.4	13.8	22.2	16.8
1835	12.6	22.6			12.4	22.3	14.3	22.9	17.8
1836	15.4	25			15.4	26.1	15.7	28.2	21
1837	11.2	17.8					12.8	18.3	15
1838	14	22	14	22	12.5	22	14	22	17.8
1839	14	22	13	21.5	12.5	20	14	22	17.4
1840	14	22	14	22.5	12	21	11.5	20	17.1
1841	10.5	19.5	10.5	19	10	18.5	9	21	14.8
1842	9	19	9.5	19	8	19	8.5	18.5	13.8
1843	8.5	18	9	18	7.8	18	10	20	13.7
1844	9.5	20	9.5	20	8.5	20	8.5	20	14.5
1845	8.5	19	8	18	8	18	9	19.5	13.5
1846	8.5	18	8.5	18	8	17	8	17	12.9
1847	8	17	6.5	15	6.5	15	6.5	15	11.2
1848	7	13.5	6.5	15	6.5	15	7	14.5	10.6
1849	7.5	13.5	6	13	7.5	13	5.5	15	10.1

| Year | Type 1 | | Type 2 | | Type 3 | | Type 4 | | Types 1–4 |
	Lowest average price s.	Highest average price s.	Lowest average price s.	Highest average price s.	Lowest average price s.	Highest average price s.	Lowest average price s.	Highest average price s.	Average s.
1850	6.5	15	6.5	16	6	17	5.5	19.5	11.5
1851	5.5	19	5.5	18.5	5.5	19	8.8	16.5	12.3
1852	6	15.5	6	16.5	6	16.5	6	16.5	11.1
1853	6	16.5	12	19	12	19	11	20	14.4
1854	11	19	9	21.5	9.5	20	7.5	19	14.6
1855	6.5	18	6.5	17	6.5	17	7	18	12.1
1856	10	19	9	23	10.5	27.5	14	33	18.3

Source: Compiled according to Thomas Tooke and William Newmarch, *A History of Prices and of the State of the Circulation* (London: P. S. King and Son, 1928), vol. 2, p. 410; vol. 3, p. 298; vol. 4, p. 431; vol. 6, p. 496. Thanks to David Chilosi for sharing the data.

*This data needs to be used with caution as it shows average lowest and average highest price of a certain type of silk. It is not clear how Tooke compiled these prices or what the quality of different types of silk was, which makes the overall average of these prices, found in the last column, problematic. Using these figures for studying the profitability of the Company's trade would be especially difficult as it is not clear what quantities of silk were sold for which price.

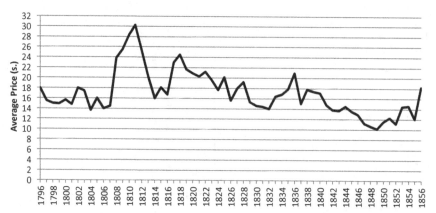

Figure B.1   Average prices of Bengal raw silk on the British market, 1796–1853

Source: Thomas Tooke and William Newmarch, *A History of Prices and of the State of the Circulation* (London: P. S. King and Son, 1928), vol. 2, p. 410; vol. 3, p. 298; vol. 4, p. 431; vol. 6, p. 496.

APPENDIX C: RETURN ON INVESTMENT ANALYSIS

In chapter 5 I have shown that the adoption of the filature system did not increase the costs of silk thread production. In fact, the EEIC was able to reel silk in filatures at lower costs than it was able to procure silk from intermediary merchants. Yet, one must also consider the initial cost of adopting the Piedmontese system. To assess the profitability of the investment I use a simple model calculating return on investment (ROI) (Table C.1). ROI is a commonly used measure of profitability. It shows the financial performance of a firm and enables informed management decisions about investment.[1] ROI is the ratio of 'net profits over the investment needed to generate the profits'.[2]

$$ROI = \frac{Profit}{Investment}$$

ROI only provides information about profitability over a specific period; therefore my analysis also calculates the Net Present Value (NPV) and the Internal Rate of Return (IRR) – measures commonly used to determine the profitability of multi-period projects.[3] NPV is the 'present (discounted) value of future cash inflows minus the present value of the investment and any associated future cash outflows'.[4] In other words, NPV is the difference between the present value of cash inflows and the present value of cash outflows over a period of time. NPV is commonly used in economics, finance and accounting to assess the profitability of investment – negative NPV denotes loss while positive NPV means that the investment is profitable. NPV is calculated by:

---

[1]   Robert Rachlin, *Return on Investment Manual: Tools and Applications for Managing Financial Results* (New York: M. E. Sharpe, 1997), pp. 3–8.

[2]   Paul W. Farris, Neil T. Bendle, Phillip E. Pfeifer and David J. Reibstein, *Marketing Metrics: The Definitive Guide to Measuring Marketing Performance* (New Jersey: Pearson Education, 2010), p. 338.

[3]   Ibid., p. 337.

[4]   Ibid., p. 346.

$$NPV = \sum_{t=1}^{T} \frac{C_t}{(1+r)^t} - C_0$$

In which C_t is net cash inflow during the period, C_0 initial investment, r discount rate, and t number of time periods.

IRR is the 'percentage return on the investment over a period of time'.[5] IRR is also used for evaluating investment and is the discount rate at which the present value of future cash flows is equal to the initial investment. The higher the IRR, the more desirable it is for a company to invest in a project.

The model includes data on the cost of setting up a filature, operational costs (the cost of producing 1 sm. lb. of silk, including charges for merchandise, freight and customs), the prices of silk on the British market, and the quantity of silk produced by the filature. The figures for the quantity of silk produced in this filature and set up costs as used in the model are based on data for the filature at Kasimbazar (a filature with 208 furnaces). The price of Bengal filature silk on the British market denotes the average price for which 1 sm. lb. was sold. It was not possible to ascertain the figure for a specific filature. The figure for operational costs is based on calculations in Table C.1. Total cost equals the operational costs (or the costs of producing 1 sm. lb. of silk) multiplied by the quantity of produced silk.[6] Revenue is the quantity of silk produced in a year multiplied by the price of filature silk on the British market. The total cash inflow is calculated as the revenue minus the total cost including set up cost. The IRR on profit streams in the period 1772–79 was 55 per cent. The NPV for investment into filatures in Bengal is positive both with a 10 per cent discount rate (NPV 1) and a 5 per cent discount rate (NPV 2). The NPV remains positive even for a 15 per cent and 20 per cent discount rate. This shows that the investment was highly profitable (Table C.1).

5   Ibid., p. 348. IRR is also referred to as the discounted cash flow rate of return, rate of return, internal yield, marginal efficiency of capital, and the investor method. M. A. Mian, *Project Economics and Decision Analysis. Volume 1: Deterministic Models* (Tulsa: PennWell Corporation, 2010), p. 316.

6   The data used comes from a filature set up by James Wiss in Kasimbazar. The only exception is the price data; these are mean prices.

Table C.1 Return on investment in setting up silk filatures, 1772–79

Year	1772	1773	1774	1775	1776	1777	1778	1779
Quantity of filature silk produced in a filature (sm. lbs.)		20,565	20,565	20,565	20,565	20,565	20,565	20,565
Price of bengal filature silk on the British market (£)		0.9	0.9	0.9	0.9	0.9	0.9	0.9
Costs								
Set up costs (£)	10,774							
Operational costs (£) = costs of producing 1 sm. lb. of filature silk		0.60	0.60	0.60	0.60	0.60	0.60	0.60
Total cost (£) = quantity × operational costs		12,339	12,339	12,339	12,339	12,339	12,339	12,339
Revenue (£) = price × quantity		18,509	18,509	18,509	18,509	18,509	18,509	18,509
Total cash inflow (£) = revenue – total cost – set up cost	(10,774)	6,170	6,170	6,170	6,170	6,170	6,170	6,170
IRR (%)	55%							
NPV 1 (£) – 10% discount rate	17,511							
NPV 2 (£) – 5% discount rate	12,405							

Source: IOR/E/4/625, 9 April 1779, pp. 131–2; IOR/E/4/630, 12 April 1786, p. 390; IOR/E/4/637, 6 May 1791, p. 429.

APPENDIX D: COMPARISON OF MANUFACTURING COSTS AT THE EEIC'S EXPERIMENTAL FILATURE AND COMMON FILATURE IN ITS VICINITY, 1832

(costs in shillings and pence per sm. lb.)

Bund	Filature	Spinners	Reelers	Water carriers	Fuel	Sweeper	Sundry charges	Petty repairs	Rent	Cocoonery	Total	
		d.	d.	d.	d.	d.	d.	d.	d.	d.	s.	d.
March, large	Experimental	8.64	5.15	0.30	3.28	0.09	0.50	0.03	0	0.17	1	6.16
	Cattorah	7.68	5.08	0.89	11.20	0.17	2.09	0.09	0.27	4.89	2	8.35
March, small and April, rainy	Experimental	7.09	4.78	0.47	3.60	0.13	0.53	0.20	0	0.60	1	5.4
	Cattorah	6.15	4.23	0.60	11.20	0.15	2.42	0.09	1.87	8.29	2	10.99
October/November	Experimental	8.87	5.00	0.57	4.07	0.13	1.00	0.27	0	0.60	1	8.5
	Cattorah	7.70	5.12	0.03	11.20	0.18	5.37	0.09	2.43	17.50	3	13.6

Source: LSE Archives, W7204, East India Company; *Reports and Documents Connected with the Proceedings of the East-India Company in regard to the Culture and Manufacture of Cotton-wool, Raw Silk, and Indigo in India* (London: J. L. Cox, 1836), pp. 210–11.

The EEIC's terminology is not clear here, but both reelers and spinners were involved in reeling.

APPENDIX E: MECHANISATION OF SILK THROWING AND WEAVING IN ENGLAND AND SCOTLAND, 1856

Table E.1   Mechanisation of silk throwing in England, 1856

County	No. of factories	No. of spindles	% of spindles	Moving power: steam (in horse-power)	Moving power: water (in horse-power)	No. of employees
Buckinghamshire	2	4,440	0.5	10		386
Cheshire	111	222,589	27.5	803	166	11,659
Derbyshire	23	74,524	9.2	368	4	3,712
Devon	2	1,630	0.2		26	133
Dorset	5	60,232	7.4	56	72	699
Essex	7	82,602	10.2	140	27	1,511
Gloucestershire	11	22,653	2.8	64	44	1,373
Hampshire	1	2,300	0.3		8	113
Herefordshire	1	768	0.1	10		35
Hertfordshire	5	36,639	4.5	78	45	1,106
Kent	1	1,200	0.1	6	8	108
Lancashire	11	45,211	5.6	271	15	1,332
Nottinghamshire	9	31,322	3.9	159	12	1,260
Oxfordshire	1	720	0.1	4		35
Somerset	8	26,548	3.3	85	29	1,069
Staffordshire	11	17,046	2.1	81	4	1,382
Suffolk	4	14,690	1.8	21		848
Warwickshire	4	9,281	1.1	31	7	443
Wiltshire	3	19,900	2.5	4	42	458
Worcestershire	12	18,296	2.3	6	77	822
West Riding of Yorkshire	17	117,164	14.5	348	68	1,592
Total	249	809,755	100.0	2,545	654	30,076

Source: Compiled from House of Commons, *Return of the Number of Cotton, Woollen, Worsted, Flax, and Silk Factories* (London: n.p., 1857), pp. 10–11.

Table E.2   Mechanisation of silk weaving in England, 1856

County	No. of factories	No. of power looms	% of power looms	Moving power: steam (in horse-power)	Moving power: water (in horse-power)	No. of employees
Cheshire	11	953	16.7	71	10	1,379
Lancashire	24	2,507	43.8	284	0	4,865
Norfolk	2	374	6.5	37	0	730
Staffordshire	1	35	0.6	3	0	59
Somerset	1	37	0.6	0	10	72
Surrey	1	69	1.2	10	0	181
Warwickshire	88	1,741	30.5	322	0	3,883
Wiltshire	1	3	0.1	4	0	7
Total	129	5,719	100.0	731	20	11,176

Source: Compiled from House of Commons, *Return of the Number of Cotton, Woollen, Worsted, Flax, and Silk Factories* (London: n.p., 1857), p. 10.

Table E.3　Mechanisation of silk throwing and/or weaving, 1856*

County	No. of factories	Moving power: steam (in horse-power)	Moving power: water (in horse-power)	No. of employees
Cheshire	11	28		721
Derbyshire	2	12		61
Dorset	1		6	82
Middlesex	11	44		419
Norfolk	1	2		20
Nottinghamshire	4	20		67
West Riding of Yorkshire	10	15	24	100
Total	40	121	30	1,470

Source: Compiled from House of Commons, *Return of the Number of Cotton, Woollen, Worsted, Flax, and Silk Factories* (London: n.p., 1857), p. 11.

*These are factories for which the Factory Commissioners did not/could not distinguish which sector they engaged in.

Table E.4 Mechanisation of silk throwing and weaving in England, 1856

County	No. of factories	No. of spindles	% of spindles	No. of power looms	% of power looms	Moving power: steam (in horse-power)	Moving power: water (in horse-power)	No. of employees
Cheshire	5	20,260	8.0	172	4.9	10	32	807
Derbyshire	6	22,895	9.0	390	11.0	153		2,333
Devon	1	2,400	0.9	80	2.3		30	259
Essex	1	25,296	10.0	569	16.1	45	8	1,089
Lancashire	9	72,403	28.5	1,263	35.7	338		4,361
Norfolk	4	78,690	31.0	655	18.5	142		2,037
Nottinghamshire	1	3,000	1.2	9	0.2	16		95
Somerset	2	15,000	5.9	179	5.1	36	10	383
Staffordshire	6	13,140	5.2	172	4.9	82	20	962
Wiltshire	1	716	0.3	47	1.3	16	12	152
Total	36	253,800	100.0	3,536	100.0	838	112	12,478

Source: Compiled from House of Commons, *Return of the Number of Cotton, Woollen, Worsted, Flax, and Silk Factories* (London: n.p., 1857), p. 11.

Table E.5   Mechanisation of silk throwing in Scotland, 1856

Scotland	No. of factories	No. of spindles	% of spindles	Moving power: steam (in horse-power)	Moving power: water (in horse-power)	No. of employees
Lanarkshire	4	14,932	49.4	88		543
Renfrewshire	2	15,312	50.6	34		204
Total	6	30,244	100.0	122		337

Source: Compiled from House of Commons, *Return of the Number of Cotton, Woollen, Worsted, Flax, and Silk Factories* (London: n.p., 1857), p. 12.

APPENDIX F: TYPES OF SILKWORM REARED IN BENGAL SILK DISTRICTS, 1818

Silk district	Type of silkworm	Bund	Quality	Further information
Bauleah	Annual			Yield does not occur every year
	Dessee	6[1]		Reared in smaller quantities than madrassie variety
	Madrassie	May–October		Madrassie better quality and higher quantity then dessee, reared in hot and rainy bunds, overall the district produced larger quantities of cocoons than the EEIC's filatures could reel
Commercolly	Dessee	5**	Varied	Best quality – March bund, November bund highest quantity, April and June/July often defective quality
	Nistry tribe	March, April	Good	Soonamooky variety: quality on par with dessee, madrassie inferior and green in colour
Kasimbazar	Annual	March	Excellent	Quality far superior to dessee worm
	Dessee	November, March	Good	November bund largest and good in quality, March bund good quality, second largest quantity
	China	April, July	Inferior	Mixed with dessee, third in quality, very long and thin filaments

Silk district	Type of silkworm	Bund	Quality	Further information
Hurripaul	Annual	March	Excellent	³/₈ of total production reeled from cocoons of annual worm
	Dessee			Introduced only in 1818
	China	every except March	Varies	Abundant, China worm produced ⁵/₈ of the total production of cocoons, quality inferior
Jungypore	Annual	January	Inferior	Yields uncertain and small
	Dessee	November, March	Varied	November bund large in quantity, March bund precarious, three times smaller than November
	China			Abundant
Malda	Dessee	November to April	Good	Dessee the best variety in Malda in terms of quality and quantity, ⁴/₅ of total production
	China		.	rare
Radanagore	Annual	March	Excellent	Abundant, profitable yield, ²/₃ of raw silk made from annual worm's cocoons
	Dessee			Not reared
Soonamooky	Annual	January	Excellent	Rearing the worm requires extra care, clear, yellow, fine and strong silk
	Dessee	5²		³/₄ of cocoons of October, November, and March bund are of dessee worm

Source: LSE Archives, W7204, East India Company, *Reports and Documents Connected with the Proceedings of the East-India Company in regard to the Culture and Manufacture of Cotton-wool, Raw Silk, and Indigo in India* (London: J. L. Cox, 1836), pp. 37–51.

[1] October, November, March, April, June/July, September.
[2] October, November, March, April, June/July.

APPENDIX G: GLOSSARY

Aurung	A textile-producing area
'Bengal Italian raw silk'	The term used by the EEIC for the raw silk produced in the Company's Bengal filatures
Board of Trade in Bengal	The principal administrative and managerial body of the EEIC in Bengal
Bund	A silk-rearing season
Country-wound silk	Silk reeled according to the local method used in eighteenth-century Bengal
Court of Directors in London	The principal administrative and managerial body of the EEIC
Cuttanie	Bengalese reeler travelling to silk-rearing villages to reel silk
Dadni	Advance payment supplied at the beginning of the season to peasants and artisans for the procurement of a specific quantity and quality of a certain commodity
Dellol	Intermediary merchant, the principal broker
Diwani	The right to collect tax revenues from Bengal, Bihar and Orissa
Filature	Factory-type establishment used for reeling silk
Filature-wound silk	Term used for the silk reeled in the EEIC's filatures in Bengal
Gomasta	Merchant agent paid by the EEIC to procure export goods
Chassars	Peasants rearing silkworms
Knotting of silk	Method proposed by the EEIC's silk specialists to rectify the unevenness of threads of country-wound silk to make the threads more round

Nacauds	Term used for reelers employed in the re-reeling of country-wound silk
Organzine	Silk yarn with a very high twist, used for warp and considered the highest-quality silk yarn
Putney	Term used interchangeably with country-wound silk
Pykars	Intermediary merchants who on behalf of the EEIC advanced money to Chassars and procured cocoons at the end of the rearing seasons
Singles	Silk yarn formed from a single thread with a single twist
'The choicest goods'	Goods procured in Bengal by the EEIC and considered having the highest potential for profit creation on the European markets
Tram	Double-twisted silk yarn
Winding	Term used interchangeably with reeling in the EEIC's documents

BIBLIOGRAPHY

Manuscript Sources

India Office Records and Private Papers (IOR), British Library, London

A. East India Company Correspondence, Bengal Despatches
IOR/E/4/616, IOR/E/4/617, IOR/E/4/618, IOR/E/4/619, IOR/E/4/620, IOR/E/4/621, IOR/E/4/623, IOR/E/4/625, IOR/E/4/626, IOR/E/4/627, IOR/E/4/628, IOR/E/4/629, IOR/E/4/630, IOR/E/4/637, IOR/E/4/638, IOR/E/4/640, IOR/E/4/643, IOR/E/4/645, IOR/E/4/645A, IOR/E/4/741, IOR/E/4/754, IOR/E/4/757, IOR/E/4/758, IOR/E/4/861.

B. East India Company Correspondence, Letters from Bengal
IOR/E/1/61, fols 355–357v; IOR/E/1/61, fols 486–487v; IOR/E/1/63, fols 19–20v; IOR/E/1/65, fols 440–441v:, IOR/E/1/66, fols 422–424v.

C. Miscellaneous Public Documents, Bombay
IOR, 1793.m.17: 'Letter from Giuseppe Mutti to John Bell Esquire on 20th October 1838', India Office Records and Private Papers.

D. East India Company Factory Records
IOR/G/23/13: 'Factory Records: Kasimbazar, 1757–59', India Office Records and Private Papers.

E. India Office Parliamentary Branch Records, Reports from the Select Committee on the Affairs of The East India Company
L/PARL/2/55: 'First – Fourth Report from the Select Committee on the Affairs of the East India Company, 1812, India Office Records and Private Papers'.

The National Archives (TNA), Kew

TNA C 12/175/27, East India Company v. Aldersey, 24 March 1789 to 11 November 1789.

Archives Nationales, Paris, France

Archives Nationales, Paris: Serie F12, F12 677A.

The Baring Archive, London

Baring Archive Series HC6.3.1, Letter 11, 1833.

Goldsmiths' Library (GL), London

GL, 1775 fol.: George Williamson, *Proposals Humbly Submitted to the Consideration of the Court of Directors, for Affairs of the United Company of Merchants of England, Trading to the East-Indies: For Improving and Increasing the Manufactures of Silk in Bengal* (London: n.p., 1775).

GL, 1795 fol. 16280, *Reports of the Committee of Warehouses of the East-India Company Relative to Extending the Trade on Bengal Raw-Silk* (London: n.p., 1795).

GL, 1796 fol. 16654, *Considerations on the Attempt of the East-India Company to Become Manufacturers in Great Britain* (London: n.p., 1796).

Royal Society of Arts (RSA), London

RSA/SC/EL/2/31, *Third Report of the Committee of Warehouses of the East-India Company Relative to Extending the Trade on Bengal Raw-Silk* (London: n.p., 1795).

London School of Economics and Political Science Archive (LSE), London

LSE Archives, W7204, East India Company, *Reports and Documents Connected with the Proceedings of the East-India Company in regard to the Culture and Manufacture of Cotton-wool, Raw Silk, and Indigo in India* (London: J. L. Cox, 1836).

Published Primary Sources

Aglionby, W., 'Of the Nature of Silk, as It is Made in Piedmont', *Philosophical Transactions* 21 (1699), pp. 184–5.

Annual Statement of the Trade and Navigation of the United Kingdom with Foreign Countries and British Possessions in the Year 1868 (London: George Edward Eyre and William Spottiswoode, 1869).

Annual Statement of the Trade and Navigation of the United Kingdom with Foreign Countries and British Possessions in the Year 1861 (London: George Edward Eyre and William Spottiswoode, 1869).

Bernier, F., *Travels in the Mogul Empire*, 2 vols (London: W. Pickering, 1826).

Brockett, L. P., *The Silk Industry in America: A History* (New York: George F. Nesbitt & Co., 1876).

Burke, E., *The Works of the Right Honourable Edmund Burke*, 12 vols (Boston: Wells and Lilly, 1826).

Child, J., *Brief Observations Concerning Trade and Interest of Money* (London: Henry Mortlock, 1668).

Child, J., *A Supplement to a Former Treatise Concerning the East-India Trade* (London: n.p., 1689).

Crawfurd, J., *An Inquiry into some of the Principal Monopolies of the East India Company* (London: James Ridgway, 1830).

East India Company, *Report of the Select Committee of the Court of Directors upon the Cotton of This Country: With Appendixes* (London: n.p., 1793).

East India Company, *Debate on the Expediency of Cultivating Sugar in the Territories of the East India Company* (London: Reporter, 1793).

East India Products, Part II: Reports on the Silk Industry in India and on the Supply of Timber in the Burmah Markets (London: George Edward Eyre and William Spottiswoode, 1874).

Gee, J., *The Trade and Navigation of Great-Britain Considered: Shewing, that the Surest Way for a Nation to Increase in Riches, Is to Prevent the Importation of Such Foreign Commodities as May Be Raised at Home* (London: Sam Buckley, 1729).

Geoghegan, J., *Some Account of Silk in India, Especially of the Various Attempts to Encourage and Extend Sericulture in that Country* (Calcutta: Department of Revenue and Agriculture, 1872).

Hadfield, *A Return of the Quantities of Silk of the Various Kinds Imported into the United Kingdom from various Countries, from 1842–56, Both Inclusive, Distinguishing Each Year's Importation, and the Countries from Whence they Came* (London: n.p., 1857).

Hansard's Historical Parliamentary Debates, 'Petition of the Merchants of London Respecting Commercial Restrictions', *House of Commons Debate 8 May 1820*, vol. 1, pp. 165–7.

Hansard's Historical Parliamentary Debates, 'Spitalfields Silk Manufacture Acts – Petition for the Repeal Thereof', *House of Commons Debate 9 May 1823*, vol. 9, pp. 143–50.

House of Commons, *An Account of the Quantity and Value of Raw and Thrown Silk Imported into, and Exported from, Great Britain, For Twenty Years, ending the 5th January 1806* (London: n.p., 1806).

House of Commons, *An Account of all Raw and Waste Silk Imported and Entered for Home Consumption in Each Year, from 1814 to the 5th day of January 1842* (London: n.p., 1842).

House of Commons, 'Fourth Report of the Secret Committee', *Reports from Committees of the House of Commons, 1715–1801* (1) IV, 1803.

House of Commons, *Minutes of Evidence Taken before the Select Committee on the Affairs of the East India Company in the Last Session of Parliament and also the Accounts and Papers Laid before the Said Committee* (London: n.p., 1831).

House of Commons, *Report from Select Committee on the Silk Trade with Minutes of Evidence, Appendix and Index* (London: n.p., 1832).

House of Commons, *Report from the Select Committee on East India Produce together with Minutes of Evidence, an Appendix, and Index* (London: n.p., 1840).

House of Commons, *Return of the Number of Persons Employed in Cotton, Woollen, Worsted, Flax and Silk Factories* (London: n.p., 1836).

House of Commons, *Return of the Number of Cotton, Woollen, Worsted, Flax, and Silk Factories* (London: n.p., 1857).

House of Commons, *Return of the Number of Power Looms used in Factories, in the Manufacture of Woollen, Cotton, Silk and Linen* (London: n.p., 1836).

House of Lords, *Journal of the House of Lords*, vol. 54, 1821.

House of Lords, *Report from the Select Committee of the House of Lords Appointed to Consider of the Petition of the East India Company for Relief* (London: n.p., 1840).

House of Lords, *The Sessional Papers, 1801–1833*, vol. 156, 1823.

Lardner, D., *A Treatise on the Origin, Progressive Improvement, and Present State of the Silk Manufacture* (Philadelphia: Carey & Lea, 1832).

Liotard, L., *Memorandum on Silk in India, Part 1* (Calcutta: Superintendent of Government Printing, 1883).

Malynes, G., *A Treatise of the Canker of Englands Common Wealth* (London: Richard Field, 1601).

Malynes, G., *The Maintenance of Free Trade, According to the Three Essential Parts of Traffique: Namely Commodities, Moneys and Exchange of Moneys, by Bills of Exchange for Other Countries* (London: William Shefford, 1622).

Master, S., *The Diaries of Streynsham Master, 1675–1680*, ed. Richard Temple (London: J. Murray, 1911).

Mun, T., *England's Treasure by Forraign Trade, or the Balance of our Forraign Trade is the Rule of our Treasure* (London: J. G., 1664).

Observations on the Ruinous Tendency of the Spitalfields Act to the Silk Manufacture of London (London: John and Arthur Arch, 1822).

Papillon, T., *A Treatise Concerning the East-India Trade: Being a Most Profitable Trade to the Kingdom, and Best Secured and Improved by a Company and a Joint-Stock* (London: n.p., 1680).

Parliamentary Papers, *Accounts and Papers Relating to Customs and Excise, Imports and Exports, Shipping and Trade, Volume 34, Session 6 December 1831 – 16 August 1832* (London: n.p., 1832), pp. 12–13.

Smith, A., *An Inquiry into the Wealth and Poverty of Nations* (State College, PA: University of Pennsylvania, 2005).

Steuart, James, *Inquiry into the Principles of Political Economy: Being an Essay on the Science of Domestic Policy in Free Nations* (London: A. Millax & T. Cadell, 1767).

Tavernier, J.-B., *Travels in India*, 2 vols (London: Macmillan & Co., 1889).

Thorp, J., *Considerations on the Present State of the Cotton and Silk Manufactories of Great Britain: And the Impropriety of Continuing to Draw the Supply of Materials for the Latter from France and Italy* (London: Lane, Darling & Co., 1807).

Tooke, T. and W. Newmarch, *A History of Prices and of the State of the Circulation*, vols 2–4, 6 (London: P. S. King and Son, 1928).

Wardle, T., *The Wild Silks of India, Principally Tusser* (London: n.p., 1880).

Secondary Sources

Books

Allen, D. W., *The Institutional Revolution: Measurement and the Economic Emergence of the Modern World* (London: University of Chicago Press, 2012).

Allen, R., *The British Industrial Revolution in Global Perspective* (Cambridge: Cambridge University Press, 2009).

Antrobus, H. A., *The History of the Assam Company 1839–1953* (Edinburgh: Constable Ltd, 1957).

Bayly, C. A., *The Birth of the Modern World, 1780–1914* (Oxford: Blackwell, 2004).

Boulnois, L., *The Silk Road* (London: George Allen & Unwin Ltd., 1963).

Bowen, H. V., *Business of Empire: The East India Company and Imperial Britain, 1756–1833* (Cambridge: Cambridge University Press, 2006).

Bowen, H. V., *Revenue and Reform: The Indian Problem in British Politics, 1757–1813* (Cambridge: Cambridge University Press, 1991).

Bowrey, T., *A Geographical Account of Countries round the Bay of Bengal, 1669–1679* (Cambridge: Hakluyt Society, 1905).

Braddick, M., *State Formation in Early Modern England, c.1550–1700* (Cambridge: Cambridge University Press, 2000).

Braudel, F., *Civilization and Capitalism, 15th–18th Century*, vol. 1: *The Structures of Everyday Life* (Los Angeles: University of California Press, 1992).

Brewer, J., *Sinews of Power: War, Money, and the English State* (New York, NY: Alfred A. Knopf, 1989).

Brock, W. R., *Lord Liverpool and Liberal Toryism, 1820 to 1827* (Cambridge: Cambridge University Press, 1940).

Casson, Mark, *Information and Organization: A New Perspective on the Theory of the Firm* (Oxford: Oxford University Press, 1997).

Carruthers, B. G., *City of Capital: Politics and Markets in the English Financial Revolution* (Princeton: Princeton University Press, 1996).

Cayez, P., *L'industrialisation Lyonnaise au XIXe siècle: du grand commerce à la grande industrie* (Lille: Universite de Lyon II, 1977).

Chandler, A. D., Jr, *The Visible Hand: The Managerial Revolution in American Business* (Cambridge, MA: Harvard University Press, 1977).

Chandler, A. D., Jr, *Scale and Scope: The Dynamics of Industrial Capitalism* (Cambridge, MA: Harvard University Press, 1994).

Chang, Ha-Joon, *Kicking Away the Ladder: Development Strategy in Historical Perspective* (London: Anthem, 2002).

Chaudhuri, K. N., *The Trading World of Asia and the English East India Company, 1660–1760* (Cambridge: Cambridge University Press, 1978).

Chicco, G., *La Seta in Piemonte 1650–1800: Un Sistema Industriale d'Ancien Régime* (Milan: Franco Angeli, 1995).

Chowdhury, B., *Growth of Commercial Agriculture in Bengal 1757–1900*, 3 vols (Calcutta: R. K. Maitra, 1964).

Coleman, D. C., *Courtaulds: An Economic and Social History*, vol. 1: *The Nineteenth Century Silk and Crape* (Oxford: Clarendon Press, 1969).

Coleman, D. C., *Courtaulds: An Economic and Social History*, vol. 2: *Rayon* (Oxford: Clarendon Press, 1969).

Coleman, D. C., *Myth, History and the Industrial Revolution* (London: Hambledon Press, 1992).

Davis, R., *England's Overseas Trade, 1500–1700* (London: Macmillan, 1973).

Ekelund, R. B. and R. D. Tollison, *Mercantilism as a Rent-Seeking Society: Economic Regulation in Historical Perspective* (College Station, TX: Texas A&M University Press, 1981).

Erikson, E., *Between Monopoly and Free Trade: The English East India Company, 1600–1757* (Princeton: Princeton University Press, 2014).

Farris, P. W., N. T. Bendle, P. E. Pfeifer and D. J. Reibstein, *Marketing Metrics: The Definitive Guide to Measuring Marketing Performance* (New Jersey: Pearson Education, 2010).

Fava-Verde, J.-F., *Silk and Innovation: The Jacquard Loom in the Age of the Industrial Revolution* (n.p.: Histancia, 2011).

Federico, G., *An Economic History of the Silk Industry, 1830–1930* (Cambridge: Cambridge University Press, 1997).

Franceschi, F., *Florence and Silk in the Fifteenth Century: The Origins of a Long and Felicitous Union* (Fiesole: Edizioni Cadmo, 1995).

Gash, N., *Aristocracy and People: Britain 1815–1865* (London: E. Arnold, 1979).

Gerschenkron, A., *Economic Backwardness in Historical Perspective: A Book of Essays* (Boston, MA: Harvard University Press, 1962).

Gordon, B., *Political Economy in Parliament, 1819–1823* (Basingstoke: Macmillan Press Ltd, 1976).

Gordon, R., *East India Company, India and China Trade* (House of Commons, 1833).

Govindan, R., T. K. Narayanaswamy and M. C. Devaiah, *Pebrine Disease of Silkworm* (Bangalore: University of Agricultural Sciences Bangalore, 1997).

Greenberg, M., *British Trade and the Opening of China, 1800–1842* (Cambridge: Cambridge University Press, 1951).

Habakkuk, J., *American and British Technology in the Nineteenth Century: The Search for Labour-Saving Inventions* (London: Cambridge University Press, 1962).

Habib, I., *The Agrarian System of Mughal India 1556–1707* (New Delhi: Asia Publishing House, 1963).

Harris, R., *Industrializing English Law: Entrepreneurship and Business Organization, 1720–1844* (Cambridge: Cambridge University Press, 2000).

Heckscher, E. F., *Mercantilism* (London: George Allen and Unwin, 1955).

Hilton, B., *Corn, Cash, Commerce: The Economic Policies of the Tory Government, 1815–1830* (Oxford: Oxford University Press, 1977).

Hoppit, J., *Britain's Political Economies: Parliament and Economic Life, 1660–1800* (Cambridge: Cambridge University Press, 2017).

Inikori, J., *Africans and the Industrial Revolution* (Cambridge: Cambridge University Press, 2002).

Jarillo, J. Carlos, *Strategic Network: Creating the Borderless Organization* (London: Routledge, 1995).

King, B. M., *Silk and Empire: Studies in Imperialism* (Manchester: Manchester University Press, 2005).

Kohli, A., *State-Directed Development: Political Power and Industrialization in the Global Periphery* (Cambridge: Cambridge University Press, 2004).

Kuhn, Dieter (ed.), *Chinese Silks* (New York: Yale University Press, 2012).

Kumar Singh, A., *Modern World System and Indian Proto-Industrialization: Bengal 1650–1800* (New Delhi: Northern Book Centre, 2006).

Lazonick, W., *Business Organization and the Myth of the Market Economy* (Cambridge: Cambridge University Press, 1991).

Magnusson, L., *Mercantilism: The Shaping of an Economic Language* (London: Routledge, 1994).

Magnusson, L. (ed.), *Mercantilism: Critical Concepts in the History of Economics*, 4 vols (London: Routledge, 1995).

Malmgreen, G., *Silk Town: Industry and Culture in Macclesfield 1750–1835* (Hull: Hull University Press, 1985).

Marsh, B., *Georgia's Frontier Women: Female Fortunes in a Southern Colony* (Athens and London: University of Georgia Press, 2007).

Mian, M. A., *Project Economics and Decision Analysis: Deterministic Models* (Tulsa: PennWell Corporation, 2010), vol. 1.

Milburn, W., *Oriental Commerce*, 2 vols (London: Black, Perry & Co., 1813).

Mitchell, B. R., *British Historical Statistics* (Cambridge: Cambridge University Press, 1988).

Molà, L., *The Silk Industry of Renaissance Venice* (Baltimore: Johns Hopkins University Press, 2000).

Mui, Hoh-cheung and L. H. Mui, *The Management of Monopoly: A Study of the East India Company's Conduct of its Tea Trade, 1784–1833* (Vancouver: University of British Columbia Press, 1984).

Mukherjee, R., *Merchants and Companies in Bengal: Kasimbazar and Jugdia* (New Delhi: India Pragati Publications 2006).

Mukherji, N. G., *A Monograph on the Silk Fabrics of Bengal* (Calcutta: Bengal Secretariat Press, 1903).

Murphy, W. S., *The Textile Industries: A Practical Guide to Fibres, Yarns, and Fabrics in Every Branch of Textile Manufacture, Including Preparation of Fibres, Spinning, Doubling, Designing, Weaving, Bleaching, Printing, Dyeing and Finishing* (London: Gresham, 1912).

Omrod, D., *The Rise of Empires: England and the Netherlands in the Age of Mercantilism, 1650–1770* (Cambridge: Cambridge University Press, 2003).

Owen, G., *The Rise and Fall of Great Companies: Courtaulds and the Reshaping of the Man-Made Fibres Industry* (Oxford: Oxford University Press, 2010).

Pariset, E., *Les Industries de la Soie* (Lyon: Imprimerie Pitrat Ainé, 1890).

Parthasarathi, P., *The Transition to a Colonial Economy: Weavers, Merchants and Kings in South India, 1720–1800* (Cambridge: Cambridge University Press, 2002).

Parthasarathi, P., *Why Europe Grew Rich and Asia Did Not: Global Economic Divergence, 1600–1850* (Cambridge: Cambridge University Press, 2011).

Pollard, S., *The Genesis of Modern Management: A Study of the Industrial Revolution in Great Britain* (London: Edward Arnold, 1965).

Porter, M. E., *Competition in Global Industries* (Boston, MA: Harvard University Press, 1986).

Porter, M. E., *The Competitive Advantage of Nations* (New York: Free Press, 1990).

Prakash, O., *The Dutch East India Company and the Economy of Bengal, 1630–1720* (Princeton: Princeton University Press, 1985).

Prakash, O., *European Commercial Enterprise in Pre-Colonial India* (Cambridge: Cambridge University Press, 1998).

Rachlin, R., *Return on Investment Manual: Tools and Applications for Managing Financial Results* (New York: M. E. Sharpe, 1997).

Ray, I., *Bengal Industries and the British Industrial Revolution (1757–1857)* (New York: Routledge, 2011).

Rayner, H., *Silk Throwing and Waste Silk Spinning* (London: Scott, Greenwood & Co., 1908).

Rawlley, R. C., *Economics of the Silk Industry* (London: P. S. King and Son Ltd., 1919).

Reinert, E. S., *How Rich Countries Got Rich and Why Poor Countries Stay Poor* (London: Constable, 2007).

Riello, G. and T. Roy (eds), *How India Clothed the World: The World of South Asian Textiles, 1500–1850* (Leiden: Brill, 2009).

Riello, G., *Cotton: The Fabric that Made the Modern World* (Cambridge: Cambridge University Press, 2013).

Robins, N., *The Corporation that Changed the World: How the East India Company Shaped the Modern Multinational* (London: Pluto Press, 2012).

Roncaglia, A., *The Wealth of Ideas: A History of Economic Thought* (Cambridge: Cambridge University Press, 2005).

Rothstein, N., *Silk Designs of the Eighteenth Century: In the Collection of the Victoria and Albert Museum, London* (London: Thames and Hudson, 1990).

Rothstein, N., *Spitalfields Silks* (London: Stationery Office, 1975).

Roy, T., *The East India Company: The World's Most Powerful Corporation* (London: Allen Lane, 2012).

Rungta, R. S., *The Rise of Business Corporations in India, 1851–1900* (Cambridge: Cambridge University Press, 1970).

Sandberg, L. G., *Lancashire in Decline: A Study in Entrepreneurship, Technology, and International Trade* (Columbus, OH: Ohio University Press, 1974).

Schmoller, G., *The Mercantile System and Its Historical Significance: Illustrated Chiefly from Prussian History: Being a Chapter from the Studien ueber die Wirthschaftliche Politik Friedrichs des Grossen* (New York: Macmillan, 1896).

Schober, J., *Silk and the Silk Industry* (London: Constable & Co. Ltd., 1930).

Schoeser, M., *Silk* (New Haven: Yale University Press, 2007).

Sebire, C. B. and J. F. Sebire, *Berisfords: The Ribbon People; The Story of a Family Business* (London: William Sessions Ltd., 1966).

Silk and Rayon Users' Association, *The Silk Book* (London: Silk and Rayon Users' Association, 1951).

Sinha, S., *The Development of Indian Silk: A Wealth of Opportunities* (London: Intermediate Technology Publications, 1990).

Slywotzky, A. J., *Value Migration: How to Think Several Moves Ahead of the Competition* (Boston, MA: Harvard Business Press, 1996).

Sonwalkar, T. N., *Hand Book of Silk Technology* (New Delhi: New Age International Ltd. Publishers, 1993).

Steensgaard, N., *The Asian Trade Revolution of the Seventeenth Century: The East India Companies and the Decline of the Caravan Trade* (Chicago: University of Chicago Press, 1973).

Sutherland, L. S., *The East India Company in Eighteenth-Century Politics* (Oxford: Clarendon Press, 1952).

Styles, John, *The Dress of the People: Everyday Fashion in Eighteenth-Century England* (New Haven: Yale University Press, 2007).

Thirsk, J., *Economic Policy and Projects: The Development of a Consumer Society in Early Modern England* (Oxford: Oxford University Press, 1978).

Thunder, M., *V&A Pattern: Spitalfields Silks* (London: V&A Publishing, 2011).

Vainker, S., *Chinese Silk: A Cultural History* (New Brunswick: The British Museum Press, 2004).

Vickery, A., *The Gentleman's Daughter: Women's Lives in Georgian England* (London: Yale University Press, 1998).

Vries, P., *State, Economy and the Great Divergence: Great Britain and China, 1680s–1850s* (London: Bloomsbury, 2015).

Warner, F., *The Silk Industry of the United Kingdom: Its Origin and Development* (London: Drane's, 1921).

Webster, A., *The Twilight of the East India Company: The Evolution of Anglo-Asian Commerce and Politics, 1790–1860* (Woodbridge: Boydell Press, 2009).

Wild, A., *The East India Company: Trade and Conquest* (London: HarperCollins Illustrated, 1999).

Wilson, C., *England's Apprenticeship 1603–1763* (London: Longmans, Green & Co., 1971).

Articles and Book Chapters

Acemoglu, D., S. Johnson, and J. A. Robinson, 'Reversal of Fortune: Geography and Institutions in the Making of the Modern World Income Distribution', *Quarterly Journal of Economics* 117 (4), 2002, pp. 1231–94.

Aldous, M., 'Avoiding Negligence and Profusion: The Failure of the Joint-Stock Form in the Anglo-Indian Tea Trade, 1840–1870', *Enterprise & Society* 16 (3), 2015, pp. 648–85.

Allen, R., 'The High Wage Economy and the Industrial Revolution: A Restatement', *Economic History Review* 68 (1), 2015, pp. 1–22.

Allen, R., J.-P. Bassino, Debin Ma, C. Moll-Murata and J. L. van Zanden, 'Wages, Prices, and Living Standards in China, 1738–1925: In Comparison with Europe, Japan, and India', *Economic History Review* 64 (S1), 2011, pp. 8–38.

Ambrosoli, M., 'The Market for Textile Industry in Eighteenth Century Piedmont: Quality Control and Economic Policy', *Rivista di Storia Economica* 16 (3), 2000, pp. 343–64.

Amsler, C. E., R. L. Bartlett and C. J. Bolton, 'Thoughts of Some British Economists on Early Limited Liability and Corporate Legislation', *History of Political Economy* 13 (4), 1981, pp. 774–93.

Arrow, K. J., 'The Economic Implications of Learning by Doing', *Review of Economic Studies* 29 (3), 1962, pp. 155–73.

Ashworth, W. J., 'Quality and the Roots of Manufacturing "Expertise" in Eighteenth-Century Britain', *Osiris* 25 (1), 2010, pp. 231–54.

Austin, G., 'The 'Reversal of Fortunes' Thesis and the Compression of History: Perspectives from African and Comparative Economic History, *Journal of International Development* 20 (8), 2008, pp. 996–1027.

Barney, J. B., 'How a Firm's Capabilities Affect Boundary Decisions', *Sloan Management Review* 40 (3), 1999, pp. 19–32.

Barney, J., M. Wright and D. J. Ketchen Jr, 'The Resource-Based View of the Firm: Ten Years After 1991', *Journal of Management* 27 (6), 2001, pp. 625–41.

Bayly, C. A., 'The Origins of Swadeshi (Home Industry): Cloth and Indian Society 1700–1930', in A. Appadurai (ed.), *The Social Life of Things. Commodities in Cultural Perspective* (Cambridge: Cambridge University Press, 1986), pp. 285–322.

Belfanti, C., 'Guilds, Patents, and the Circulation of Technical Knowledge: Northern Italy during the Early Modern Age', *Technology and Culture* 45 (3), 2004, pp. 569–89.

Berg, M., 'In Pursuit of Luxury: Global History and British Consumer Goods in the Eighteenth Century', *Past and Present* 182 (1), 2004, pp. 85–142.

Berg, M., 'Small Producer Capitalism in Eighteenth-Century England', *Business History* 35 (1), 1993, pp. 17–39.

Berg, M., 'Passionate Projectors: Savants and Silk on the Coromandel Coast 1780–1798', *Journal of Colonialism and Colonial History* 14 (3), 2013, pp. 1–24.

Berg, M., 'Useful Knowledge, 'Industrial Enlightenment', and the Place of India', *Journal of Global History* 8 (1), 2013, pp. 117–36.

Bertucci, P., 'Enlightened Secrets: Silk, Intelligent Travel, and Industrial Espionage in Eighteenth-Century France', *Technology and Culture* 54 (4), 2013, pp. 820–52.

Bhadra, G., 'The Role of Pykars in the Silk Industry of Bengal (c.1765–1830)', *Studies in History* 3 (1), 1987, pp. 155–85.

Bhadra, G., 'The Role of Pykars in the Silk Industry of Bengal (c.1765–1830) Part 2', *Studies in History* 4 (1/2), 1988, pp. 1–35.

Bhadra, G., 'Silk Filature and Silk Production: Technological Development in the Early

Colonial Context, 1768–1833', in Deepak Kumar (ed.), *Science and Empire: Essays in Indian Context, 1700–1947* (Delhi: Anamika Prakashan, 1991), pp. 59–87.

Bhattacharya, S., 'Cultural and Social Constraints on Technological Innovation and Economic Development: Some Case Studies', *Indian Economic and Social History Review* 3 (3), 1966, pp. 240–67.

Bonner, J. C., 'Silk Growing in the Georgia Colony', *Agricultural History* 43 (1), 1969, pp. 143–8.

Bowen, H., 'Lord Clive and Speculation in East India Company Stock, 1766', *Historical Journal* 30 (4), 1987, pp. 905–20.

Bowen, H., 'Investment and Empire in the Later Eighteenth Century: East India Stockholding, 1756–1791', *Economic History Review* 42 (2), 1989, pp. 186–206.

Bowen, H., 'Sinews of Trade and Empire: The Study of Commodity Exports to the East India Company during the Late Eighteenth Century', *Economic History Review* 55 (3), 2002, pp. 466–86.

Bowen, H. V., 'British Exports of Raw Cotton from India to China during the Late Eighteenth and Early Nineteenth Centuries', in Giorgio Riello and Tirthankar Roy (eds), *How India Clothed the World: The World of South Asian Textiles, 1500–1850* (Leiden: Brill, 2009), pp. 115–38.

Broadberry, S. and B. Gupta, 'Lancashire, India, and Shifting Competitive Advantage in Cotton Textiles, 1700–1850: The Neglected Role of Factor Prices', *Economic History Review* 62 (2), 2009, pp. 279–305.

Buchan, B., 'The Emergence of the Technostructure: Lessons from the East India Company, 1713–1836', *Journal of Management History* 41 (1), 2003, pp. 105–16.

Cannadine, D., '"Big Tent" Historiography: Transatlantic Obstacles and Opportunities in Writing the History of Empire', *Common Knowledge* 11 (3), 2005, pp. 375–92.

Carlos, A. M. and S. Nicholas, 'Giants of an Earlier Capitalism: The Chartered Companies as Modern Multinationals', *Business History Review* 62 (3), 1988, pp. 398–419.

Carlos, A. M. and S. Nicholas, 'Theory and History: Seventeenth-Century Joint-Stock Chartered Trading Companies', *Journal of Economic History* 56 (4), 1996, pp. 916–24.

Chapman, S. D., 'British-Based Investment Groups before 1914', *Economic History Review* 38 (2), 1985, pp. 230–51.

Chapman, S. D., 'The Agency Houses: British Mercantile Enterprise in the Far East c. 1780–1920', *Textile History* 19 (2), 1988, pp. 239–54.

Chapman, S., 'Vanners in the English Silk Industry', *Textile History* 23 (1), 1992, pp. 71–86.

Chaudhuri, K. N., 'India's Foreign Trade and the Cessation of the East India Company's Trading Activities, 1828–40', Economic History Review 19 (2), 1966, pp. 345–63.

Chaudhury, S., 'International Trade in Bengal Silk and the Comparative Role of Asians and Europeans, circa. 1700–1757', *Modern Asian Studies* 29 (2), 1995, pp. 373–86.

Chaudhury, S., 'Merchants, Companies and Rulers: Bengal in the Eighteenth Century', *Journal of the Economic and Social History of the Orient* 31 (1), 1998, pp. 74–109.

Chen, Juanjuan and Nengfu Huang, 'Silk Fabrics of the Ming Dynasty', in D. Kuhn (ed.), *Chinese Silks* (New York: Yale University Press, 2012), pp. 369–430.

Choi, Eugene, 'Entrepreneurial Leadership in the Meiji Cotton Spinners' Early Conceptualisation of Global Competition', *Business History* 51 (6), 2009, pp. 927–58.

Clapham, J. H., 'The Spitalfields Acts, 1773–1824', *Economic Journal* 26 (104), 1916, pp. 459–71.

Coase, Ronald, 'The Nature of the Firm', *Economica* 4 (16), 1937, pp. 386–405.

Coleman, D. C., 'Mercantilism Revisited', *Historical Journal* 23 (4), 1980, pp. 773–91.

Cottereau, A., 'The Fate of Collective Manufactures in the Industrial World: The Silk Industries of Lyons and London, 1800–1850', in C. F. Sabel and J. Zeitlin (eds), *World of Possibilities: Flexibility and Mass Production in Western Industrialization* (Cambridge: Cambridge University Press, 1997), pp. 75–152.

Das Gupta, Ashin, 'India and the Indian Ocean in the Eighteenth Century', in Uma Das Gupta (ed.), *The World of the Indian Ocean Merchant, 1500–1800: Collected Essays of Ashin Das Gupta* (Oxford: Oxford University Press, 2001), pp. 188–224.

Davini, R., 'Bengali Raw Silk, the East India Company and the European Global Market, 1770–1833', *Journal of Global History* 4 (1), 2009, pp. 57–79.

Davini, R., 'A Global Supremacy: The Worldwide Hegemony of the Piedmontese Reeling Technologies, 1720s–1830s', in A. Guagnini and L. Molà (eds), *History of Technology*, vol. 32 (London: Bloomsbury Publishing, 2014), pp. 87–105.

Dyer, J. H. and H. Singh, 'The Relational View: Cooperative Strategy and Sources of Interorganizational Competitive Advantage', *The Academy of Management Review* 23 (4), 1998, pp. 660–79.

Endrei, W., 'The Italian Contribution to the Development of Sericulture in Hungary', in S. Cavaciocchi (ed.), *La Seta in Europa Secc. XIII–XX* (Prato: Istituto Internazionale di Storia Economica, 1993), pp. 301–13.

English, W., 'The Textile Industry: Silk Production and Manufacture, 1750–1900', in Charles Singer (ed.), *A History of Technology IV: The Industrial Revolution, c.1750–c.1850* (Oxford: Clarendon Press, 1958), pp. 308–27.

Flanagan, J. F., 'Figured Fabrics', in C. Singer (ed.), *A History of Technology III: From the Renaissance to the Industrial Revolution, c.1500–c.1750* (Oxford: Clarendon Press, 1957), pp. 187–205.

Flynn, D. O. and A. Giráldez, 'Silk for Silver: Manila, Macao-Nagasaki Trade in the 17th Century', in Debin Ma (ed.), *Textiles in the Pacific, 1500–1900. The Pacific World: Lands, Peoples and History of the Pacific, 1500–1900* (Aldershot: Variorum, 2005), pp. 33–50.

Furuta, Kazuko, 'Silk-Reeling in Modern East Asia: Internationalization and Ramifications of Local Adaptation: In the late 19th Century', in Debin Ma (ed.), *Textiles in the Pacific, 1500–1900. The Pacific World: Lands, Peoples and History of the Pacific, 1500–1900* (Aldershot: Variorum, 2005), pp. 191–220.

Gereffi, G., M. Korzeniewicz and R. P. Korzeniewicz, 'Introduction: Global Commodity Chains', in G. Gereffi and M. Korzeniewicz (eds), *Commodity Chains and Global Capitalism* (Westport, CT: Praeger, 1994), pp. 1–14.

Ghemawat, Pankaj, 'Competition and Business Strategy in Historical Perspective', *Business History Review* 76 (1), 2002, pp. 37–74.

Goodman, J., 'Cloth, Gender and Industrial Organization towards an Anthropology of Silkworkers in Early Modern Europe', in Simonetta Cavaciocchi (ed.), *La Seta in Europa Secc. XIII–XX* (Prato: Istituto Internazionale di Storia Economica, 1993), pp. 229–47.

Grossman, S. J. and O. D. Hart, 'An Analysis of the Principal–Agent Problem', *Econometrica* 51 (1), 1983, pp. 7–46.

Gupta, B., 'Competition and Control in the Market for Textiles: Indian Weavers and the English East India Company in the Eighteenth Century', in G. Riello and T. Roy (eds), *How India Clothed the World: The World of South Asian Textiles, 1500–1850* (Leiden: Brill, 2009), pp. 281–308.

Habib, I., 'The Technology and Economy of Mughal India', *Indian Economic and Social Review* 17 (1), 1980, pp. 1–34.

Hannah, L., 'Marshall's "Trees" and the Global "Forest": Were "Giant Redwoods"

Different?', in N. R. Lamoreaux, D. M. G. Raff and P. Temin (eds), *Learning by Doing in Markets, Firms, and Countries* (Chicago: University of Chicago Press, 1999), pp. 253–93.

Hao, Peng, 'Sericulture and Silk Weaving from Antiquity to the Zhou Dynasty', in D. Kuhn (ed.), *Chinese Silks* (New York: Yale University Press, 2012), pp. 65–113.

Hashino, Tomoko, 'Institutionalising Technical Education: The Case of Weaving Districts in Meiji Japan', *Australian Economic History Review* 52 (1), 2012, pp. 25–42.

Hatch, C. E., Jr, 'Mulberry Trees and Silkworms: Sericulture in Early Virginia', *Virginia Magazine of History and Biography* 65 (1), 1957, pp. 3–61.

Hayami, Yujiro and V. W. Ruttan, 'Factor Prices and Technical Change in Agricultural Development: The United States and Japan, 1880–1960', *Journal of Political Economy* 78 (5), 1970, pp. 1115–41.

Hejeebu, S., 'Contract Enforcement in the English East India Company', *Journal of Economic History* 65 (2), 2005, pp. 496–523.

Hertz, G. B., 'The English Silk Industry in the Eighteenth Century', *English Historical Review* 24 (96), 1909, pp. 710–27.

Hills, R., 'From Cocoon to Cloth: The Technology of Silk Production', in S. Cavaciocchi (ed.), *La Seta in Europa Secc. XIII–XX* (Prato: Istituto Internazionale di Storia Economica, 1993), pp. 59–90.

Hilt, E., 'Incentives in Corporations: Evidence from the American Whaling Industry', *Journal of Law and Economics* 49 (1), 2006, pp. 197–227.

Hopkins, T. K. and I. Wallerstein, 'Commodity Chains in the World-Economy Prior to 1800', *Review Fernand Braudel Center* 10 (1), 1986, pp. 157–70.

Hopkins, T. K. and I. Wallerstein, 'Conclusions About Commodity Chains', in Gary Gereffi and Miguel Korzeniewicz (eds), *Commodity Chains and Global Capitalism* (Westport, CT: Praeger, 1994), pp. 48–50.

Hupfel, Simon, 'The Spitalfields Acts and the Classics: Ricardo, J. S. Mill, Bowring, and Senior on the London Silk Industry, 1823–1841', *European Journal of the History of Economic Thought* 19 (2), 2012, pp. 165–95.

Hutková, K., 'Technology Transfers and Organization: The English East India Company and the Transfer of Piedmontese Silk Reeling Technology to Bengal, 1750s–1790s', *Enterprise & Society* 18 (4), 2017, pp. 921–51.

Hutková, K., 'Transfer of European Technologies and their Adaptations: The Case of the Bengal Silk Industry in the late-eighteenth century', *Business History* 59 (7), 2017, pp. 1111–35.

Iredale, J. A. and P. A. Townhill, 'An Early Silk Comb', *Textile History* 2 (1), 1971, pp. 57–64.

Iredale, J. A. and P. A. Townhill, 'Silk Spinning in England: The End of an Epoch', *Textile History* 4 (1), 1973, pp. 100–8.

Itoh, Motoshige and Masayuki Tanimoto, 'Rural Entrepreneurs in the Cotton-Weaving Industry of Japan', in Y. Hayami (ed.), *Toward the Rural-Based Development of Commerce and Industry: Selected Experiences from East Asia* (Washington: World Bank, 1998), pp. 47–68.

Johnson, H. G., 'Mercantilism: Past, Present and Future', *The Manchester School* 42 (1), 1974, pp. 1–17.

Jones, S. R. H., 'Technology, Transaction Costs, and the Transition to Factory Production in the British Silk Industry, 1700–1870', *Journal of Economic History* 47 (1), 1987, pp. 71–96.

Kawagoe, T., 'Technical and Institutional Innovations in Rice Marketing in Japan', in Y. Hayami (ed.), *Toward the Rural-Based Development of Commerce and Industry: Selected Experiences from East Asia* (Washington: World Bank, 1998), pp. 23–46.

Kiyokawa, Yukihiko, 'Transplantation of the European Factory System and Adaptations in Japan: The Experience of the Tomioka Model Filature', *Hitotsubashi Journal of Economics* 28 (1), 1987, pp. 27–39.

Klose, N., 'Sericulture of the United States', *Agricultural History* 37 (4), 1963, pp. 225–34.

Knight, P., 'The Macclesfield Silk Button Industry: The Probate Evidence', *Textile History* 35 (2), 2004, pp. 157–77.

Kranton, Rachel E. and Anand V. Swamy, 'Contracts, Hold-up, and Exports: Textiles and Opium in Colonial India', *American Economic Review* 98 (3), 2008, pp. 967–89.

Kuhn, D., 'Textile Technology: Spinning and Reeling', in J. Needham (ed.), *Science and Civilization in China: Chemistry and Chemical Technology* (Cambridge: Cambridge University Press, 1988), vol. 5, part 9.

Lemire, B. and G. Riello, 'East & West: Textiles and Fashion in Early Modern Europe', *Journal of Social History* 41 (4), pp. 887–916.

Li, L. M., 'Silks by Sea: Trade, Technology, and Enterprise in China and Japan, *The Business History Review* 56 (2), 1982, pp. 192–217.

Lin, J. and Ha-Joon Chang, 'Should Industrial Policy in Developing Countries Conform to Comparative Advantage or Defy It? A Debate Between Justin Lin and Ha-Joon Chang', *Development Policy Review* 27 (5), 2009, pp. 482–502.

Liu, G. K. C., 'The Silkworm and Chinese Culture', *Osiris* 10, 1952, pp. 124–94.

Lopes Cordeiro, J. M., 'A Technology Transfer in Portugal's Late Eighteenth Century: The Royal Silk Twisting Mill of Chacim', *Textile History* 23 (2), 1992, pp. 177–88.

Ma, Debin, 'Between Cottage and Factory: The Evolution of Chinese and Japanese Silk-Reeling Industries in the Latter Half of the Nineteenth Century', *Journal of the Asia Pacific Economy* 10 (2), 2005, pp. 195–213.

Ma, Debin, 'The Modern Silk Road: The Global Raw-Silk Market, 1850–1930', *Journal of Economic History* 56 (2), 1996, pp. 330–55.

Ma, Debin, 'Why Japan, Not China, Was the First to Develop in East Asia: Lessons from Sericulture, 1850–1937', *Economic Development and Cultural Change* 52 (2), 2004, pp. 369–94.

Ma, Debin, 'The Great Silk Exchange: How the World was Connected and Developed', in Debin Ma (ed.), *Textiles in the Pacific, 1500–1900. The Pacific World: Lands, Peoples and History of the Pacific, 1500–1900* (Aldershot: Variorum, 2005), pp. 1–32.

Magnusson, L., 'Introduction', in L. Magnusson (ed.), *Mercantilism: Critical Concepts in the History of Economics*, 4 vols (London: Routledge, 1995), vol. 1, pp. 1–48.

Margrave, R. D., 'Technology Diffusion and the Transfer of Skills: Nineteenth-Century English Silk Migration to Paterson', in P. B. Scranton (ed.), *Silk City: Studies in the Paterson Silk Industry, 1860–1940* (Newark: New Jersey Historical Society, 1985), pp. 9–34.

Marshall, P., 'Private British Investment in Eighteenth-Century Bengal', in P. Tuck (ed.), *The East India Company, 1600–1858* (London: Routledge, 1998), vol. 4, pp. 127–44.

Mass, W. and W. Lazonick, 'The British Cotton Industry and International Competitive Advantage: The State of the Debates', *Business History* 32 (4), 1990, pp. 9–65.

Miller, L., 'La Cultura de la Manufacture: Les Marchands Fabricants', in M.-A. Privat-Savigny (ed.), *Lyon au XVIIIe Siècle: Un Siècle Surprenant!* (Lyon: Musée Gadagne/Sogomy, 2012), pp. 109–21.

Miller, L., 'Material Marketing: How Lyonnais Silk Manufacturers Sold Silks, 1660–1789', in J. Stobart and B. Blondé (eds), *Selling Textiles in the Long Eighteenth Century: Comparative Perspectives from Western Europe* (Basingstoke: Palgrave Macmillan, 2014), pp. 85–98.

Minard, P., P. Gervais and J. Le Goff, 'Colbertism Continued? The Inspectorate of

Manufactures and Strategies of Exchange in Eighteenth-Century France', *French Historical Studies* 23 (3), 2000, pp. 477–96.

Morris, M., M. Schindehutte and J. Allen, 'The Entrepreneur's Business Model: Toward a Unified Perspective', *Journal of Business Research* 58, 2005, pp. 726–35.

Moss, D. J., 'Birmingham and the Campaigns against the Orders-in-Council and East India Company Charter, 1812–13', *Canadian Journal of History* 11 (2), 1976, pp. 173–88.

Mukherjee, R., 'The Story of Kasimbazar: Silk Merchants and Commerce in Eighteenth-Century India', *Review Fernand Braudel Center* 17 (4), 1994, pp. 499–554.

Mukhia, H., 'Social Resistance to Superior Technology: The Filature in Eighteenth-Century Bengal', *Indian Historical Review* 11 (1/2), 1984, pp. 56–64.

O'Brien, P., T. Griffiths and P. Hunt, 'Political Components of the Industrial Revolution: Parliament and the English Cotton Textile Industry, 1660–1774', *Economic History Review* 44 (3), 1991, pp. 395–423.

Özveren, E., 'The Shipbuilding Commodity Chain, 1590–1790', in G. Gereffi and M. Korzeniewicz (eds), *Commodity Chains and Global Capitalism* (Westport, CT: Praeger, 1994), pp. 20–33.

Page, W., 'Industries: Silk-weaving', in W. Page (ed.), *A History of the County of Middlesex: Volume 2, General; Ashford, East Bedfont With Hatton, Feltham, Hampton With Hampton Wick, Hanworth, Laleham, Littleton* (London: Victoria County History, 1911), pp. 132–7.

Parthasarathi, P., 'Great Divergence: Article Review', *Past and Present* 176 (1), 2002, pp. 275–93.

Parthasarathi, P., 'Cotton Textiles in the Indian Subcontinent, 1200–1800', in G. Riello and P. Parthasarathi (eds), *The Spinning World: A Global History of Cotton Textiles, 1200–1800* (Oxford: Oxford University Press, 2009), pp. 17–42.

Patterson, R., 'Spinning and Weaving', in C. Singer (ed.), *A History of Technology II: The Mediterranean Civilizations and the Middle Ages, c.700 BC to c.AD 1500* (Oxford: Clarendon Press, 1956), pp. 191–220.

Peers, D. M., 'Gunpowder Empires and the Garrison State: Modernity, Hybridity, and the Political Economy of Colonial India circa 1750–1860', *Comparative Studies of South Asia, Africa, and the Middle East* 27 (2), 2007, pp. 245–58.

Perlin, F., 'Proto-Industrialization and Pre-Colonial South Asia', *Past and Present* 98 (1), 1983, pp. 30–95.

Pincus, S., 'The Making of a Great Power? Universal Monarchy, Political Economy, and the Transformation of English Political Culture', *European Legacy* 5 (4), 2000, pp. 531–45.

Pincus, S., 'Whigs, Political Economy, and the Revolution of 1688–89', in D. Womersley, P. Bullard and A. Williams (eds), *'Cultures of Whiggism': New Essays on English Literature and Culture in the Long Eighteenth Century* (Newark, DE: University of Delaware Press, 2005), pp. 62–82.

Poni, C., 'Comparing Two Urban Industrial Districts: Bologna and Lyon in the Early Modern Period', in P. L. Porta, R. Scazzieri and A. S. Skinner, *Knowledge, Social Institutions and the Division of Labour* (Cheltenham: Edward Elgar, 2001), pp. 199–228.

Porter, Michael E., 'Changing Patterns of International Competition', *California Management Review* 28 (2), 1986, pp. 9–40.

Porter, M. E., 'Changing Patterns of International Competition', in D. J. Teece (ed.), *The Competitive Challenge: Strategies for Industrial Innovation and Renewal* (Cambridge, MA: Ballinger, 1987), pp. 27–57.

Porter, M., 'What Is Strategy?', *Harvard Business Review* 74 (6), 1996, pp. 61–78.

Prakash, O., 'The English East India Company and India', in H. V. Bowen, M. Lincoln and N. Rigby (eds), *The Worlds of the English East India Company* (Rochester, NY: Boydell Press, 2002), pp. 1–18.

Ramaswamy, V., 'Silk and Weavers of Silk in Medieval Peninsular India', *Medieval History Journal* 17 (1), 2014, pp. 145–69.

Ray, I., 'The Silk Industry in Bengal during Colonial Rule: The 'De-Industrialisation' Thesis Revisited', *Indian Economic and Social History Review* 42 (3), 2005, pp. 339–75.

Rees, R., 'The Theory of Principal and Agent, Part I', *Bulletin of Economic Research* 37 (1), 1985, pp. 3–26.

Reynard, P. C., 'Manufacturing Strategies in the Eighteenth Century: Subcontracting for Growth among Papermakers in the Auvergne', *Journal of Economic History* 58 (1), 1998, pp. 155–82.

Richards, J. F., 'Fiscal States in Mughal and British India', in B. Yun-Casalilla and P. O'Brien (eds), *The Rise of Fiscal States: A Global History, 1500–1914* (Cambridge: Cambridge University Press, 2012), pp. 410–42.

Ricardo, D., *The Works and Correspondence of David Ricardo: Volume 5 Speeches and Evidence 1815–1823*, ed. P. Sraffa and M. H. Dobb (Indianapolis: Liberty Fund, 1951).

Riello, G., 'Asian Knowledge and the Development of Calico Printing in Europe in the Seventeenth and Eighteenth Centuries', *Journal of Global History* 5 (1), 2010, pp. 1–28.

Riello, G., 'Strategies and Boundaries: Subcontracting and the London Trades in the Long Eighteenth Century', *Enterprise & Society* 9 (2), 2008, pp. 243–80.

Rössner, P. R., 'Heckscher Reloaded? Mercantilism, the State, and Europe's Transition to Industrialization, 1600–1900', *Historical Journal* 58 (2), 2015, pp. 663–83.

Rothbarth, E., 'Causes of the Superior Efficiency of USA Industry as Compared with British Industry', *Economic Journal* 56 (223), 1946, pp. 383–90.

Rothstein, N., 'Canterbury and London: The Silk Industry in the Late Seventeenth Century', *Textile History* 20 (1), 1989, pp. 33–47.

Roy, T., 'Where Is Bengal: Situating an Indian Region in the Early Modern World Economy', *Past and Present* 213 (1), 2011, pp. 115–46.

Schäfer, D., G. Riello, and L. Molà, 'Introduction: Silk in the Pre-Modern World', in D. Schäfer, G. Riello and L. Molà (eds), *Threads of Global Desire: Silk in the Pre-Modern World* (Woodbridge: Boydell Press, 2018), pp. 1–18.

Sickinger, R. L., 'Regulation or Ruination: Parliament's Consistent Pattern of Mercantilist Regulation of the English Textile Trade, 1660–1800', *Parliamentary History* 19 (2), 2000, pp. 211–32.

Sinha, S., 'Development Impact of Silk Production: A Wealth of Opportunities', *Economic and Political Weekly* 24 (3), 1989, pp. 157–63.

Steele, M., 'The Comparative Economics of Government and Guild Regulation in the European Silk Industry in the Early Modern Period', in S. Cavaciocchi (ed.), *La Seta in Europa Secc. XIII–XX* (Prato: Istituto Internazionale di Storia Economica, 1993), pp. 193–207.

Stern, P. J., 'History and Historiography of the English East India Company: Past, Present, and Future!', *History Compass* 7 (4), 2009, pp. 1146–80.

Stewart, D. W. and Qin Zhao, 'Internet Marketing, Business Models, and Public Policy', *Journal of Public Policy & Marketing* 19 (2), 2000, pp. 287–96.

Styles, J., 'Clothing the North: The Supply of Non-Élite Clothing in the Eighteenth-Century North of England', *Textile History* 25 (2), 1994, pp. 139–66.

Teece, D. J., 'Business Models, Business Strategy and Innovation', *Long Range Planning* 43, 2010, pp. 172–94.

Varadajan, L., 'Silk in Northeastern and Eastern India: The Indigenous Tradition', *Modern Asian Studies* 22 (3), 1988, pp. 561–70.

Ward, J. R., 'The Industrial Revolution and British Imperialism, 1750–1850', *Economic History Review* 47 (1), 1994, pp. 44–65.

Webster, A., 'The Political Economy of Trade Liberalization: The East India Company Charter Act of 1813', *Economic History Review* 43 (3), 1990, pp. 404–19.

Wilkins, M., 'The Free-Standing Company, 1870–1914: An Important Type of British Foreign Direct Investment', *Economic History Review* 41 (2), 1988, pp. 259–82.

Williamson, Oliver E., 'The Vertical Integration of Production: Market Failure Considerations', *American Economic Review* 61 (2), 1971, pp. 112–23.

Williamson, Oliver E., 'Transaction Cost Economics: The Governance of Contractual Relations, *Journal of Law and Economics* 22 (2), 1979, pp. 233–61.

Williamson, Oliver E., 'The Organization of Work: A Comparative Institutional Assessment', *Journal of Economic Behaviour & Organization* 1 (1), 1980, pp. 5–38.

Williamson, O. E., 'The Economics of Organization: The Transaction Cost Approach', *American Journal of Sociology* 87 (3), 1981, pp. 548–77.

Yelle, L. E., 'The Learning Curve: Historical Review and Comprehensive Survey', *Decision Sciences* 10, 1979, pp. 302–28.

Yonekawa, Shin'ichi, 'University Graduates in Japanese Enterprises Before the Second World War', *Business History* 26 (2), 1984, pp. 193–218.

Zanier, C., 'Silk Culture in Western India: The 'Mutti Experiment' (1830–47)', *Indian Economic and Social History Review* 21 (4), 1984, pp. 463–96.

Zanier, Claudio, 'Japan and the "Pébrine" Crisis of European Sericulture during the 1860s', *Bonner Zeitschrift für Japanologie* 8, 1986, pp. 51–63.

Zanier, C., 'Pre-Modern European Silk Technology and East Asia: Who Imported What?', in Debin Ma (ed.), *Textiles in the Pacific, 1500–1900. The Pacific World: Lands, Peoples and History of the Pacific, 1500–1900* (Aldershot: Variorum, 2005), pp. 105–90.

Zhao Feng, 'Silk Artistry of the Yuan Dynasty', in D. Kuhn (ed.), *Chinese Silks* (New York: Yale University Press, 2012).

Unpublished

Ambedkar, B. R., 'Administration and Finance of the East India Company' (unpublished M.A. thesis, Columbia University, 1915).

Davini, R., 'Una Conquista Incerta. La Compagnia Inglese delle Indie e la Seta del Bengala, 1769–1833' (unpublished Ph.D. thesis, European University Institute, 2004).

Davini, R., 'The History of Bengali Raw Silk as Interplay between the Company Bahadur, the Bengali Local Economy and Society, and the Universal Italian Model, c.1750–c.1830', *Commodities of Empire Working Paper* 6 (2008), pp. 1–22.

Hoffmann, M. and Toshihiro Okubo, '"By a Silken Thread": Regional Banking Integration and Pathways to Financial Development in Japan's Great Recession', *Center for Economic Studies & ifo Institute Working Paper* No. 4090, 2013, pp. 27–34.

Johnson, D. C., 'Silk in Mughal India' (unpublished paper presented at the conference 'Historical Systems of Innovation: The Culture of Silk in the Early Modern World (14th–18th Centuries)', Berlin, December 2010).

King, B. M., 'The Transformation of Tusser Silk' (paper presented at the conference 'Textile History of America Symposium', Lincoln, Nebraska, January 2004), pp. 285–6.

Mau, Chuan-Hui, 'Silk Industry: Technology and Human Capital Formation in France and China' (paper presented at the 'Epstein Memorial Conference: Technology and Human Capital Formation', London, June 2008), pp. 1–20.

Ray, I., 'Long Waves Of Silk Prices In Bengal During 17th–18th Centuries' (paper presented at the conference 'Global Economic History Network Conference: Cotton Textiles', Pune, December 2005).

Richards, J. F., 'The Finances of the East India Company in India, c. 1766–1859', *London School of Economics Working Papers* 153 (11), 2011, pp. 1–29.

Rothstein, N., 'The Silk Industry in London, 1702–1766' (unpublished M.A. thesis, University College London, 1961).

Styles, J., 'Fashion, Textiles and the Origins of the Industrial Revolution' (paper presented at the conference 'Anglo-Japanese Conference of Historians', Osaka, August 2015).

Zanier, C., 'Silk and Weavers of Silk in Medieval Peninsular India' (unpublished paper presented at the conference 'Historical Systems of Innovation: The Culture of Silk in the Early Modern World (14th–18th Centuries)', Berlin, December 2010).

INDEX

WORLDS OF THE EAST INDIA COMPANY